INDIAN ECONOMY : RETROSPECT AND PROSPECTS

INDIAN ECONOMY :
RETROSPECT AND PROSPECTS

Edited by:
Dr. L.S.N. Prasad
Dept. of Economics,
Hindu College, Guntur (A.P.)

SERIALS PUBLICATIONS
DELHI (INDIA)

Indian Economy: Retrospect And Prospects

First Published, 2003

ISBN 81-86771-08-5

Published by:

SERIALS PUBLICATIONS
4830/24, Prahlad Street,
Ansari Road, Darya Ganj,
New Delhi-110002
Ph.: 3245225, 3811659
Fax: 91-11-3812678
E-mail: serials@satyam.net.in

CONTENTS

ACKNOWLEDGEMENTS

India achieved independence with peaceful cooperative efforts. The fore fathers of India like Dadabhai Nouroji, the grand old man of India, discussed the drain of wealth from India in 1880. Mahatma was interested not only in social development but also in economic development. The first prime minister Sri Jawahar Lal Nehru was very much interested from the beginning in planning and development.

If we go through the economic history with independent India, there were many hurdles rather than growth in Indian Economy. We adapted the decentralized planning and we are at the end of the implementation of the 9th plan. We formulated the first industrial policy in 1948 even before, we adapted the constitution. After that we formulated seven industrial policies till 1991, which was the latest, the industrial development was not up to mark.

There was some kind of satisfaction in the production of food grains in India, still 35 crores of population are illiterates. In the external sector we were not able to mobilize foreign exchange resources and we are depending on IMF loans for structural adjustments.

India is the 18th poorest country. The per capita income increased from Rs. 230 to Rs. 9,330 during the last 50 years which is less than the per capita income of Sri Lanka and of Pakistan. It is very regrettable thing that the GDP growth rate inanely 3.5 percent in five decade period, where as it is 7 per cent in China. China doubled it is GDP in 10 years and Japan in 17 years. For India it took 35 years.

Another problem in Indian Economy is there is high cost of subsidies given by the government in the area of power, petroleum and to some extent in food grains. Recently in Andhra Pradesh there was a tremendous agitation in the hike of electricity prices.

The fiscal deficit of the center is 6% of the GDP. The IMF and the international organizations suggesting that India should reduce its fiscal deficit at 1.5%. The union government depending on disinvesting the public sector industries to reduce its fiscal deficit.

The environment of external trade is very conducive to economic growth. Internationally the prices of manufactured goods are falling. Prices of major imported items such as oil, fertilizers are also decreasing. Inspite of all the above there was an increase in negative balance of trade.

Deregulation of Indian customs rules and allowing the good os foreign origins will lead to destruction of cottage and rural industries. It will hamper the employment opportunities in the economy, particularly in rural areas.

In the last 50 years there is no sustainable economic development along with macro economic stability. There was no impressive achievement in any sector. By international standards the growth rate of our economy is not good. The fiscal management in the economy by different governments in the last 52 years is not so good. Fiscal deficit is in alarming state. In this context an aggregate analysis is required to discuss the correct picture of the economy and to underline the areas of strength and identify the areas of correction. The main intention in organizing this seminar is to bring out solutions to the burning problems of the economy.

I am really thankful to Honourable Sri P.V. Narasimha Rao for inaugurating the seminar. I am grateful to the president of the Hindu College Committee Sri Madhavapedi Radhakrishna Murthy, and the Secretary and Correspondent Dr. Mannava Radha Krishna Murthy for their encouragement. I also thank Sri B. Raghavendra Rao, Principal of the College for his support. I also thank Sri P.

Murali Krishna in charge of the department, for his constant support for the success of the seminar.

I thank Dr. Y. Sivaji Ex. MP for his constant encouragement, Prof G. Raghava Reddy, (Retd), Professor of economics, Sri Venkateswara University, Prof. N. Sudhakara Rao, of Nagarjuna University for their support in organizing the seminar.

I thank Dr. A. Rajasekhar, Smt. L. Alivelu, Sri P. Vassudeva Rao, Smt. K. Videhi, Mr. P.Venugopal, Miss S. Sulochana, member of the department for their involvement in organizing the seminar. I thank Mr. A. Satish, Mr.. T. Naga Raju for their help in typing and assistance. I thank the SERO- UGC of Hyderabad for sanctioning the seminar. I also thank my wife and my son for their co-operation.

I thank Mr. S.K. Jha of serials publications, New Delhi for bringing out the book in a beautiful way.

Text of the Speech of Honorable Sri P.V. Narasimha Rao, Former Prime Minister of India at the inauguration of the UGC Sponsored National Seminar on 'Indian Economy Retrospect and Prospects', in AD Hall, Hindu College, Guntur. 24th March, 2002

I am very happy that you are organizing a Seminar on Economy. You may know that I have been asking for this kind of review all over the country from all people who can think. Because we started in a uncharged sea. Not many people know that 1991 has a special significance in the economic history of India. As much as 1947 had on the political side. We became free in 1947 but we did not know which way to go on the economic side. We had two great models before us one was the capitalist model and the other was becoming communist model. You look at this, you found it beautiful. So your attention was divided between two things which, from a distance, looked very attractive. You did not have the occasion to go and look it from close quarters. So, Panditji, the great visionary that he was, he said, "I will neither accept this 100% or that 100% so he started what is called mixed economy. In this and just relating the history as it has happened, mixed economy has had several up and downs and there was a time when every body said this is no economy at all." There was a time because Panditji's personality was great, everybody said, this is the greatest thing. Neither of them understood the details of the mixed economy, I am sorry to say. I have lived from these times so I know from year to year, from stage to stage, from issue to issue how mixed economy has been moulded to confront with the existence of the life of the people. You can write very very detailed history of the mixed economy, I don't know whether it has really been undertaken by economists or economic historians, but this is a unique experiment, very successfully undertaken under conditions which were totally confusing at the time it was undertaken. I am not aware of any other country where such a thorough going experiment was undertaken and had succeeded to the extent it has succeeded here. I have visited at least 150 countries in the world. Wherever I went, I tried to understand what is the poor mans' life like. As Foreign Minister we did not have to go anywhere, even all kind of treatment and all, but when we ask for these things, even the protocol people in those countries were little taken aback why this man was going to poor quarters. From my very first visit to Zimbabwe what Zimbabwe, today it was called by another name Rhodesia, every time I have been looking into the lives of the people and if you do not look into the lives of the people no economist can give you a formula which will ever have any chance of succeeding. So if economists are meeting here for the next few days to go into the details of liberalization started in 1991 I am very happy about it. You have no answer. Life is too complex to admit of simple answers; it is not like brick and mortar, it is not inanimate. If I am doing something the next man is doing against what I am doing, not necessarily because he is against me, but he holds a different view. I can't blame him if he holds a different view. So anyone who starts a system, any one who starts a programme, will run into these difficulties every minute of his existence and the existence of the programme. In 1991 it so happened that in a way both the big systems, the grinding stones between which our own economy was getting ground and had to take different turns in different areas we need going for total nationalization. Agriculture, which is the biggest economic activity in India, was in private hands. The small trader again, that is as critical because he is in every village in every country, is again in private hands. But they were no one to give me a 5000 crore steel factory. We went to other countries. Panditji also met personal appeals that we want for India a few steel plants: You know what they say, why you want a steel plant will you give steel. You do not need steel plant; he was trying to tell India what India needs and the essence of sovereignty that I know what I need even if I go wrong. I have the right to go wrong; so Panditji said this won't do. If you do not give I will go to some other." That is how Bhilai came. After Bhilai came everybody started coming, because it was business for them. So this is the history which one has to keep in mind, how the whole thing developed one after the other, one after the other. You will not have this kind of pattern in any other country; either you have the entire thing, the whole lives of the people controlled centrally or nothing controlled centrally, everything left to itself. This is the middle path. The middle path given to us in our own culture by the Great Buddha. Look at the wisdom. There has been avoiding extremes. There is always a middle path and you have to find it. Nobody is going to prescribe the middle path for you. Nobody. So this is how our culture, our heritage has helped us to carry on with the mixed economy given by Panditji because it is in line with our genius. Came 1991, Soviet Union collapsed. Not many people know the implication of the USSR's collapse for India. It was tremendous. It was not even possible to compute it in proper terms. It was political, non-political, economic, non-economic. It has a dimension all of its own, because we were not a communist country. It is not Bulgaria; it is not like Rumania, it is not like South Korea, it is not like Singapore. So the relationship between us, India and USSR was multi-dimensional and something which you cannot calculate in any terms. So when the USSR collapsed, it so happened that I was at the helm of affairs in India.

What do I do? I am a Congress worker. I am not an economist; I am not a leader of that caliber; I was going home; I had not asked for a ticket; I did not contest in 1991 election and suddenly I find myself with this huge mechanism and I have to run it. So you can understand the dimension of the problem in 1991. So we went into it. We have brought out something, which is called liberalization. Why do we liberalize? I remember when Rajiv Gandhi was Prime Minister, he was almost worried to the extent of talking about it every day, the industrial pattern of the country. He was a young man with new ideas. He found that new ideas were knocking against so many things, whenever he wanted to advance them, not against this, not against that, he was not able to find a way easily, but he was trying to find the way. So on the public sector undertakings and this public sector as I said is the result of what we had to do because nobody else was prepared to do. It came as a necessity; the whole public sector came as a necessity to India and we had to do it. It is our child. You cannot possibly say my child is bad, I don't want to feed him. No mother would say it. So it is our concern; we have started it because we wanted it, we needed it. So let us not forget that the public sector in India which is a part of the mixed economy given by, and conceptualized by, Panditji, was the creature of necessity and not because anybody has any fancy for it. So we started with that. It went on increasing and increasing. You will be surprised to know, I headed a small cabinet committee on the public sector undertakings and we find to our horror that 30% of the loss making units were those which we had taken from the private sector. So the losses come from the private sector, and today everybody says public sector is in loss. Just the opposite of what happened; why did we take them? We took them only because we do not want labour to be thrown out of employment. So it was a not profit and loss question at all. It was a human question and if you do not have the human question before you in India you can inform we have successfully planned for anything in India. That is how we took this 30%, 27-30%. Now today they do not seem to understand this, unfortunately because the economists of today, maybe they have come from institutions which themselves, who have not studied this is inside and out side of India, itself of the economy of India and therefore we find that they are taking economy to one side where there is a polarization between the rich and the poor. We never wanted. If it was not the intention in 1991 at all. So, where did it go wrong? I wish I had been sitting with these friends and trying to explain what went wrong, and why it needs to be considered what went wrong. You have to go into very minute details. This has not been done and Hindu College is going to take lead in this. I would be very happy. I would like to congratulate you for making bold to do this. It is not going to be easy. What you see before you is not reality, there is something beyond, there is something behind and you have to penetrate this virtual reality to go to the real reality. It is going to be a difficult exercise, but I am sure you are serious enough to go into it. And you will devote the time and attention needed. So we had one great difficulty. We were trying to spread our money to thin, to wide for too many things; government was the only employer. Delhi or Hyderabad, anywhere a matter of normal daily occurrence was a black flag demonstration by the youth. NOUKARI DO WARNA GADDI CHOD DO. Thousands and thousands. It is not their fault. We have given them education, you have to provide employment to them. You are the only employer, you have nothing to spare, you don't know to allow to go and search for some employment elsewhere. What kind of social justice is this? What kind of public policy is this? So the first thing, we have to do was... Yes to tell them we are not able to give you employment but we will remove all the restrictions that bind you today and make you incapable in getting employment elsewhere. You start anything you wish, you do not have to take permission, you don't have to take a license, you do not have to go and go round people and the offices, that was the situation. Indira Gandhi had given a programme in 1975 through which 25,000 young men, boys or girls doing any venture would get money. You would get it but you would not get the permission to do that. He would get the money but not the permission. If the money is given, why should we deny him the permission? It is that simple. It is so illogical. The whole thing looked logical so we said remove. But once you remove something you also run into several other situations where you have to dismantle the existing rules, existing regulations and anybody who is running the regulatory machinery wants the machinery to be dismantled because he would be dismantled. So there is so much of human obstruction taking place because one thing leads to another and it affects a lot of people in the bureaucracy and so on. We have to contend with those things one after other, one after the other. While the political muscle was supplied by me and Dr. Manmohan Singh did the rest, it was a very good combination. If he said this cannot be done according to our interests I did not push him to do much, and I never said you cannot go beyond this. Otherwise there will be a difficulty. Then he would not go so we both observed the Lakshman Rekha. Neither he crossed it nor I crossed it. The industrialization pattern has completely changed. Today we wanted substitution. As I said we were spreading our money too wide. You are running schools, you are running hotels, you are running shops, you are running industries. Now is it necessary to do this. If you do, they you don't have money. So what suffered? Education suffered, rural development suffered. Therefore the sufferers were the young boys and the primary school, the primary education suffered. We decided to spend 6% of the GNP on education in the year 1968, 34 years ago. We are still now somewhere near 4 per cent. Can you imagine a greater example of inadequacy not because there was anything wrong with our intentions. The simple fact is you do not have the money, you are a poor country. I remember in Karimnagar, when India became free, we had 2 high schools. Good, only that many people were becoming matriculates, others nobody bothers. Today there are 200 and are still asking more, so the way we have extended the education facility, we have expanded health facility; this phenomenon, no other country has done it from that stage to this stage. But still we are inadequate because the needs are growing. Our population has become tripled what it was in 1947's population. So what is the idea, it is just the matter of common sense. You are spending on this, this..... Somebody has to take the burden of one or two so that you can give your money directly to those who need it. No western country or no industry is going to come and run schools for you, so you have to run schools; but they run, they can start industries. We said OK. We have public sector which is catering to the needs of India, on the whole, about 30%; the remaining 70% is Virgin soil. Please come start your industry there. There will be competition between public and your private sector. They will get technology from you. You will be able to do some joint work and in course of time we will see what to do with the public sector. Ultimately public sector is not just an industry, it is an evidence of self reliance. It flows the flag of self reliance for any country. India has to have the self reliance. It is too big for anyone to come and manage. It is like an elephant which has to stand on its own legs. Once the elephant falls down, no other elephant will not be able to come and lift it. So India has no business to fall from the level of self reliance which is it needed for it. It doesn't mean, as economists, that you have to produce every thing as economist states. I have to pay for every thing that I want in foreign exchange. Where do I get foreign exchange? You are getting your exchange from one or two sources today, that's what economist tells me. I am not an economist myself. I am only a commonsense worker. That's how I understand. There is a time you are sending raw material, only today we are sending finished goods. But it's not enough, it's not enough. Therefore your manufacturing sector has to be sustained here. That will be sustained by foreign means, not necessarily American, German, Britain or from any other country. Foreign means what is outside the

Government is foreign. That is how we defined FDI. It did not mean coming from any another country. From the same society necessarily. But from outside the government. A source, it is an addition to the government source, that is what we thought, didn't happen why if you are changing the government every year at the center who is going to come to invest in the country? Tell me, be serious, I am not talking as a congressman. I am talking as a person sitting in New York who has to take out a cheque book and write out a cheque for $1 billion and then he looks at India, what is the political stability in India, and he doesn't find it. We may still say we are stable, but if he doesn't find it he will be the master. His cheque book goes into pocket, it doesn't come out. This is the position. So this is what we really planned in 91. It certifies to some extent. For 2 and half years I did nothing but sell this idea of liberalization telling them that your money will be safe, we have a legal system which is akin to yours. There is a huge market, which everybody is seeking. So you do not have to bother. Please come, there is 70 per cent virgin soil. You please put yours. Meanwhile, governments changed and this, which had become a steady trickle, dried up. Today what they are doing is: they are selling the public sector undertaking. What do you get? They are not able to get anything. Why should you sell? The point is if you have not given up mixed economy, then you have no right to sell any of the public sector undertakings. Come on, give us a new policy. Say this will not be mixed economy, there will be something else. That is the kind of economy that we want to develop. You do what you like. I do not know even if I am not sure whether they can do they like. Radhakrishna Murthyji is a very eminent lawyer. You have to tell me. I make a distinction between government property and people's property. It is a very valid distinction. The Charminar belongs to the people of India, Taj Mahal belongs to the people of India. It does not belong to the trustees or it does not belong to the state government. If the government has bought something, yes, I agreed. You inherited after 500 years and you say you sell it. Can you do this? Looking it at from the very narrow legal point, maybe no court will set it aside. But the peoples court will have to set it aside, that is what I am really appealing to, in the name of disinvestments if you want to deprive yourselves of the ownership. People will not forgive you for it because you are actually tampering with their ownership, not your ownership; this is the distinction, this distinction has to be understood and appreciated. But this is not solving any problem. In the Small Sub committee which I headed in 1989 & 1990, we came to the conclusion that much of the sick units were taken over from the private sector and ultimately even then, those who are in 215 or 230 units, where on the whole giving profits some of the units went into loss, some of the units into profits. So what is the point in selling them? On the whole, the public sector has not burdened you. With anything which you cannot bear. You have to justify it, if you can justify it only on this ground that because of this the whole Government is going downhill, but that is not the case. So the rationale of these disinvestments to the extent is of doing away with your ownership. This is not quite clear to me. Those who are studying this, I would like them to go deep into this matter. This a very important question. This is juridical a question. It is a question of property. It is a question of public policy and also a question of reversing the policy which has come for the last 50 years. No single person or no single government has the right to do it. There has to be a national consensus on this. There was a national consensus which the Congress Government built up. Not that everybody agreed with it but there was a consensus, consensus does not mean unanimity. But to that extent consensus was available. Is the consensus available today on whatever is being done? I am not blaming anyone. This is not by way of criticism, this is not by finding fault since you are going into the question. I am pointing out this. If this seminar you had not planned, I won't have said even this, because there are others who said, who are saying what needs to be said. Some are saying even what doesn't need to be said. The styles are different, the contents are different, and that's not my job now. I am on the fringe. So I don't have to get in the frame I said and I ask not getting into it. Since you as intellectuals are going into this, as scholars are going in to this. I just wanted to tell you that these are, just some of the aspects which you go into. New government is not a permanent debating society. You have to take a decision. You have a situation to face, you have to take a decision. You have to go ahead. Somebody says it is right, somebody says it is wrong; you go on answering questions later, but you cannot say that I will answer all the question later, but you cannot say that I will answer. Answer all the questions and then take a decision, that will not be yes, possible, you can consult people. Yes, number of people you can consult. You make your own assessment, but you have to take a decision. Government depends on decisions, not on debates. So the decisions that have been taken have to reviewed against the background of the circumstances when they were taken. Then if you have something to suggest better, nothing like it. I have been wanting it for the last 4 or 5 years, since 1997. I made the first appeal that there would be a reassessment of all these policies and if anybody can suggest anything much better than this, but that is not happening. Without doing that they take the policy in a direction it was not intended and they tell me that it is all yours, you tell me what is the improvement you have brought on this. I am prepared to be convinced, because when I was convinced in 2002 also, I will not close my mind? but I didn't see anyone even telling me one argument why the things that are being done are being done, that is my difficulty. May-be they are going thoroughly in to it because I have had the opportunity of going into the all these questions thoroughly and it is only from the periphery I am looking at this. So if at the end of this you come to any conclusions, suggestions, any critique of what is being done and if you tell me I would like to be in touch with those who are running, who are conducting the seminar. There will be different opinions, absolutely no difficulty about that. And therefore, I would like this dialogue to go on but at the same time decisions also taken are being side by side. The dialogue cannot be interminable and endless. While you are taking dialoque, then you can also be making mid course change. India is on the move. The net result of liberalisation is that India is on the move, that ice has been broken. Today, I found a young fellow who has got some IT ideas, and he has got some telephone, some something; he is feeling he is getting up, he is trembling, he is falling down. I am feeling so happy about even the falling down because he is making an effort. So, this generation, this young generation is not a dependent generation, it is an independent generation; they are bound to fall, they are bound to succeed ultimately. The country will go ahead as a result of this national effort.

I have not come across but such huge national effort in the last 50, 60 years. We were only following it and suffering sometime also but that was a static situation. Today is completely dominant, we do not know what is going to happen because in this era where technology is changing so fast, we are not able cope with the change. We are not able to manage this, even understand the change before you understand one change over the other. So they are doing something which is in line with the times. The 21st century is going to be qualitative from the 20th century. It is not a continuation of the 20th century at all. Time wise it is a different matter. The calender changes day by day but there is a quantum jump between 20th and 21st century. Values are going to change, beliefs are going to change, techniques are going to change and probably recognize this country. So this is the measure of what you have to study and I would like you to go into as many aspects as you can. I am sure the aspects cannot be gone into because you are meeting in Guntur. There are areas where conditions are totally different from Guntur. They will have to come to different conclusions, at least different angles in the situation. So with this effort, go on in the whole country starting from the northeast. I know something about the northeast, the problems of that area are totally mind-boggling. You just cannot imagine how that area is groaning under those problems from many many decades. Try to do something. You cannot change all these things. Insurgency, the continued insurgency where I cannot describe how difficult it is, life is for those people there. So each area has its own social difficulties, but you are meeting here at a place where you can have some view of what is happening in the country and I hope you will be able to come to useful conclusions. Please let me know, I am engaged in this inquiry; it is not a government's inquiry, it is an inquiry of a seeker, just say in the spiritual field. I am a seeker in the economic field....

Thank you very much.

SESSION–1

INDIAN AGRICULTURE AND MAJOR CHALLENGES

1

IRRIGATION DEVELOPMENT: SOME ISSUES OF EFFICIENCY AND EQUITY

P. Kothandarami Reddy
G. Raghava Reddy

Introduction

Irrigation is one of the surest ways of promoting agricultural development. It is well established by empirical investigations and historical experience that agricultural development should either precede or simultaneously occur with industrial development. Progress in major irrigation works is necessary for both agricultural and industrial development as it provides water for crop production and power for industrial operations as well as lift irrigation. That is why major irrigation projects have been accorded a pride of place in India's development strategy. Irrigation is generally classified into two types: (1) surface and (2) underground. The former is again classified into 3 types: (1) major (2) medium and (3) minor irrigation. It is also classified into protective and productive. Each category of irrigation has its own merits and demerits. The choice of one does not exclude the other. It is a question of choice of an appropriate combination of irrigation projects of different categories with a view to optimizing the utilization of water, land and labour resources and thereby maximize production and productivity. An attempt is made here to elucidate the role of irrigation in agricultural development and comment on some of the connected issues such as efficiency and equity in irrigation development on the basis of Indian experience in general and Andhra Pradesh (A.P.) in particular.

Irrigation and Production Possibility Curve

The role of irrigation in agricultural development can be illustrated with the help of one of the standard tools of economics, namely the production possibility curve. A concave production possibility curve demonstrates the presence of an increasing opportunity cost as production moves along the frontier in any direction from one extreme to the other. In our hypothetical case we show the production of commercial crops on the X axis and food crops on the Y axis. A glance at figure 1 will indicate that it is possible to produce OP quantity of food or OG quantity of commercial crops by fully and efficiently utilizing all the resources in agriculture under given conditions of technology. If there is inefficiency or under utilization of resources including irrigation, it is not to possible to operate on the production possibility frontier by better utilization of resources and thereby increase the production of both the crops as in the case of a movement from A to B. By harnessing water resources for irrigation, it is possible to shift the production possibility curve from PG to RF and thereby increase production in accordance with the community preferences as shown by points such as C, D, E on the RF frontier. As is well known under given conditions, it is not possible to operate on any point to the right of the RF frontier such as N. The task of agricultural growth is to continuously push the production possibility curve to the right.

The purpose of irrigation development in India is to push up the proportion of gross irrigation area in the total cultivated area and thereby increase agricultural production and productivity. The possibilities of extending irrigation by all means is to be explored consistent with the requirements of efficient allocation of financial resources.

Irrigation Potential and Use

Irrigation potential created as a percentage of ultimate irrigation potential is 67 in India. Gross irrigated area as a percentage of cross cropped area is 31 in the country. In respect of Andhra Pradesh these percentages are 66 and 37 respectively.[1] In respect of the latter, namely the proportion of area irrigated, A.P.'s position is slightly better than that of the nation as a whole, where 1/3 of the cultivated area is exposed to the vagaries of the monsoon with all its consequences for risk and uncertainty in farm production. One-third of the ultimate irrigation potential remains to be exploited. Even the created potential is wasted due to defective maintenance or no maintenance of works and canals.[2] Therefore, the task of irrigation policy is to ensure the full use of the crated potential and exploit the ultimate potential in future to meet the challenge of growing demand for agricultural production.

Issues of Efficiency and Equity

The estimated loss of water flow in the canal system of major and medium irrigation projects is 30 to 40 per cent due to evaporation and seepage. There are innumerable drainage problems. Water does not reach the tail end farms. Production is adversely affected. This is an issue of equity across farms of different locations and therefore access to canal water system. The foregoing issues are receiving some attention of late and World Bank assistance is sought to tackle these issues. Loss of production due to water shortage in tail end farms and those subject to water logging leads to a high capital-output ratio and it has a depressing effect on the growth rate of the economy as is well noted in the contributions of Harood and Domar. Delays in irrigation project planning, execution and completion and poor maintenance, cost escalation, low budget allocations constitute a vicious circle, which is to be broken.

Excessive concentration of investment in a few major projects, not taking equity concerns explicitly into consideration while designing irrigation systems, paying little attention to the design of new institutions for sharing water and policy failures to ensure optimum cropping pattern have resulted in the inefficient use of water resources. Evidence suggests that minor irrigation which is cost efficient and whose spread effects are strong has been neglected.[3] Inter-regional variations in irrigation endowment, as in the case of the country, are very glaring in A.P. In 1985-86, the irrigation ration was as high as 82 per cent in West Godavari, 77 per cent in Nellore, 73 per cent in Krishna but as low as 8 per cent in Adilabad, 10 per cent in Medak and 13 per cent in Anantapur and Mahabubnagar. It is also worth noting that 4 districts viz. Guntur, Nellore, Prakasam and Karimnagar accounted for 81 per cent of the increase in the net irrigated area during 1970-71 to 1984-85 in Andhra Pradesh.[4] Due to neglect of minor irrigation, the area under tank irrigation declined sleepily by over one-third and the deterioration was at most by half in drought-prone areas and under utilization in command areas of major irrigation projects. Conjunctive irrigation is the solution in irrigated areas. There are serious ecological and environmental problems associated with the planning and execution of not only major irrigation works like the Sardar Sarovar across river Narmada, but also the exploitation of underground water in drought-prone Rayalaseema. The government of A.P. has declared 1993 as the year of minor irrigation development. This seems to be a beginning of the awareness on the part of the State and the public to ensure efficiency and equity in the development of irrigation systems and their effective management.

REFERENCES

1. Sahetiya Srichand: The Economic Times, Survey of States: Andhra Pradesh Nov. 1, 1993.
2. T.R. Prasad, Development of Andhra Pradesh: Problems and Prospects, CESS, Hyderabad, p. 72.
3. R. Radhakrishna, The Economic Times, Op. Cit., p. 11.
4. D. Narasimha Reddy, The Economic Times, Op. Cit., p. 11.
5. Govt. of A.P., Statistical Abstract of A.P., 1990-91.

2

INDIA'S FOOD SECURITY: SOME ISSUES

I. Satya Sundaram

In a densely populated Third World country like India food security is very important. Though the foodgrain stocks in India are growing, all is not well with the agricultural sector. It is facing a number of serious problems. Hence, food security cannot be taken for granted.

Food security has two aspects: (i) availability of food, and (ii) accessibility to the foodgrain stocks. The household ought to have freedom to choose what to buy from the available foodstock.

The Indian Situation

The foodgrain production is still fluctuating. It reached a peak of 208.87 million tonnes in 1999-2000, but fell to 196.07 million tonnes in 2000-01 (revised estimates). The production of pulses has been fluctuating around 13 million tonnes.

The per capita net availability of foodgrains per day has been fluctuating. It was 444 grams in 1955, 480.1 grams in 1965, but fell to 405.5 grams in 1975. In 1991, it was high at 510.1 grams, but declined to 466 grams in 2000.[1] This means that our food security is quite tenuous.

Another disturbing development is the shift from staples to each crops. During the period 1960-61 to 1998-99, the area under coarse grains has gone down from 45 million hectares to 29.5 million hectares. Since the introduction of new economic policies in 1990-91, the area under foodgrains declined by 2 per cent and area under coarse grains by 18 per cent. Area under non food cash crops like cotton and sugarcane has increased.

In 1997, the revamped PDS (RPDS) was replaced by the Targeted PDS (TPDS) which provided 10 kg of wheat or rice per month to families below the poverty line (BPL) at highly subsidized prices, and withdrawal of all subsidies for families above the poverty line (APL). As a result, food prices increased, off-take decreased and stocks grew.

Experts say that the BPL/APL categories were arbitrary and the BPL beneficiaries who were to be targeted were artificially reduced. In fact, 12 states informed the Supreme Court that they could not identify people in the BPL category. Instead of targeting the poor, the World Bank driven policies made the poor end their food entitlements.[2]

Recently, India's food grain stocks reached a level of 60 million tones. A World Bank report states that half the stock with the Food Corporation of India is at least two years old and 30 per cent up to four years old. This calls for immediate disbursal of grain to achieve the twin goals of preventing its wastage and feeding the millions who do not have access to food.

Thus, India is in no happy position. The reason for this is the over exploitation of natural resources which led to the degradation of land, deforestation, water depletion and contamination, and loss of biodiversity—that is, a major drain on the resource base.[3]

Measures Needed

Food security needs enough purchasing power with the poor. Hence, the antipoverty programmes should be effectively implemented. Also, because of huge food grain stocks available, the food-for-work programme should be taken up seriously. A part of the wage can be paid in kind. This solves the problem of poverty, and also strengthens rural infrastructure.

Experts say that we must shift from a commodity—centered approach to a farming systems based approach built on the foundation of integrated natural resource management to produce more from every unit of water, land and other imputes one sustainable basis.

The emphasis should be not merely on quantity but on quality too. Improving post-harvest technologies would go a long way in improving quality. This assumes importance with the removal of quantitative restrictions (QRS) on imports.

In the agricultural sector, priority should be given to:[4]

- Augmenting availability of seeds/planting materials of High Yielding Varieties (HYV);
- developing and promoting HYV, specially for rain fed eco-systems;
- small farm mechanization;
- transfer of technology through continuous assessment and refinement, and
- developing infrastructure for post-harvest management, processing, marketing and agri-business.

Also, millets should be recognized as 'nutritious cereals' instead of coarse cereals. Special interest should be shown in the conservation and cultivation of such crops.

There is a need for bringing more and more wastelands under cultivation by improving their productivity.[5] Data relating to wastelands is not reliable. The estimate range from 38.4 million ha. to 187 million ha.

The use of chemical fertilizers has serious limitations. Hence, the growing importance of organic farming. In organic farming, oilcakes and oil meals play a key role as natural fertilizers. Vermi composing needs to be encouraged as the earthworms are used in land reclamation, soil improvement and organic waste management. Of course, organic farming requires crop rotation.

Also, recycling of crop residue may be done by burying farm wastes in the field itself. We should give importance to integrated Nutrient Management. In organic farming, cost of production is low. It is also eco-friendly.[6]

The PDS should be confined to the poorest of the poor; others can purchase foodgrains in the market at reasonable prices when foodgrain stocks with the government are kept at a reasonable level. The PDS should also be used as an anti-poverty programme.

Community food banks (CFB) can be started at the village level, with initial food supplies coming as a grant from governments and donor agencies like the World Food Programme. Later, such CFBs can be sustained through local purchases and from continued government and international support for food for eco-development and food for nutrition programmes.[7]

We should have a decentralized community grain banking system which would ensure local level food security.[8]

There is need for change in food habits. Indians depend too much on cereals like rice, and less on vegetables and fruits. Almost three-thirds calorie of an average Indian comes from cereals. A change in the food habits would reduce the severity of food shortage.

REFERENCES

1. Ministry of Finance, Government of India. Economic Survey 2000-01.
2. Vandana Shiva: 'At the Mercy of Globalisation,' The Hindu, September 23, 2001.
3. Asha Krishnakumar: 'Food Security: For a World Free of Hunger,' Frontline, August 17, 2001. p. 80.
4. Bhagirath Singh: 'New Horizons of Indian Agriculture: An Analysis,' Southern Economist.
5. I. Satya Sundaram: 'Food Security: Need for a Pragmatic Approach,' Civil Services Chronicle, December, 2000. pp. 30.
6. I. Satya Sundaram: 'Organic Farming: Towards Sustainable Agriculture,' Civil Services Chronicle, February, 2001. pp. 18-19.
7. M.S. Swaminathan: 'Eliminating Hunger: A Challenge,' The Hindu (Magazine Section) October 7, 2001, p. 11.
8. Asha Krishnakumar: op. cit., p. 82.

3

ROLE OF AGRICULTURAL DEVELOPMENT IN INDIAN ECONOMY: SOME BASIC ISSUES

M.R.S. Babu and
B.S. Rao

Agriculture is not a mere technological phenomenon. In India, it is a way of life. It was so in past, continues to be so today and it will continue to be so in future. Agriculture will remain a central core of development. Its contribution to National Income is substantial.[1] Agriculture is not only cultivation, it is a social and cultural phenomenon which provides a bedrock to the entire process of socio-economic development. Agriculture produces resources, which generate many productive cycles with multiplier effects extending to all facets of life in the rural society. From this viewpoint, agricultural research should not be confined to technocratic research. It should give greater attention to its contribution to rural development. To realize such multiplier effect of agriculture, it should become the main stream of the rural development. It should become an effective instrument for the development of the entire rural society through meaningful linkages between agriculture and village industries. Separation of agricultural research from industrial activities of rural society in non-agricultural sector has not helped the quicker transformation of the rural society. Agriculture and rural technology should be made inseparable.

While everybody is looking forward to some novel polices, our polices on agriculture have turned out to be an anti-climax. Competition is increasing day by day and the task is becoming more daunting because of the increasing productive efficiencies of the developed countries. In such a scenario, it is but natural, our attention is drawn towards the agricultural sector because of its prominence. With this background, this paper attempts to analyse:

(a) Status of Agricultural progress in the Indian Economy.
(b) the share of public investment in Indian Agriculture.
(c) the state of Agricultural productivity in the context of new Agricultural technology.

The very nature of Indian rural society divided into more than 5,75,000 villages[2] with nearly 4,50,000 villages having a population of less than 1,000 requires an indigenous strategy of development. Majority of the rural poor belongs to the categories of small and marginal farmers, agricultural labourers.[3] The rural society in India has a predominant place, as even after four decades of planning, it still constitutes over 74 per cent of population, 90 per cent of rural population depending on agriculture holdings 51 per cent of the holdings still constitute less than 1 hectare size and 90 per cent holdings are less than 2 hectare size. In terms of gain full work 30 per cent are land less agricultural labourers and 51 per cent are cultivators, many of whom do not have land of their own. It is not a question of mere transfer of technology or extending merely urban facilities to villages but it is a question of reconstructuring rural society on certain foundations which with reinforce their capacity to withstand the onslaught of urbanization which flourishes on exploitation of villages. Mahatma Gandhi had warned as back as 1929 when he stated: "To serve our villages is to establish Swaraj, every thing else is but an idle dream."

For the last 15 years the investment in agricultural sector has decreased enormously, during the decade of 1990 investment for the development of agricultural sector, and for the irrigation facilities. Even the growth/share of the public sector investments were decreased to a greater extent.

From 1980 to 1997 the ratio of investment of public and private sector is shown in the Table 1. If we observe the table it reveals that the share of private sector investment is greater than the public sector investment. It gives us the idea that the Government wants to privatize the agriculture by removing subsidies and etc., to the agriculture. But majority of the people in rural areas are poor and they are unable to investing the agriculture even if it is main source of livelihood. On the other hand the proportion of investment in the agricultural sector is decreasing year by year. This clearly indicates us the negligence of the Government towards the agricultural sector. Better performance of agriculture has been a major factor in reducing the incidents of the rural poverty.[4]

It is true that rice yields in Andhra Pradesh are low compare to Tamil Nadu and Punjab. This is despite the fact that the state is the second highest, and the highest in consumption of the NPK and pesticides respectively. The low yields cannot be attributed to a single factor of low ground water usage. It is native to compare the actual yields and experimental station on yields to stay that there is a scope for doubling the yield rate. During 1999-2000 the production of food grains in 209 million tones and it is fall down to 109 million tones in 2000-2001. This is due to lack of proper irrigation facility and depending on monsoons.

A serve pest infestation is presently driving farmers to spray huge doses of pesticides in an attempt to save the their crop. The cost of cultivation of cotton have increased so dramatically that in some villages the debt accumulated over the last 2 or 3 years has risen to Rs. 5,000 per house hold.[5] It is no longer rare in these parts for women to mortgage their "Mangala Sutra," or for land-owning farmers to sell an acre are two to start at repaying their debt.

To conclude agriculture and rural development are increasingly recognized as important segments in our planning; it is not yet the foundation of planning. What we social scientists–need to work for is to establish the inescapability of the foundational nature of holistic rural uplift in our process of development. This may be possible by the agriculture an instrument of uplift of the entire rural society with all its segments. Rural development, thus, is an alternative strategy to the prevalent development model which continues to foster new disparities rather than reducing them. In this alternative strategy, agriculture will not be an end in itself but will be a paddling source of development process. This is a daylight revelation.

REFERENCES

1. Dr. B.B. Singh (2000): "Challenges to agricultural lending." Financing Agriculture July-Sept, p. 8.
2. Shah G.S. and Chaturvedi, H.R. (1983): Gandhian approach to Rural development, The valid experiment, Ajantha publications, New Delhi, p. 2.
3. World Bank (1975): "Rural Development: Sector policy paper," Washington, D.C., February, p. 3.
4. Missra S.N. (1997): Agricultural Liberalisation and Development Strategy in IX plan: Economic and Political Weekly, Vol. XXXII, No. 13, March 29, P.A. 19.
5. Carine Pionetti and Ramanjaneyulu (2001): Wither Transgenic agriculture. The Hindu, November 27.
6. Y.V. Krishna Rao (2001): A broken hand to Agriculture sector, Visalandra Daily, March 10.

4

CHALLENGES IN INDIAN AGRICULTURE

T. Susilendra Sarma

Agriculture in India is more than a profession, it is rather a way of life to nearly twenty crore farmers in India, even in this twenty-first century. Though the contribution of agriculture to National G.D.P. is now only 30 per cent, 60 per cent of the population of India out of its 1 billion depend on agriculture for their livelihood. Nearly one crore new livelihoods will have to be created every year and these must come largely from the farm and rural sector only. All this indicates the unique place that agriculture has in the Indian Economy. Nearly 30 crores of population live below poverty line, who mostly belong to the categories of landless and resource poor small farm families.

The role of agriculture is highly crucial in solving the major problems of Food security, Poverty and Livelihood in the country with 1 billion people, which makes the problems of very large magnitudes.

Though agricultural sector achieved conspicuous results in production after 60s through technological change, the challenges in the new millennium are no less.

Achievements in Indian Agriculture

A famine ridden Indian Economy of the past transformed into self-sufficient Economy in food, the credit of which goes to the use of HYV crops along with large doses of fertilizer, pesticide and water, which termed as

Green Revolution during 70s. In Post Green Revolution phase, though public sector investment reduced from 18 per cent, private investments increased in Agriculture, their real incomes increased. Besides there were subsidies and other support. As a result, foodgrain production increased significantly particularly in cereals and oil seeds. Yield per hectare doubled in paddy and tripled in wheat in the forty years span from 60s. Government measures to raise irrigated area, area under HYV seeds and fertilizer and expansion of Credit facilities led to substantial increase in foodgrains. Irrigated area increased from 24% in 1970-71 to more than 40% by the end of the century. The area under HYV seeds increased 5.6 to 32.2 million hectares in paddy and from 6.5 to 23 million hectares in the case of wheat. Fertilizer consumption increased from 2.2 million tonnes to 16.2 million tonnes during the period from 1970-71—2000-01. Foodgrain production crossed 200 million tonnes with an annual buffer stock of 20 to 30 million tonnes during 90s. Oil seed production has gone up to 26 million tonnes and Potato to 25 million tonnes from 10 million tonnes each in 1970-71.

In the meanwhile, population reached 1 billion by the end of the century. It is estimated that the demand for foodgrains which was at 197 million tonnes in the year 2000, will rise to nearly 235 million tonnes in 2015 and to 264 million tonnes by 2030.

In 2000, the demand for milk was at 80 million tonnes, vegetables 84 million tonnes, fruits 50 million tonnes, meat 5.5 million tonnes, eggs around 2 million and fish 6 million tonnes.

In 2030, the demand is likely to be 130-158 million tonnes for milk, 151-193 million tonnes for vegetables, 84-106 million tonnes for fruits, 10-14 million tonnes for meat, 3.6 to 4.8 million eggs and 10-14 million tonnes for fish.

Keeping this magnitude of demand, achieving food security for the huge additions of population is one of the major challenges in the coming years. There will be pressure to produce more diversified foods at a much accelerated pace compared to our past.

Will it be possible for Indian Agriculture to face this challenge? If we observe India's current position in the world, it stands second highest in the production of the major food crops rice and wheat. In the case of pulses and groundnut it occupies first place. India is the largest producer of milk in the world. Aquaculture also made significant progress and reached to sixth place in fish production. Export earnings from live stock products are nearly Rs. 2000 crores and the contribution from livestock sector to GDP has increased to 25 per cent.

However, the high position India holds in the production of several crops in due to the large area under these crops. It is a striking fact the yield per acre for these crops has been very much low compare to that of other countries. For example in the case of rice the world average yield per hectare is about 3000 kg, whereas in India it is less than 2000 kg, which is far lower than 6000 kg of Japan and 5500 kg of China. In the case of pulses, we occupy first position in production, but 118th position regarding productivity. Similar is the situation with other crops also. In India, there is only merge scope to increase production through area expansion. The per capita availability of land which was 0.48 hectare in 1952 has declined to 0.15 hectare now. The area under food grains has more or less remained constant around 125 million hectares since 1970-71. This area may go down to 123.3 million hectare in the coming years due to soil degradation. Deterioration of land and water resources, loss of biodiversity, large scale deforestation, global climatic changes, effects of globalisation such as intellectual property rights, intensified competition in international trade, diversified food consumption pattern, large growing population clubbed with widening economic inequalities pose serious challenges to Indian Agriculture in the coming years.

Considering the land scarcity, yield improvement should be our goal in every crop to achieve food and nutrition security. It is estimated that we need to produce 110 million tonnes of wheat by 2020. To recollect the trend in the past, the annual growth rate in food production was hardly 0.1 per cent between 1900 and 1947. During the period 1970-1999, the annual growth rate was 2.8 per cent, which was higher than the growth of population and this was the outcome of successful application of science and technology in agriculture. But during 90s, Environment has become the most important subject of debate. The UN conference on Environment and Development of 1992 focused on the ensuring catastrophe, if efforts to bring about harmony between nature and mankind is not given top priority in future policies.

In view of growing water scarcity, and declining soil fertility, technology should seek for raising productivity with less amount of water in fragile soils. Hence the following aspects are to be considered in the field of agriculture in the coming years:

1. Science and technology in various spheres to be applied in Agriculture. Information and Communication system, Genetic Technology, Research on developing seeds and farm techniques for dry lands and pest resistance etc.
2. In view of the change in global trade policies and regulations, it is necessary to develop domestic scientific research, and encourage the scientists of the country so as to meet challenges.
3. Government must give proper attention for the technology progress in Agriculture through appropriate policies and implementation.
4. Investment on agricultural research from all agencies i.e., Government, Private Sector and N.G.Os., is a must. The present investment in agricultural research is only 0.46 per cent in agricultural G.D.P. as against 2 percent in advanced countries.
5. It is desirable that the investment in agricultural research activities to be undertaken by Government, so that there will not be monopoly trends and vested interests.
6. The Government in developing countries having

budget deficits are not able to spend enough financial resources for Agriculture. In federal system, the responsibility of progress of agriculture and providing necessary infrastructure lies on the State Government. Avoiding wastage of water, and energy resources, use of recycling methods, ecofriendly agricultural practices are to be promoted by the State Government. Technology should be in such a way that the goal of Food Security to be activated with reasonable prices affordable by the common man. Towards this both the central and state governments should take action.

7. Technology should be developed in such a way that there is sustainable growth in agriculture. For this, there is need for the blend of traditional knowledge regarding agricultural practices and bio-diversity with the modern techniques, so that ecological balance of the earth is concerned. Measures to restore soil fertility, better and fuller utilization and conservation of water, at individual farm level as well as at the level of medium and major Irrigation Dams. Use of modern irrigation methods such as sprinkle and drip irrigation will have to be expanded for better yields in dry areas.
8. Improvement in agricultural marketing services, storing facilities, agro-extension services and appropriate pricing policies will provide incentive to the farmer to increase production as well as marketable surplus.
9. In recent times, the need for agro-processing services has immensely increased. Large investments in these become crucial for the expansion of agricultural exports by stopping the wastage of large proportions of horticulture and other products.
10. In view of the severe competition on external front, Government should take proper measures and make agriculture a cost-effective and profitable business and successful trade partner in the world market.

Lastly, it can only be said that there is no time for relaxation. It is time for bold decisions and quick and efficient implementation, in the right direction on the part of the Governments, both Center and States. Our country must stand firm in facing the liberalization and globalization pressures and exploitary strategies imposed by the advanced countries in the guise of W.T.O. Our ultimate goal will be the well-being of the farmer and the entire society, through sustainable progress in Agriculture.

5

INDIAN AGRICULTURE AND MAJOR CHALLENGES

I. Annapurna

Introduction

The basic need of a human being is air, water and food. We need not procure air and water, which are abundant on the globe. The only thing is we should not pollute and waste them, and the next essential is food which can be obtained only from agriculture. Majority of nations that gave importance to agriculture profited optimum. For example: US is able to dominate the world primarily through agricultural suppliers only. China has built 40% of the world's total agricultural dams and reservoirs. Though Israel is geographically situated in a harsh and scarce area with respect to rains it can manage the minimum available water with highest efficiency with the support of sprinklers and drip irrigation with optimum government subsidies. In all these cases government subsidised 40 to 80% of the investments needed in agriculture. At this juncture of the best developing stage, India is being misguided by western influential nations through World Bank not to invest on agriculture and electricity with the government funds, and this may adversely affect our Indian agriculture, productivity may result in negative targets and hence it may lead to dependence from a self reliance state.

Water Management

The total volume of water rains on India is equivalent to

total rainfall on USA. But, the difference here is USA is 2½ times bigger in area than India. That is, the rainfall in India is 2½ times denser, i.e. 400 million hectare meters of rain water is falling on India and the river basins are catching an estimated volume of 187 million hectares of water. But, the reservoir capacity at present in India is only 17.4 million hectare meters. That is, we can tap only 4.35% of our rain resource. In addition to the rainfall, we have 43.2 million hectares of ground water sources. Out of this only a fraction has been in actual utilisation. It is a natural gift to the Indian subcontinent. But our farmers, the planners or the government are not able to utilise properly. One of the examples regarding farmers—(1) Indian farmers are using 25 times more water than American farmers (California) for the production of cotton, (2) One ton of paddy needs 1000 tonnes of water but our people use a number of times more. Now taking into consideration the actual land under irrigation is 91 million hectares out of 320 million hectares aerable land.

In order to rectify today's masor economic problems of India we have to deal with the situation suitable to our nation. But running after the advanced nations in the name of globalization, market economisation, liberalisation, privatisation and so on and so forth. Because India is the denser popular country, majority population in this country are lying below poverty line and more than 70% are in agricultural sector. And we can synchronise our economy with that of the Global only by improving the productivity of the agriculture, only with the available resources in the country itself, so that we can stand competitively in the world agriculture commodity market and money markets. This is the only real alternative to compete with the fast depleting Indian fiscal situation.

In my opinion if we want to rebuild our economy through industrialisation, it needs latest advanced technology which is in the grip of developed nations. Our technological infrastructure is not at par with them. So the only alternative to stabilise present economic doldrums is through sustainable agricultural practices only, as nature has given the best resources to India.

Production Challenges

At present the population of the nation is estimated around 1000 millions and 53% of the population is under 5 years of age i.e. around 550 million excluding the population growth ratio. If you take the present population as standard total, the food demand of adult is 4 times that of a child of below 5 years i.e. the demand for foodgrains by 2020 will be four times to that of present day demand. That is if the present day demand is 200 million tonnes, by 2020 it will became 600 million tonnes. But at the present rate of production, this is almost impossible because the government is not able to take positive steps to improve the incentives for better agriculture production. The rate of growth of population is becoming faster and faster. Since we are not able to control the population growth because of the region, political reasons are interfering with the family welfare programmes of the government and the result is failure in population regulation and it will lead to food crisis and nutritional deficiencies.

In order to overcome these surmounting demands we have to modernise our agricultural system, consolidate the rate of production, increase the aerable land to irrigational land because irrigational lands can only give the standard estimated productions overcoming weather anamolies.

In my observation I found that the production rate of agriculture is stable and at par with average world standards in irrigated areas. But it is only less than 30%, but the remaining cultivation is rain fed. To improve systematic irrigation the foremost thing is to curb the river water disputes between states. This problem is preventing speedy completion of irrigation projects at estimated costs. Because of the river water disputes and court interventions, the planned projects are delayed decades together, sometimes half centuries. Because of this constraint we are loosing millions of tonnes of production and trillions of rupees. To deal with this menace the whole water in India should be nationalised and the planning and execution should be under a national level autonomous corporation, without any interference and influences from politicians and State Governments. Simultaneously the Government should act in a systematic long-termed planned way keeping in mind the long term direct and indirect economic benefits of overall production. I am specifically mentioning this opinion because today's Governments are thinking that supply of electricity to agricultural sector is a burden to the States. But these Governments are forgetting the facts that the agriculture produce generated through farming with the help of electricity is also a major raw material for the industry, which is again a livelihood for lakhs of people. And I have already mentioned that control and regulated irrigation can only optimise the agriculture production at competitive levels. This is the need of the hour. The other incentives which are carefully to be subsidised for the agricultural sector are irrigation equipments like drippers, sprinklers and ploughing equipment etc., and better seeds and fertilizers.

If we can manage to improve the productivity of agriculture by implementing the above said reforms, we can reduce the cost of production of the agricultural commodities which in turn can contribute to cheaper industrial raw materials. In turn the industry can produce essential commodities at lesser production costs and in turn the market will show positive index, so that the Government's burden of Dearness allowances and other variable expenditure comes down and with that the budgetary deficits can be reduced considerably.

This is the way through which we can improve our fiscal position by rendering proper encouragement to our agricultural sector. It is the only option left to India, which is technologically underdeveloping nation. This relief in expenditure of Government maintenance can be diverted to agriculture subsidisation sector so that it can again extra vitalise total production sector i.e. agriculture and industry.

Aqua Culture

The basic element to improve the overall health and vigour depends upon required intake of all the 21 amino acids i.e. in terms of proteins, until 60's. Indian population is deprived because of inadequate production and supply of protein food. To meet this deficiency the Indian farmers have taken up aqua culture on a massive scale for the production of fish, latter the prawn. In India the farm community is highly unorganised and uneducated majority with very small land holdings. The National level planning and production is out of their intellectual limit. So the burden of planning solely lies with the Government and its advisory boards. But, to my analysis and survey in building fish tanks or prawn ponds, there is no uniform planning or pollution control in case of incoming water or outgoing water and roads for transportation. It appears everything is irregular. With the same amount of water, land resources, if the tanks and ponds are constructed in a planned and orderly way facilitating with fresh water canals, drains, roads and trsnportation the production can be four-fold at International standards with minimum hassle of infection and diseases. But, unfortunately things are leading to the wrong direction. Soon after the first phase of reforms, every sector is attaining the commercial and corporate culture. The same situation is prevailing in aqua culture too. Here to my expectations, the Government institutional research and guidance is not able to cope up with the world aqua cultural trends.

For example: (1) When there is high incidence of viral infection in prawn in Taiwan, we have not have able to identify the threat of the disease on our farms; unknowingly we have imported prawn feeds from Taiwan and acquired the viral contamination from it too. (2) About the fresh water prawn, Isreal is an expert in this area and they have developed better strains and mechanisms of developing Neelakanta prawn and other advanced high yielding varieties. But, we are not able to guide farmers in this direction successfully.

Since ancient times, the population of Indian sub-continent is mainly dependent upon agriculture. Artisonary i.e. production of clothing, domestic utilities, cosmetics, sculptures and other goods and implements making is a part time job for the same agricultural workers during off-season time. After the entry of the British the rural cottage industry was completely destroyed and mass production systems evolved and organisation started to grow. Even after the organisation and industrialisation 70% of the population are still directly depending upon agriculture. Due to organisation and its white collar jobs the agriculture lost its glory and importance. Because of the urban nature of the administrations the farming community deprived from all its rights. The major deficiency in law production rates is lack of importance in the profession and management, while calculating the agricultural commodity prices the Government is reluctant to recognise the managerial remuneration in the production of the agricultural sector. And the agricultural investment finances are totally inadequate, the technology available to the farmers not up to the global standards. And the investment which are needed to update the agricultural system for higher production at par with the better production nations are not at all competitive. The limited resources of the nations are diverted to the non-planning and unproductive sectors. For example: unproductive subsidies and advertisements of the government.

In order to increase the irrigation facilities from river waters, the topography of land should be positive to the canal systems from irrigation river projects. So it has its own limitations. The next alternative is the ground water; to lift ground water from under ground sources, electricity supply is the main infrastructure needed. Because of the Government's non-planning expenditures and social welfare schemes they neglected the electrical production sectors due to lack of funds. At least even now itself if the Governments and political parties as a whole by stopping the election strategies with welfare programmes by tax payers money, we can improve the bleak and gloomy situations to the brightest production targets.

To improve the food production the other inputs needed are fertilizers and pesticides. The chemical fertilizers nitrogen, phosphorous and potassium are the main ingredients needed as the main plant nutrients. Since the Nitrogen fertilizer's production is directly dependent on petroleum, it is a deficient raw material in India, so the major part of the nitrogen fertilizers is imported. The prices of Nitrogenous fertilizers are always fluctuating and it always needs government subsidy or protection to keep their prices standard. Unfortunately we are lacking the phosphorous and potassium raw materials also. So India has to depend upon imports for all its fertilizers needs. To minimise the situation the Government is undertaking bio-fertilizers improvement programmes.

Pesticides are another major input needed for plant protection and better yields, even adverse pathological conditions. Though it is an important sector India has not able to produce its own chemicals for its own environment and pests. Since 1930's we are dependent on European and American research pesticides and chlorinated hydro carbons, for example: DDT, BHC and endrins etc. Organo phosphorous chemicals, Ex: monocrotophose, endosulphones etc. Synthetic pirathroides etc., almost all the compounds related to these groups are formulated at their atmospheric and pathological conditions, which are not 100% equivalent to our conditions. That is why we are not getting optimum results at the use of these chemicals. So our farmers are deprived of health and wealth, a poor farmer is committing suicide. It is a definite failure and a challenge on the part of the Government policy-makers and our agricultural scientists.

Credit, Finance and Marketing

Due to globalisation we are facing competition in price and quality in agricultural products, for example, the International prices of rice are below 200 dollars per ton but our farmer can seu his product at above 250 dollars a ton only because of higher cost and lower rate of production. And we are also behind many countries in market techniques. For example, the processed Cashew kernels to Europe are marketed through Singapore and Malaysian agents which are exported from our country. Though we are producing millions of tonnes of mangoes we are in a position to export only a few thousands of tonnes. Though we produce the world class Basmati Rice we are facing stiff competition from Pakistani Jasmin rice in International markets. These examples show that there is a lot more to be done by the Indian Government and the corporate sector for the marketing of our agricultural products. Because the individual Indian farmer is a poor peasant to promote his produce in International markets. While receiving imports too we are showing some weaknesses in commanding, balancing and synchronising the domestic prices with that of imported one's. For Ex: Taking the edible oil market into consideration, while importing palm oil from Malaysia and Nigeria, Soyabean oil from USA and sunflower oil from CIS countries under WTO condition the Government has shown its inability to increase the import duty upto the mark. So that our domestic oils can compete with foreign oils in order to keep the Indian farm economy at balance. That is why domestically produced oils are facing dwindling markets. So all these examples are reminding us that we must adopt more scientific and wholehearted approaches to reach the global competitive commercial atmosphere.

As India is one of the denser populous country we have to consider too many things while making economic policies of agriculture, financing and industrialisation, marketing, subsidising etc. Here we have achieved a lot in creating a healthy atmosphere in the credit structure of farming community by nationalisation of banks and opening up agricultural bank branches in rural areas, by starting NABARD and the co-operative land mortgage system and rural agricultural co-operative credit societies system. Essentially the loaning policy has been devised keeping in view the overall employment and development of the farming community. Though the system has been developed the allotments are too meagre to encourage the gigantic agricultural sector of India at international standards.

Inspite of these measures our agriculture is not supported by the Government at par with the developed nations. The developed nations are heavily protecting their agriculture, so that they can produce optimum level, and command the World markets and prices with quality and quantity. At the same time the developing countries are discriminating the agricultural sector against the domestic industry and over valued exchange rates (Bautista and val des 1989). The terms of trade are deliberately kept unfavorable to agriculture in keeping with the prevailing wisdom to "extract" surpluses from this sector for promoting industrialization.

6

INDIAN AGRICULTURE—MAJOR CHALLENGES

P. Sai Latha

Introduction

The year 1991 saw the emergence of the 'crisis-driven' economic reforms in our country with the three pious *mantras* of Liberalisation, Privatisation and Globalisation with ambitious goals of high growth rate, enlargement of employment potential and reduction of incidence of poverty. But the reforms failed to make an appreciable impact on the latter two.

- The growth rate during 1993-'94 to 1997-'98 was over 7%, which is not a mean achievement; but this growth failed to make its dent on poverty and employment.
- The rate of growth of employment declined to 1.1% during 1990-'91 to 1997-'98 as against a growth of 2.41% achieved between 1983 and 1990-'91.
- The percentage of people living below poverty line declined from 44.48% in 1983 to 35.11% in 1990-'91; but in the post reform period (1991-'97) it increased from 35.1% to 37.23%.

However, the most undesirable flaw of the first generation of economic reforms was the neglect of the backbone of our economy—Agriculture. The very success of economic reforms in an agrarian economy like India is dependent on agricultural development, which has a vital role to play in

- raising the standards of living

- reducing the incidence of poverty
- achieving food security
- achieving economic growth
- expansion of the secondary and tertiary sectors.

As a consequence of the neglect of this sector, the average annual growth rate in agriculture and allied sectors, which was 3.9% during 1980-'81—1990-'91, fell to 3.6% during the post reform period 1992-'93—1999-2000.

The new international economic order that is evolving under the aegis of the World Trade Organisation (WTO) and the state of rural economy in the domestic front call for a set of agricultural reforms. Such reforms can help the sector become globally competitive and domestically more progressive and sustainable. The Government of India announced the National Agriculture Policy (NAP) on July 28, 2000 to this effect. "The policy seeks to promote technically sound, economically viable, environmentally non-degrading and socially acceptable use of country's natural resources-hand, water and genetic endowment to promote sustainable development in agriculture." The Finance Minister in his Budget speech (2001-'02) stated that the Government intends to proceed with the reform process by implementing the second generation of reforms with agricultural and rural development as one of the main objectives. However, it is easier said than done.

Major Challenges

Agriculture has been the prime mover of Indian economy. For centuries, agriculture in India influenced the various facets of human life—traditional, cultural and economic. It would be no exaggeration if we say 'Indian economy means Indian agriculture.' Agriculture continues to be a dominant sector contributing approximately 27.5% to GDP at factor cost and employing 61% of India's working population. Agricultural research brought significant improvements in terms of growth in production and productivity. Green revolution in crops, yellow revolution in oil seeds, white revolution in milk production, blue revolution in fish production and golden revolution in horticulture bear ample testimony to the contributions of agricultural research and development efforts undertaken in the country (Economic Survey 2000-2001). Today, India can boast of being the largest producer of tea, milk, cashew nuts, coconuts in the World, second largest producer of wheat, vegetables, sugar and fish and third largest producer of fruits, tobacco and rice.

Despite the achievements mentioned above, Indian agriculture faces certain challenges on account of the emergence of the new international economic order and rapid growth of population. The major challenges as viewed by eminent agricultural scientists and policy makers are

- Food security
- Urbanisation resulting in increased demand for processed foods
- Generation of employment opportunities
- Environmental degradation
- Globalisation of agricultural trade

Food Security

Increase in population and laws of inheritance result in reduction of per capita availability of land for cultivation and water for irrigation. According to the Economic Survey 1999-2000, the area under food grain production ranged between 123 million hectares and 130 million hectares during the 10 years period 1990-2000. So the area devoted to food grain production has reached stagnation. Further increase in food grains can be achieved only through higher yields per unit of land, water, energy and time. India with its population of 102.7 crores ranks second in the world. India's landscape is only 2.4% of the total world area while its population is approximately 16.7% of the world population. India receives only 1% of the total rainfall in the world.

Given these input constraints, it is now left to science to find ways of raising biological productivity without causing harm to ecology. At this moment, what Indian agriculture needs is not just 'Green Revolution' but **'Evergreen Revolution'** as put forth by Prof. M.S. Swaminathan. The increase in productivity should be sustainable overtime. But it is even more important to ensure that the fruits of this revolution reach the farmer of small means (small and marginal farmers).

Honourable Prime Minister in his speech at the Conference of Chief Ministers on WTO and Agriculture and Food Management stated that we have moved away "from an economy of scarcity to an economy of plenty." It is important to remind ourselves of the pathetic cries of 30 Crore Indians suffering with hunger and starvation while we boast of self-sufficiency in food grain. With the average population growth rate of 1.9% per annum and food grain production growth rate at 1.7% a serious threat to food security is imminent in years to come. If the present levels of food consumption (14 Kg./per capita/month in rural and 11 Kg./per capita/month in urban areas) and present rate of population growth continue, the challenge would be on how to provide 300 million tonnes of food grains to feed the country's population which would reach 1350-1400 million by 2020. But if our teeming population is to be properly fed then we will need 330 million tonnes food grains by the year 2006-2007 itself.

This challenge of food security can be met with the help of substantial **public investment** in agricultural assets, marketing and storage facilities, irrigation, power, rural infrastructure, agricultural research and extension rather than subsidies on agricultural inputs. But there has been a considerable decline in public investment in agriculture during the post-reform period on account of fiscal compression. At constant prices (1993-'94 prices), Gross Capital Formation (GCF) in agriculture fell from Rs. 4467 crores in 1993-'94 to Rs. 3846 crores in 1998-'99, but rose to Rs. 4668 crores in 1999-2000 which is only 25% of total GCF in agriculture. The National Agriculture Policy aims at increasing the public investment for development of rural infrastructure, which can bring about agricultural and rural development.

Considering the **irrigation** needs in Indian agriculture, emphasis has to be given to promote the proven cost-reducing micro-irrigation technology of drip irrigation which helps conserve water, reduce fertiliser inputs and ensures higher productivity. The available irrigation potential should be utilised to the optimum level. At present, the created irrigation potential is estimated to be 94.7 million hectares of which the actual utilisation is only 84.7 million hectares.

Urbanisation

Urbanisation brings down the land available for cultivation on the one hand and increases the demand for processed food and semi processed foods on the other. The latter is because both the husband and wife of nuclear families go out for work.

There has been an increase in purchasing power and more money is available for spending on food. The increasing awareness of the need for balanced nutrition has led to changes in eating habits. There is a growing demand for scientifically processed ready-to-eat foods.

An attempt to meet the demand for processed foods will minimise the wastage taking place on harvested foods due to inadequate storage, improper mode of transportation and packing on one hand while enhancing income and employment opportunities on the other.

Therefore in July 1998 government of India gave the food processing industry the status of 'Sunrise' Industry.

Generation of Employment Opportunities

Agriculture continues to enjoy a dominant place in employment generation. The Ninth Five Year Plan projected the employment growth rate in the three sectors of economy taking into consideration their employment elasticities and projected GDP growth rates. The data reveals that employment is likely to grow from 391.4 million in 1997 to 441.5 million in 2002—an increase of 50.1 million work opportunities. Of this, 24.2 million would be created in agriculture alone. The planning commission emphasises "it is necessary to increase public investment in agriculture especially for strengthening irrigation and other rural infrastructure in backward areas so that sustained agricultural growth and therefore acceleration of employment growth is facilitated." The Planning Commission considers horticulture also to be an employment intensive sector.

National Agriculture Policy seeks to tap the employment potential from agriculture and allied activities such as animal husbandry and fisheries. Programmes like afforestation, regeneration and restoration of degraded land need attention as they generate more employment opportunities while making additions to GDP. As Prof. Swaminathan opines, generation of employment opportunities would also be possible by creating an atmosphere of contract farming, which is of greater relevance in high value crops such as sugarcane, fruits, vegetables, etc.

Since the generation of opportunities for gainful employment is the most challenging task facing us now, and as the agricultural sector will have to provide most of the jobs as stated by the Planning Commission, our approach to agricultural growth should henceforth be more income and employment oriented and not just production oriented.

Environmental Degradation

In a haste to achieve high rates of growth in various sector of the economy, little attention was paid to the damages that the development projects would cause to the environment. There has been an increasing damage to the ecological foundations of agriculture such as land, water, forest, bio-diversity and the atmosphere. This can have adverse effects like global warming, erratic weather conditions, acid rains etc.

Exploitative agriculture offers great possibilities if carried out in a scientific way but poses great dangers if carried out with only an immediate motive. The spread of green revolution resulted in over exploitation of land and water resources and extensive use of chemical fertilisers and pesticides. The latter is an important source of contamination of water bodies. Intensive agriculture and irrigation contribute to land degradation, particularly salination, alkalisation and water logging. Over exploitation of ground water has led to intrusion of saline water making it unfit for drinking and irrigation.

Forests have an important role to play in checking soil erosion, conserving water, controlling floods, balancing carbon-di-oxide and oxygen levels in atmosphere. Unfortunately, the rich forest belt in our country is dwindling due to *Jhum* farming, overgrazing, over exploitation and indiscriminate siting of development projects in forest areas.

India is one of the twelve mega bio-diversity centres in the world; but this wealth is being lost due to expansion of agriculture and impoundment of water in the areas of rich bio-diversity.

The subsidies on power, water and fertilisers have resulted in wasteful and indiscriminate use of these resources causing threat to environment and should therefore be provided only where they are most needed. Environmental degradation challenges the very existence of human race unless serious thought is given to control it.

Globalisation of Agricultural Trade

Agriculture is one of the areas in which India has an inherent strength to dominate the global markets. A major challenge before us is to reduce the costs and raise the productivity and quality of agricultural produce to global standards.

After industry, it is now the turn of the agriculture sector to experience the removal of restraints and controls. The Quantitative Restrictions (QRs) are dismantled, the Aggregate Measure of Support (AMS) is reduced and the agricultural sector of our country is thrown open for international competition. Liberalisation and globalisation of agricultural trade draws our attention to three important subjects

- Trade liberalisation
- Reduction in input subsidies
- Intellectual property rights.

Trade Liberalisation

Trade liberalisation can have significant improvement in the overall income distribution in favour of agricultural sector. Improvements in terms of trade in favour of agriculture will promote faster agricultural growth.

Prof. Ashok Gulati estimated that between 1987-'88 and 1993-'94, prices of wheat, rice cotton and sugarcane were well below prices prevailing in the international market. This study raises a strong argument in favour of trade liberalisation in agriculture. It would however depend upon the policies that would be adopted by other countries and also the future trends in agricultural production in India.

Reduction in Input Subsidies

The member nations of WTO are required to reduce the trade distorting subsidies if they are above permissible levels. Certain subsidy practices in developing countries, which are generally made available to low income, or resource poor farmers were however exempted from reduction commitments. The Agreement on Agriculture (AoA) requires each member to compute AMS, the annual level of support expressed in monetary terms leaving out the exempted subsidies. As per the AoA, India does not have to reduce its domestic support and subsidy to agriculture except for its own fiscal reasons. The present level of support is well below the permissible level of 10% of the value of agricultural production. Prof. Swaminathan hopes that if the developed nations stop giving subsidies to their agro-sector, then, there will be lot of scope for the Indian agro-sector. Global agricultural trade will then be an instrument of prosperity to India.

Intellectual Property Rights

Introduction of Intellectual Property Rights (IPR) regime

for seeds and plant varieties as a part of globalisation of Indian agriculture brought in Multi National Companies (MNCs). Bio-technology advance has helped the MNCs in evolving new hybrid varieties of seeds. They are leaving no stone unturned for tapping the vast market opportunities in developing countries like India. If the MNCs incorporate genetic use restriction mechanisms known as 'Terminator' seeds in hybrids, then the small farmers will experience genetic enslavement since their agricultural destiny will be in the hands of a few companies. The impact of Genetically Modified Organisms (GMOs) on human health and environment is not fully understood. So the farmers should be warned against the use of such seeds.

Bio-piracy: India should be alert about bio-piracy. To prevent huge losses it will have to undertake huge documentation about the use of its herbal wealth. For instance Indian ancient use of turmeric was sought to be patented under the American Law in 1995. Fortunately, Dr. R.A. Mashelkar, Director General of CSIR, prevented it. An American company has been granted a patent right for *Neem* as a pesticide. *Basmati* rice, which was universal variety in India, was patented as *Kasmati* and *Texmati*.

The Government of India, so as to protect its plant varieties and farmers' rights had introduced a bill called Indian Plant Variety and Farmers' Rights Bill (Indian PVFRB) in 1999. This bill has unique features such as:

- Opportunity for registration of extant varieties
- Registration of farmers' traditional varieties by communities of NGOs on their behalf and
- Constitution of National Gene Fund.

Knowledge should be made an important resource to make Indian agriculture globally more competitive and domestically more progressive. India should not look at the challenges thrown by WTO with pessimism that it would remain forever an importing country and that it is incapable of offering intellectual property to the international market. In addition to the potential Indian Scientists have, ten thousand entries of innovations, outstanding examples of traditional knowledge with Honey Bee Network provide ample evidence of our substantial intellectual property.

Conclusion

With more than 80% of India's poor living in rural areas, boosting agricultural growth is critical to raising rural incomes and living standards. The challenge is to create a link between the world of science and the poor. Given the input constraints, small farm holdings and growing proprietary science, it is very crucial to step up "public good" research supported from public funds. Such an effort can make the fruits of scientific research accessible to the poor farmers and improves their incomes. This will be helpful in improving productivity in agriculture.

India with its diverse soil and climatic conditions has ample scope to harness the opportunities emerging on account of globalisation of agricultural trade. Demand for fruits, vegetables, flowers and herbs is fast growing in advanced countries. Adoption of precision farming in production of these commodities will reduce the costs. Opportunities emerging in the area of processed and semi processed foods both in the internal and external markets should be tapped. As our Honourable Prime Minister stated 'India can avoid pitfalls and seize the prospects of freer global trade in agriculture only if we treat this as a *'National Mission.'* In this context he called for collective and coordinated action by Central and State Governments, agricultural universities, farmers, Krishi Vigyan Kendras and all those associated with agriculture. **In the new millennium, the nature, the humanity and the technology must work in harmony to make agriculture sustainable.**

It would not be over ambitious to hope that India with its enormous intellectual property—traditional and contemporary—and rich biological diversity should transform from being a technology recipient country to a global leader in offering sustainable technologies.

"Whenever you are in doubt, or when the self becomes

too much with you, apply the following test. Recall the face of poorest, and the weakest man whom you may have seen, and ask for yourself, if the step you contemplate is going to be of any use to him. Will he gain anything by it? Will it restore him to a control over his own life and destiny? In other words it will lead to Swaraj for hungry and spiritually starving million."

—Mahatma Gandhi

These were the words of wisdom by the Father of our Nation seventy years ago. Translation of these words into actions will make the people less selfish and socially and morally responsible.

REFERENCES

1. Agricultural and Processed Foods Export Development Authority (APEDA): *Indian Agriculture 2000.*
2. Ashok Gulati, IFPRI, 2001: *Trade Liberalisation and Food Security.*
3. Bhandare, S S, Business Line, June 26, 2001: *Agriculture sector—Paradox of plenty.*
4. Department of Agriculture and Co-operation: *National Agriculture Policy.*
5. Editor, Indiaagronet.com: *Indian Agriculture—Challenges and potential.*
6. Government of India: *Economic Survey 1998-'99 and 2000-'01.*
7. Hanumantha Rao, C H, Economic and Political Weekly—Special Articles, September 8, 2001: *WTO and Viability of Indian Agriculture.*
8. http://www.sristi.org/, *Implications of WTO for Indian Agriculture—The case of intellectual property rights and emerging bio-safety protocol.*
9. http://www.worldbank.org/data/, The World Bank Group: *India at a glance.*
10. Jha, Dr. Satish C., Observer Research Foundation—Seminar Report: *India's Food Security Remains Vulnerable.*
11. Kalyana Sudaram, M, Deccan Herald, November 4, 2001: *Need for action.*
12. Kohinoor Mandal, News Report in the Financial Express, January 12, 2000: *Agriculture sector to face five major challenges, says M S Swaminathan.*
13. Misra, S K and Puri, V K, 2001: *Indian Economy.*
14. Prime Minister Sri Vajpayee's speech at the Conference of Chief Ministers, New Delhi, May 21, 2001: *WTO and Agriculture and Food*

Management.

15. Ruddar Dutt and Sundharam, KPM, 2001: *Indian Economy.*
16. Sahay, Prof. K.B., Observer Research Foundation—Seminar Report: *Foodgrain Production in India Myth and Reality.*
17. Swaminathan, Dr. M S, ASCI Foundation Day Lecture, 1979: *From Begging Bowl to Bread Basket.*
18. Swaminathan, Dr. M S, CGIAR/NAS Biotechnology Conference, October 21-22, 1999: *Genetic Engineering and Food, Ecological and Livelihood Security in Predominantly Agricultural Developing Countries.*
19. The World Bank Group, News Release No. 98/1681/SAS: *India to bridge agriculture technology gap with World Bank support.*
20. Vyas, V S, Economic and Political Weekly—Perspectives, March 10, 2001: *Agriculture: Second Round of Economic Reforms.*

7

TOWARDS ASCERTAINING A SUSTANABLE PATHWAY FOR INDIAN AGRICULTURE

G. Sudhakar

India, predominantly an agriculture economy has to certainly rely on agriculture for higher growth rate of economy. Unless atleast a minimum moderate growth rate in agriculture is supported, the overall growth rate of the economy will no longer be sustained at expected heights. This is quite clear from the past ten years experience of economic reforms and Globalisation. The complementarities between the present goals of efficiency, equity and sustainability in Indian agriculture outweigh the trade-offs, if any between them. India has adopted two different development statergies until now for faster economic growth, based on two different idealogies. One was under Nehru's socialism, in which, "state enterprises were expected to attain the commanding heights of economy." But that ended in a fiasco. Now a new startegy has been adopted, under the name of "Economic Reforms." The ecstasy of this idea is now subdued due to lopsided economic reforms.

Indian agriculture is now experiencing a paradox of sorts, sluggish growth, long term decline in public investment, declining yield rates, mounting stocks of Cereals and lower offtake from the PDS, shattering food security, input illusions, decline in employment and natural calamities leading to increased underemployment. The poor performance of agriculture turned the agriculturists become poorer not only in comparison with non-agriculturists but also in absolute terms and per capita availability of foodgrains has also been declined. If the largest population of the country become poorer and undernourished then what is there to rejoice? Removal of malnourishment among children and consequent deaths, removal crude poverty in rural sector, increasing employment potential inversely reducing the numbers depending on agriculture and use of natural eco-systems more efficiency.

Withering Growth Rates

Falling rates in Indian agriculture have greater concerns on policy modulations for growth of the economy. No doubt the long term track record of agriculture growth is fluctuating but as encouraging rates. During the eighth plan period under the regime of early liberalisation, the country's G.D.P. is poised to be above 6.5 per cent per annum only true to the sustainable growth rate of 2.9 per cent growth in agriculture sector. While G.D.P. during ninth plan (1997-2002) is expected to come down to 5.1 per cent due to fail in growth rate in agriculture to below 1.6 per cent in the first four years of the plan period. But in these four years agriculture population has increased by no less than 1.9 per cent per annum.

Growth rate of food grains and non-food grains production in 1990s compared to 1980s from 3.5 per cent to 1.8 per cent and from 4 per cent to 3.2 per cent respectively. The importance of fertiliser relative to irrigation as a source of growth has increased considerably in recent years. But the per hectare utilisation is still far below that of in developed countries. As no further expansion of suitable land for national primary productivity for human consumption of 40 per cent has been stepped up and the per capita land with rise in population has declined from 0.48 h. In 1950 to 0.15 ha. in 2000. The growth rate of capital formation in agriculture at 1980-81 prices is at 6.05 per cent per annum, whereas its share in total gross capital formation declined from 16.86 per cent to 10.85 per cent during the period from

1989-90 to 1994-95. And in the public sector capital formation in agriculture showed a negative growth rate of 0.13 per cent. Employment in agriculture and allied sectors has registered an overall increase of only 2.5 per cent during 1993-2000. This low growth has serious repurcussions on absolute and relative incomes in agriculture. The per worker value added in agriculture at 1993-94 prices is just around Rs. 12200 compared to Rs. 57559 in non-agriculture in 1999-2000, while the respective figures for 1993-94 being Rs. 10416 and Rs. 42040 respectively.

New Dimension of Food Security

Food security is the major objective of our agriculture policy. The advent of green revolution eased the production front to achieve the self sustainability in food grains and oil seeds production. But the reforms initiated in the country dragged a new dimension to the problem of food security.

Demand for foodgrains is facing a downward shift during the past decade or so leaving more stocks in the godowns unmoved to market, perhaps this is because of change in consumer tastes and preferences as a result of the increasing availability of a wide variety of food items other than food grains. During 1993-2000 food grains prices rose by 76 per cent compared to 37 per cent in the manufactured products. The poor have been confronted with adverse relative prices of foodgrains even with a drop in output of foodgrains and also cash crops in 2000-2001, procurement purchases of both rice and wheat were on an unprecedented scale and buffer stocks of foodgrains rose embarrassingly to 62m. tonnes, by the end of June 2001 from 42.3m. tonnes on the same date in the previous year.

Decline in Public Investment

The most disappointing feature of Indian agriculture is a gradual decline in gross capital formation at constant prices, by both public and private enterprenuers. Gross fixed capital formation in agriculture by the public sector has been declining in all states including resource available rich states.

Decline in private investment may be explained with adverse terms of trade in agriculture. But there is no substantial reason for decline in public investment. Growth rate of the economy depends more on the capital formulation in different sectors. Achieving an expected growth rate of 4 per cent in agriculture can be materialised with 15 per cent capital formation, in the farm sector. But capital formation in the sector come down to just 6.05 per cent of G.D.P. for the last 10 to 15 years. On the investment front the macro-economic stabilisation process launched in July 1991 lead to a fiscal sieze in agriculture sector. Investments on irrigation projects, Research and Development, information and transportation become almost negligible.

It is observed that after implementation of green revolution, the rate of return to public investment in research and extension has been quite high at 60 per cent and 50 per cent respectively. It further stresses the need for increase in public and private investment towards research, extention, gross capital formation and institutional framework. These are the basic pre-requisites for the proper development and diffusion of new technology. These are best ensured by a rational demacration of the relative roles of the state and markets in agriculture. The adverse affect of less public investment has been already depicted by the lower growth rate in agriculture. Unless the situation of slackness in public investment is reverted, it may effect the future growth of sector and jeopardise food security as pressure on the available infrastructure increase and the productivity of current inputs begins to decline.

Soil Conservation and Productivity

Soil erosion and loss of fertility due to floods, cyclones, chemical input use are causing great concerns in the agriculture over the decades. Fluctuating monsoons, rains and irrigation activities led to pumping of more ground water resulting in ridiculous water management, the unregulated exploitation of natural resources is somehow developing environmental problems. Soil erosion or degradation due to salinity, alkalinity, acidity, waterlogging etc. is upto 32 per cent (47 m.ha.) of the net cultivated area of 150 m.ha. Excessive care of using more water and fertiliser without adequate drainage on irrigated lands accounts for the largest decrease in productivity in nearly 20 m.ha. While utter neglect of the rain fed areas cost much of productivity for want of adequate attention to supply of both fertiliser and water. The productivity loss due to the above both amounts to 30-35 per cent.

Protections and Outcomes

Since the means and ends are weak in agriculture, it requires strong support from all sections of the society. Diversity in soils and its fertility, culture practices, irrigation potentials, economic backwardness, market practices, the sector always looked for proper coordinated activity both by public and private sectors. Contrary to the supports expected to agriculture sector, it received a step-motherly treatment. Probably the unorganised nature and widely-spread activity of the sector might not be capable of getting due support. Protections given to agriculture are very thin both in pre-liberalisation and post-liberalisation when compared to concessions to industry. Many studies revealed that expenditure, tax and trade policies have favoured industry and discriminated against agriculture. The once given favours in plan allotments to agriculture were removed in subsequent plans. The cost effective incentives and subsidies given are mis-directed and the benefits were not reached to the poor peasant, who ultimately failed in cost-effective production and stood before Government and private trader with folded hands for want of minimum support price. The apathy of agriculture pricing policy did not save the Indian farmers from debt suicides.

Our efforts to safeguard the interests of agriculture sector at W.T.O. are facing infant obstacles. Transparencies in agriculture procurement, pricing allocations, subsidies and legislations as demanded by developed and E.U. countries during Singapore round and Doho round talks are ready to punish our agriculture interests.

The Tasks Ahead

1. The task ahead for the government is to kick-start the agricultural economy once again to achieve targeted growth rates in G.D.P. at 8 per cent level during tenth plan period and maintain a sustainable growth in order to keep the face of growth of economy. Sustainability as defined requires a dynamic balance among three mutually interdependent components:
   (a) Protection and enhancement of interdependent elements
   (b) Economic productivity and
   (c) Social infrastructure such as jobs, housing, education, health and cultural opportunities. An equitable and sustainable growth can be expected by stepping up output in diversified areas such as dairy production and other animal production, horticulture and floriculture, where demand is more elastic than that for foodgrains. A good harvesting season along with a planned investment only could help in achieving a fairly high growth rate in agriculture.
2. Growth in agriculture can be picked up by reverting slackened public investment in agriculture. More investment is needed in rural infrastructure, especially irrigation, rural roads, in skill development, improving health status of agriculture labourers, marginal and small farmers, rural artisans and assetless farmers. Agriculture subsidies presently exist on critical inputs such as fertilisers, water, electricity and credit. Though not subsidies be lifted for agriculture, but have to be reviewed for their efficient allocation and give impetus to the evolution of cost-reducing innovations and for market competitiveness.
3. In the present shattering situation on the foodgrains front, most cautious and rigid steps are required to

achieve the goal. Foremost is concentrating in the exports of foodgrains as the country has comparative advantage in the production of rice and wheat. The exports will strengthen food security at home since exports can always be adjusted to buffer fluctuations in production for the domestic market. Changing the domestic trade restrictions in order to open up agricultural trade. Opening up of agricultural trade is now treated as boost for overall economic growth rate as the country has a comparative advantage in agriculture. Increased trade will help modernise production, processing and marketing in these sectors.

4. It is not conceivable that agriculture can deliver the expected output without using modern technology like bio-technology. To improve the sustainability of existing farm lands and also to improve the quality and quantity of food supply. Genetic Modification Technology is inevitable. The current initiations in the bio-technology in India are oriented to the needs of large-scale commercial agriculture. This warrants urgent intervention for redirecting the course of investigation, research towards subsistent and substantial farming. The bio-tech research in the public sector have to be furthered inorder to solve the cost factor involved in Genetic Modification seed production to make it affordable to the marginal and small farmers.
5. India has to head the timely advice of international academic bodies to change to a new pathway of improving productivity with available technologies in a way that is environmentally compatible; economically viable and socially equitable for economic yield maximisation with adequate Job opportunities. It may be argued that productivity of inputs is improved through dissemination of new technologies, inputs and input subsidies to the less developed areas.
6. The process of economic reforms should stride over

supply side factors such as technology, fertilisers, irrigation, infrastructure, credit, trade, research and extension that rise aggregate supply response and are the prime movers behind accelerated and sustainable growth of Indian agriculture. The conniving native collaborators with national Governments prior to and after liberalisation and with imported plant breeders after liberalisation are creating all fiascos in agriculture sector in the areas of seed, patent, research, trade and bureaucracy. The best example for it is the recent Basmati rice fiaso. If these betrayals are allowed without checks, there will be no hopes of better performance of agriculture and the hungry farmer has no choice except to tighten his belt on an already very thin waistline.

REFERENCES

Books

1. 'Gatt Agreement, its impact on agriculture, industry: Trips and Trims,' D. Bhorali, Mittal Publications.
2. 'My vision for India's Rural Development,' Jagannath Misra, Vikas Publishing House Private Limited.
3. 'Political Economy of Reforms and Liberalisation,' Edit by V.S. Mahajan, Deep and Deep Publications.
4. 'Indian Economy since Independence,' Edit by Uma Kapilla, Academic Foundation.
5. 'Sustainable Agriculture'—towards Food Security, M.S. Swaminathan, Konark Publishers Private Limited.
6. 'Recent Developments in India Economy,' Edit by Uma Kapilla, Academic Foundation.
7. 'Rural Development,' I. Satyasundaram, Himalaya Publishing House.

8

INDIAN AGRICULTURE AND MAJOR CHALLENGES

V. Saravanan

India is primarily an agricultural country. The importance of agriculture in Indian economy is evident. Agriculture is the largest and most important industry in India nearly 65 per cent of the people in India depend on agriculture either directly or indirectly for their living. It provides 29 per cent of Gross Domestic product and accounts for a sizeable share of total value of the exports.

A massive application of science and technology can enable Indian agriculture to face the serious challenges of poverty, food insecurity and malnutrition.

There is a well-known proverb that *"the Indian farmer is born in debt, lives in debt, dies in debt and bequeaths debt and the 'indebtness' is the only compulsion of the farmer from cradle to grave."*

Our Indian agriculture often faces monsoon crisis and other natural calamities due to climatic change. Even scientists are not able to foresee exactly the change in monsoon.

Salient Features of Agriculture in India

(i) Stagnation and low productivity

Agriculture stagnation has been a bane of the British rule in India. The Britishers never made any serious effort to develop the agrarian economy of India. They only brought about some reorganization in this field mainly to meet the raw material requirements of their own industry. And further under the growing pressure of population on the one hand and lack of investment on the other, Indian agriculture started showing distinct signs of decay. Productivity in Indian agriculture is among the lowest in the world and the provision of land use, the organization of farming, the tools and implements used are all outmoded there by persisting stagnation in this sector.

(ii) Uneconomic land-holdings

Land holdings in Indian agriculture are very small and uneconomic continued process of subdivision and fragmentation have made the land holding ridiculously small, in many cases, unfit for cultivation. And those holdings upon which cultivation is carried on, do not provide enough income to the farmers even to meet their basic minimum requirements. Between 1985-86 and 1990-91, the operational land holdings had increased by 8.1 million or 8.3 per cent operational area, on the other hand rose only marginally by 0.6%; indicating clearly the pressure of population on land.

(iii) Subsistence nature of agriculture

Since over three-fourths of operational holdings are small and uneconomic and productivity in agriculture is extremely low the Indian farmers takes to farming more as a way of life. Rather than any commercial or profitable activity. The tiny farms in agriculture are in the nature of subsistence of forms because the meager production is hardly sufficient for self consumption of the cultivators. There is no scope for commercialization or profit oriented production in a large segment of Indian agriculture.

(iv) Gamble in monsoon

Indian agriculture is aptly described as a gamble in monsoon. Inspite of continuous expansion in irrigation potential, nearly 68 per cent of area under cultivation is still dependent on rainfall which is uncertain, erratic and confined to about four months in a year. Any year of bad rains spells disaster to agriculture and brings misery to millions of people engaged in dry farming areas. Lack of assured irrigation deters agricultural production and restricts the possibility of double or multiple cropping.

(v) Unemployment and poverty

Low productivity and lack of necessary inputs perpetuate the backwardness of agriculture which fails to accommodate the mounting pressure of population on its weak infrastructure. Consequently there is widespread unemployment in this sector which is estimated to be of the order of 20 million persons. Due to lack of farm inputs and in the absence of progressive farm, practices, cultivators do not operate their forms intensively and this results in unemployment on the farms.

Agriculture During the Plans

The place assigned to agriculture in the five-year plans can be best judged from the sum of money allocated to this sector in each one these plans. How much importance an economy attaches to a particular sector is reflected in the scheme of its expenditure and the amount of money allocated to this sector. Judged by this criterion, agriculture has been occupying a very important place in the successive programmes of India's economic development.

The outlay of agriculture has been rising steeply during the successive plans from Rs. 601 crore in the first plan, it rose to Rs. 950 crore in the second, Rs. 1754 in the third, Rs. 36568 crores in the seventh five year plan. Under the Eighth plan, outlay on agriculture and allied activities, irrigation, rural developments and special area programs is proposed as Rs. 96168 crore.

During the first plan, agriculture was given 31% of total public sector outlay. During the second plan, it came to 20%. For the third plan it was 20.5%. The fourth plan outlay on agriculture works out at 23.3% of the total public sector outlay of the plan. In the fifth plan outlay on agriculture and irrigation accounted for 24% of the public sector outlay.

During the seventh plan, outlay on agriculture and irrigation accounted for 22% of the public sector outlay. The proposed outlay on agriculture including rural development, special area programmes and irrigation flood control during the Eighth plan is 96468 crore which is about 22% of the total public sector outlay. During the Ninth plan agriculture and rural development have been accorded quite high priority with a share of 19.4% of the over all allocations.

Food Productions in India

Food grain production in India has reached 200 million tons and moving towards self sufficiency in food grain production. According to the central statistical organization (CSO) the production of rice during Kharif season 1999-2000 was expected to show a grate of 4.2% over the same period.

The country was the second largest producer of vegetables, fruits and flowers in the world.

The agriculture sector has boosted the growth of GDP. It recorded a significant growth contributing to about 2.8% of the GDP as estimated by the central statistical organization. In the export front, the plantation sector generates a massive foreign exchange of Rs. 390 crores is contributed by exports from south India.

Sugarcane is cultivated in more than 110 countries and India stands first in sugar production with around 450 established sugar factories. The biggest hurdle now faced by sugar industries is that due to the open market purchase system adopted by government and controlled supply from the Indian sugar manufactures, massive imports are made by Indian purchases for low price and consequently the domestic sugar manufacturer's market has eroded. Some relief is now required from the government to list up the sugar industry which is purely based on agriculture. In India, 270 lakh hectares of land is used to cultivate oil seeds. It has the distinction of having the largest area under oilseed cultivation in the world. Some of the places have yielded a harvest of 10 ton per hectare against the expected yield of 70 tons per hectare.

Major Challenges in the Indian Agriculture

The India agriculture faces a lot of challenges which need timely consideration so as to enable the country to become self-sufficient in food grains production. They are:

- The total loss of foodgrains suffered in the post-harvest period has been estimated to be 9.33% of total production, of which loss offered in storage accounted for 6.58% and damage caused by insects to food grains accounted for 2.55%. This was an enormous national loss which is equivalent to Tamil Nadu state's two years food grain production.
- Nearly 40% of the land under cultivation in the country has fallen due to decline in rainfall and monsoon disorder.
- Soil erosion affects the quality of the soil, which leads to decrease in nutritional values of food. The food grains loses the capacity of withstanding the storage period due to the poor soil quality.
- The increase in population has made a lot of pressure on the cultivation, on the other side cultivable lands are converted into 'real estates.'
- Migration of the rural population to urban areas has caused decline in the total area under cultivation as they switchover from their agricultural employment to urban labour.
- The hesitation shown by the educated is also a major cause for decline in the cultivation. The rural educated neither do the job of their parents (agricultural labours) nor they are willing to take up agriculture related jobs.
- Lack of adequate procurement center at the required places has been a handicap for the farmers to sell their produce for a fair price.

Suggestions for Promoting Indian Agriculture

- To create awareness among the agriculturists and to introduce latest technological developments in cultivation and irrigation, the mass media, newspaper, street plays, etc., could be used as the effective way to educate them. And the existing strategies adopted on the same line has to be strengthened to suit the practical needs.

- Traditional wisdom in cultivation should be integrated with modern technologies to attain self-sufficiency in food production.
- The decline in the area of cultivable land should emphasize the need to augment production of food production.
- The decline in the area of cultivable land should emphasize the need to augment production of food crops to match the state's population. Efforts should be made to convert wastelands into fertile by allying suitable technology.
- Reducing losses of stored foodgrains and the need to protect foodgrains from pest and other attacks by enhancing effective storage models. It will enable the farmers to protect the grains both quantitatively and qualitatively, retain nutritive value of foodgrains and so on. Large-scale open storage system can be done in closed storage systems.
- More concentration on water management may be made in order to utilize available water effectively and to boost the yield by using modern cultivation methods.
- In order to preserve the natural capacity of the soil and to prevent ground water contamination, frequent use of fertilizers should be avoided and alternative techniques needs to be substituted.
- Government has to establish more procurement centers to protect farmers from distress sale. They could neither sell it nor stock it for a better price. Sometimes, farmers could not meet even their expenses on cultivation as they do not have facility of storing their produce in good condition.
- In India, the dry land/rain area is about 65% of the cultivated land. Effective implementation of watershed

development in a systematic and scientific manner has to be done.
- Post harvest technologies and effective cropping system/pattern are to be adopted on soil type and water availability which gives food security.
- Seed quality test should be carried out at every stage by different test like genetic purity, disease test and physical purity before they are planted.

Conclusion

Jawaharlal Nehru declared in early in 1948 that "everything else can wait but not agriculture." Thus he emphasized the importance of agriculture in nation's development. The nation's economy lies on the core sector, namely agriculture and the industry. As India is basically an agricultural country much importance is given by the government to it. However, due to the large scale non-utilisation of land resources and the poor agricultural practices, the government could to succeed in its efforts. Our country will prosper only if modern agricultural methods, techniques are followed, proper storage facilities are provided and agricultural produces are permitted to be sold for a fair price.

REFERENCES

1. Dr. Ganesamurthy V.S. "Role of Agricultural Technology and Environmental Management in Agriculture" Third Concept, Vol. 14, No. 167, Jan 2001, pp. 21-24.
2. Sahul Hameed S. "Food Grains Production in India: Problems and Prospects" Third concept. Vol. 13, No. 56, February 2000, pp. 34-36.
3. Competition Success Review Yearbook 2000, pp. 18-20.
4. Prof. Swaminathan, M.S. "Growing the food we need," Manorama Yearbook 2001, pp. 554-557.

SESSION–2

INDIAN INDUSTRIAL GROWTH

1

INDIA'S INDUSTRIAL GROWTH—RETROSPECT AND PROSPECTS

K. Nageswara Rao

Though Indian Industrial System has been functioning under the rule of licenses, some relaxations were introduced in the mid-seventies and mid-eighties to accommodate the changing industrial environment. The new Economic Policy and the package of trade policy reforms aimed at (a) declining, deregulating, decontrolling and debureaucratisation of industrial licensing system, (b) encouraging private enterprise by reducing the reservation of priority areas of public sector mainly to promote efficiency and productivity of future industrial growth and (c) opening up Indian Economy to attract investment and technology.

These programmes aimed at access to high technology and world markets for strengthening export activity by the elimination of a substantial volume of import licensing and optional import compression, of course, by protecting the essential imports of sensitive items like petroleum, fertilizers etc. However, India was compelled to accept some conditionalities which were reflected in the structural adjustment programme. As a result, Indian Industrial growth experienced a series of mixed trends during the period of liberalization compared to earlier decades.

Purpose of the Study

In view of this dynamic scenario, an attempt is made in this paper to examine the changes in the Industrial production, to analyse the trends in the industry-wise annual growth rate of industrial production, to explain the composition of industrial employment in public and private sectors, to estimate the effects of dis-investment in public sector units and to suggest some measures to sustain higher rate of industrial growth.

For the purpose, data relating to the industrial production for two decades 1980-90 and 1990-2000 are collected and the average annual values are estimated to describe and compare the industrial performance. Further, to analyse industrial growth during the period of liberalization data relating to 1994-2001 with 1993-94 base year are used.

Industrial Performance during 1980-90

The rate of growth of industrial production was low during 1966-75 because India's planning strategy was conceived in the frame work of a closed economy. It staged a smart recovery during 1975-79 and suffered negative growth rate in 1979-80 due to the second oil shock, the drought conditions and the constant savings proportion to GDP at 16.0 per cent. Hence, the period 1965-80 was treated as the period of industrial stagnation.

Industrial sector launched into a high growth phase during 1980-90, Table 1 shows the industry-wise index of Industrial production and its annual growth rates. It is seen that the general index of industrial production increased significantly during 1985-90. This was mainly due a higher growth performance of mining sector (40.0 per cent), Electricity (60.0 per cent) and manufacturing sector (30.0 per cent).

During 1990-94 the index of industrial production declined by (6.0 per cent) every year. Due to the dismal performance of manufacturing sector and severe import compression. It is reported that export industries suffered a recession and the industrial demand declined significantly. The depressed conditions of 1991-92 of the manufacturing sector were reversed and positive growth rate of 0.6 per cent was recorded in the next year. Cement, machinery, ship-

TABLE 1
INDEX OF INDUSTRIAL PRODUCTION AND GROWTH RATES

Period/ Year	*Mining Quarrying*	*Annual growth rate*	*Manu-facturing*	*Annual growth rate*	*Electricity*	*Annual growth rate*	*General*	*Annual growth rate*
1981-85	139.7	12.7	114.4	5.8	123.1	8.9	118.3	7.0
1985-90	188.1	5.7	146.7	8.8	183.9	9.4	167.9	8.5
1990-94	224.7	2.3	212.5	4.1	191.6	7.2	161.9	4.3
1994-99	121.9	3.3	139.9	6.3	130.8	9.0	137.1	6.0
1994-95	109.8	9.8	109.1	9.1	108.5	8.5	109.1	9.1
1995-96	120.5	9.7	124.5	14.1	117.3	8.1	123.3	13.0
1996-97	118.2	-1.9	133.6	7.3	122.0	4.0	130.8	6.1
1997-98	126.4	6.9	142.5	6.7	130.0	6.6	139.6	6.7
1998-99	125.7	-0.8	148.8	4.4	138.9	6.5	145.2	4.1
1999-00	126.7	1.0	159.4	7.1	141.8	6.6	154.7	6.6
2000-01*	126.6	4.0	162.0	6.2	152.8	4.6	157.3	5.7

Not: *April to December
Growth rates in percentages

Source: Govt. of India, Economic Survey, 2000-2001, S. 37.

building, sugar, cloth, polyester, railway wagons etc., recorded a growth rate over 10.0 per cent.

The general index of industrial production changed by 2.3 per cent in 1992-93 over the proceeding year because the intermediate goods, capital goods, consumer durable and basic industrial achieved a positive growth. The mining sector also registered the same rate of growth while the growth rate of electricity sector was positive (5.0 per cent) but less than the previous year.

During 1994-98 the general index of industrial production staggered because of the inconsistent performance of mining and electricity. Later, the performance of these sectors experienced ups and downs. The recession in the capital goods industries and a fall in the demand for exports due to international recession are responsible for the slower growth rate of industries.

The growth rate of general industrial production was 7.0 per cent per annum during 1980-85 and increased to 8.5 per cent per annum in the next five years. The was attributed to the high rate of growth in manufacturing and electricity industries.

The external debt and foreign exchange crisis of 1991 and the programme of stabilization measures and structural adjustments led to severe import compression and hence industrial growth recorded a steep fall from 8.2 per cent in 1990-91 to 0.6 per cent in 1991-92. Thus, the period of economic reforms began with stagnation of industrial production.

Industrial production staged a steady recovery from 1992-93 and registered a high growth rate in 1994-95 and 1995-96 mainly due to better performance of mining and manufacturing industries. As a result of the positive measures like delicencing of several industries, simplification of procedures, opening-up more areas to the Private Sector, steep reduction in personal and corporate income-tax rates and customs and excise duties. Industrial production recovered to 6.0 per cent in 1993-94 and recorded a high 9.8 per cent in 1995-96. However, it suffered a setback in the following years due to infrastructural bottlenecks, demand recession for consumer durables etc.

Trends in Industrial Employment

Table 2 shows the branch-wise employment in public sector industries during the pre and post liberalization periods. The annual average level of employment in public sector units was 164.94 lakh persons during 1981-85 and it increased to 183.91 lakhs persons during 1985-90. In other words, public sector employment registered an increase of 12.0% during the pre-liberalization period. State Governments have been providing employment opportunities on a large scale followed by quasi-governmental units Public sector annual average employment was nearly 40.0 lakhs before the phase of liberalization.

TABLE 2
INDUSTRIAL EMPLOYMENT IN PUBLIC SECTOR

(Fig. in Lakhs)

Period/ Year	*Central Govt.*	*State Govt.*	*Quasi Govt.*	*Local Govt.*	*Total*
1981-85	32.75	60.37	50.72	21.11	164.95
Percentage	19.85	36.60	30.57	12.80	100.00
1985-90	39.74	67.46	59.18	22.15	183.91
Percentage	21.61	36.68	32.17	12.04	100.00
1990-94	33.95	72.33	64.05	22.18	192.51
Percentage	17.64	37.57	33.27	11.52	100.00
1994-99	31.69	74.18	64.45	22.23	194.55
Percentage	17.32	38.13	33.12	11.43	100.00
1994	33.92	73.37	65.14	22.02	194.45
1995	23.95	73.55	65.20	21.97	194.66
1996	33.66	74.14	64.58	21.94	194.29
1997	32.95	74.84	65.35	22.44	195.59
1998	32.53	74.58	64.61	22.66	194.18
1999	33.13	74.58	3.85	22.59	194.15

Source: Govt. of India, Economic Survey, 2000-2001, S. 52.

A closer examination of the table reveals that public sector employment showed a positive but very low rate of increase during 1990-99. In fact, it increased from 197.51 lakh persons in 1990 to 194.55 lakh persons in 1999. Inspite of delicencing and liberalization the employment in public sector industries was a little more than 2.0 per cent during 1990-99.

Further, it is noted that employment by state and quasi Governments accounted for 37.0 per cent and 33.0 per cent of the total employment after 1991. Except in 1994 the share of employment provided by central government was around 17.0 per cent during 1991-99. The tempo of generating additional employment received a set back during the liberalization phase and infect the average annual employment by Central Government in public sector units declined to 32.58 lakh persons compared to 39.74 lakh persons during 1996-99.

Industry wise employment in public and private sectors during the pre and post liberalization periods is shown in Table 3. Manufacturing units have been the major source of industrial employment in public sector followed by mining and quarrying. In fact, the level of employment opportunities in manufacturing sector has been equal to the level of employment opportunities provided combined by the mining and electricity sectors.

It is noted that employment in mining and manufacturing sectors remained stagnant during 1990-93 and declined afterwards. On the contrary the employment in electricity sector showed a marginal increase during 1994-99. In all, employment in mining and electricity accounted for 5.0 per cent of the total employment during 1990-99 while that of manufacturing sector's share was around 10.0 per cent.

During 1991-99 the average annual employment level in manufacturing sector declined by 0.58 lakhs, it increased by the same rat in mining and electricity sectors. During the post liberalization phase the performance of manufacturing sector has been fluctuating and discouraging, while that of mining sector growth has been encouraging.

Manufacturing sector is the only major area providing

TABLE 3
INDUSTRY-WISE EMPLOYMENT IN PUBLIC SECTOR

(Fig. in Lakhs)

Period/Year	*Mining Quarrying*		*Manufacturing*		*Electricity*		*Total*	
	Public	*Private*	*Public*	*Private*	*Public*	*Private*	*Public*	*Private*
1981-85	9.01	1.04	16.54	45.24	7.24	0.38	164.95	74.29
Percentage	5.46	1.40	10.03	60.90	4.39	0.51	–	–
1985-90	9.57	0.98	18.55	44.19	8.38	0.40	183.90	73.98
Percentage	5.20	1.32	10.08	59.73	4.56	0.54	–	–
1990-94	9.87	1.00	18.58	45.12	9.12	0.40	191.64	77.39
Percentage	5.15	1.29	9.70	58.30	4.76	0.51	–	–
1994-99	9.77	0.97	16.87	50.00	9.49	0.41	194.55	84.39
Percentage	5.02	1.15	8.67	59.25	4.88	0.49	–	–
1994	10.15	1.01	17.84	46.30	9.38	0.40	194.45	79.30
1995	10.16	1.03	17.56	47.06	9.35	0.40	194.66	80.59
1996	9.93	1.07	17.38	50.49	9.46	0.42	194.29	85.12
1997	9.78	0.92	16.61	52.39	9.58	0.41	195.59	86.86
1998	9.37	0.91	16.16	52.33	9.54	0.42	194.18	87.48
1999	9.26	0.87	15.69	51.78	9.62	0.41	194.15	86.90

Source: Govt. of India, Economic Survey, 2000-2001, S. 52.

large scale employment in private sector. The average annual employment in this sector was around 45.0 lakh persons during the pre liberalization phase as against the total employment of 74.0 lakh persons in private sector. During this period employment in mining industry was less than 1.0 lakh persons while that of electricity sector was around 0.40 lakh persons.

In the post liberalization period the average annual employment in mining sector showed a gradual increase. More towards privatization resulted in an increase of employment in manufacturing sector from 44.57 lakh persons in 1990 to 52.39 lakh persons in 1999. On an average manufacturing industry provided 58.0 per cent of total employment in private sector. The level of employment in electricity remained unchanged while that of mining industry showed an increasing trend.

Dis-investment and Trends in Employment

The government strategy towards the public sector has been to encompass a judicious mix of strengthening strategic units, privatizing non-strategic units through gradual dis-investment or sale of weak units. The main elements of the Government policy towards public sector undertakings are (a) to bring down or lower (b) closed own public sector units that can not be revived. On the recommendations of the disinvestments commission thrust was given to the process of dis-investment. The targets and achievements of dis-investment in public sector undertakings during 1991-00 is shown in Table 4.

Though there was no clear strategy and a defined plan for finalizing the level of dis-investment amount, at the beginning of liberalization period the achievement exceeded the target of dis-investment in 1991-92. Surprisingly, no dis-investment took place in 1993-94. Later, less than 8.0 per cent of the targeted amount was dis-invested during 1995-97. With an offer of voluntary retirement scheme, the level of dis-investment was placed at Rs. 10000 crores in 1999-2000. However, the achievement was only 18.0 per cent. It is interesting to note that for the period as a whole (1991-2000) the size of dis-investment was only 42.07 per cent of the targeted amount.

TABLE 4
DIS-INVESTMENT IN PUBLIC SECTOR UNDERTAKINGS

(Rs. in Crores)

Year	*Target*	*Achievement*	*Percentage to Total*
1991-92	2500	3038	121.52
1992-93	2500	1913	76.52
1993-94	3500	Nil	Nil
1994-95	4000	4843	121.07
1995-96	7000	362	5.17
1996-97	5000	380	7.60
1997-98	4800	902	18.79
1998-99	5000	5371	107.42
1999-2000	10000	1829	18.29
Total	**44300**	**18638**	**42.07**

Source: Govt. of India, Economic Survey, 2000-2001, S. 135.

The efforts of dis-investment resulted only in a slower place of withdrawing capital from public sector units, mainly due to the non-cooperation of the bureaucrats. The policy of dis-investment and the voluntary retirement scheme had their effects on the structure of industrial employment. Table 5 shows that sector-wise industrial employment during 1981-99.

It is seen from the table that more than two-thirds of industrial employment was in public sector and the rest was in private sector. The first four years of the liberalization period itself experienced a shift in the share of employment from public sector to private sector. Later, this trend continued every year. This is mainly due to gradual dis-investment in public sector units and encouragement for the scheme of voluntary retirement.

Conclusion

In its process of development India adopted the import substitution strategy at the beginning and later on the

TABLE 5
SECTOR-WISE INDUSTRIAL EMPLOYMENT

Period/ Year	*Public Sector*	*Percentage*	*Private Sector*	*Percentage*	*Total*
1981-85	164.95	68.95	74.29	31.05	239.24
1985-90	183.90	71.31	73.98	28.69	257.88
1990-94	191.64	71.23	77.39	28.77	269.03
1994-99	194.55	69.75	84.39	30.25	278.94
1994	194.45	71.03	79.30	28.97	273.75
1995	194.66	70.72	80.59	29.28	275.25
1996	194.29	69.54	85.12	30.46	279.41
1997	195.59	69.24	86.86	30.76	282.45
1998	194.18	68.94	87.48	31.06	281.66
1999	193.15	68.72	87.90	31.28	281.05

Source: Govt. of India, Economic Survey, 2000-2001, S. 52 & S. 53.

strategy of self-reliance and minimum dependence on foreign resources for production. The performance of industrial sector was not bad and the economic growth was positive after 1966. As a result here was a shift from the import substitution industries strategy to export oriented industries strategy. The 1981 IMF loan and 1985-88 Exim policy confirmed the shift in this strategy. It was particularly during seventies and eighties potential exporters got high export assistance from Government of India.

The industrial growth rates in some sectors, during 1991-95, slowed down indicating an industrial recession. Industrial output fluctuated in a cyclical pattern as a part of normal business cycle and dynamism of the development process. The slowdown in the capital goods industry, and declining annual growth rates mining industry were the causes of concern.

Since 1996-97 the industrial recovery was significant with accelerated growth rates in various sectors of the economy. A good harvest in 1998-99 resulted in greater consumer demand for industrial products, improved capacity utilization, fiscal package including rationalization of excise and customs duty anomalies, tax holiday awarded to infrastructure industries, new programme of rural industrialization and specific measures for the small scale sector are the major factors that are behind the industrial recovery.

However, the average annual industrial growth rate achieved after liberalization is lower than that achieved in the decades before liberalization. The following are some of the measures that sustain higher industrial growth rate:

1. Additional infrastructure facilities commensurate with the increasing requirements of industry are to be created at a faster rate.
2. Priority areas for foreign direct investment need to be clearly demarcated.
3. Enunciation of unambiguous policies and promotion of small scale and ancillary sector is the need of the hour.
4. Cut in the corporate and personal income-tax may rejuvenate industrial demand.
5. Modification of excise duties on intermediate goods and reduction of customs duty on imported raw materials may promote the growth of manufacturing industry.
6. Withdrawing restrictions on maximum permissible bank finance and granting a little more freedom to banks in assessing credit requirements for borrowers may eliminate the shortages of investment funds in industrial sector.

REFERENCES

1. K.C. Sharma, "Perspects in industrial sector since Independence," Indian Economic Journal, Vol. 46, Oct-Dec 1998, Bangalore.
2. Govt. of India (1991), "India's New Economic Policies," New Delhi.
3. B. Majumdar, "From import substitution to open door industrialization, An evaluation," Productivity, Vol. 33, No. 2, July-Sep, 1992.
4. Ahluwalia, Isher Judge, "Industrial growth in India—Stagnation since the Mid-Sixties," Oxford University process, New Delhi, 1985.
5. Govt. of India, Economic Survey 1997-98, New Delhi.
6. Kapila, U., Indian economy since independence 6th Edn., Academic Foundation, New Delhi, 1995.

2

INDIAN ECONOMY—PROSPECTS & RETROSPECT

A CASE STUDY OF HANDLOOM INDUSTRY

K. Kanaka Durga

Handloom Industry—Retrospect

Our country has a rich cultural heritage and the art of hand weaving formed part of it. Handloom industry is an age-old source of livelihood for millions of people in our country. The industry has vast inherent potentiality and has had a glorious past. In skills the handloom weaver is second to none. Being highly labor oriented as it is, the handloom industry, which has a legacy of unrivalled crafts-manship, is an ancient cottage industry with a decentralized set up, spread throughout the length and breadth of the country. There are at the moment, as many as 3.5 million handlooms functioning in various parts of our country. About ten million people are said to be directly depending on this industry to eke out their livelihood, while many more millions of people are dependent up on the subsidiary occupations connected with the handloom industry. India's handlooms are today manufacturing about one third of total cotton cloth required for consumption in the country and for export abroad. Though widely dispersed, a major chunk of this industry is concentrated in the southern states of Tamil Nadu and Andhra Pradesh. Andhra Pradesh has rich heritage of Dravidian traditions. It also absorbed some of the central Asian traditions; the first Morse was built in Machilipatnam by the Muslim trader in the 10th and 11th century A.D.

History has recorded that the handloom fabrics of India not only received popular patronage and adorned regal personages but also won acclaim. Shrouds for the Egyptian Mummies were said to have been supplied by India. In the royal courts of France and England our handloom fabrics were held clear. In the annals of history the travel agents of Fahiyan, Huan Tsang, Warthima, Bernier, Curriri, Tavernier, General Ormi, Marcopolo spell out the glory of the handloom industry of the bygone days.

From the state of glory the industry, step-by-step, limped to a stage where the once lauralled artisan weavers are facing a variety of problems and they even find it difficult to ekeout their livelihood depending full time on the handloom solely. The following are the main causes for the reported position of handloom industry.

Causes of Retrospect

The competition from power looms and textiles has led to the decimation of the handloom sector, which has taken place in both the input and output market. The main reason for this situation is the textile policy of 1985 which permits anybody anywhere in the country to install power looms after collecting a nominal fee it allowed the mushroom growth of powerlooms, and Pvt. 1.39 million handlooms out of work, robbing 5.54 million person of livelihood.

Second reason is the lopsided cotton yarn distribution policy. Handloom industry is once again in serious crisis with the unprecedented rise in the prices of yarn, dyes and chemicals. Non availability of yarn at required quality and quantity too is an endemic problem for the weavers.

The handloom industry requires working capital finance at low rate of Internet, as is the case with other industries, small and big. The weaver co-operatives are tagged only to NABARD.

The fragile nature of weavers' survival is also related to the complex organisational structure of the handloom sector. The agencies for marketing handloom cloth are diverse and numerous. This diversity of the marketing agencies arises chiefly from the unorganized state of the industry itself.

The main strength of the handloom sector lies in the development of new designs with various color combinations. The effort for design development in handloom sector is sporadic and insufficient.

The advertisement in this field has so far been fragmented and is of a local nature.

Absence of Marketing Research is another hurdle for the growth of handloom industry. Co-operatives need fresh concepts on how to organize business and marketing in response to the significant changes that have occurred in the business environment in recent years.

In effective handling of export markets is another cause. This is mainly due to ban imposed on imports, political climate and competition from countries like Japan and China.

Inadequate funds have affected the development of handloom industry. There appears to be a yawning gap between the Governments promises and their fulfillment's. The plight of the handloom weavers who are under the co-operative fold is even worse.

From the above study I may suggest the following suggestions:

The Government of India may revise its textile policy in consultation with the State Governments so as to ensure full employment to all the 3.5 lakhs of handlooms in the Country.

There should be a Commissioner for Handlooms equal in rank of the Textile Commissioner to be exclusively in charge of the development of Handloom industry.

The Government may provide financial assistance to the weavers' co-operative societies to enable them to purchase improved appliances.

The Governments should purchase all their requirements of textiles from the weavers' co-operative societies.

The Co-operative Spinning Mills should produce standard quality of yarn of such counts and required quantity by weavers' co-operative societies.

The RBI should raise the credit limits to primary societies.

There shall be a body of Handloom interests to decide upon the nature and extent of cash incentives to be given on exports of Handloom cloth. Encourage weavers to produce exportable varieties by providing adequate incentives.

Quality is a basic factor. It is a major marketing element. The interest of marketing lies in the fact that the applications of value engineering in the operation of handloom will enable the handlooms to manufacture items to required quality levels. Quality is built best in products, in relation of yarn and all through production and no amount of advertising and sales promotion can sell an interior or poor quality product.

Exchange of information from the weaver to the consumer and *vice versa by* inspecting the production process also useful to maintain acceptable level of quality.

Design has to be proved to be a powerful instrument in the exploitation of the market. If the product is right for the consumer, he or she wants to buy it. It is obviously very important to design a product that is satisfactory and desirable to the customer.

Handlooms should stress the importance of consumer research. In the Research consumers are asked to make all the objections they can about products.

The weavers should be able to face the challenges in the rapidly changing technology. New production and marketing techniques should be developed by the marketeer in maintaining the existing customer and increasing the new ones, because marketing begins with the assessment of customer concerns and ends up with the evaluation.

Restructuring the marketing strategies is the most influential factor in meeting the challenges of the new millennium.

Taking note of the new challenges and opportunities presented by the rapidly changing global environment the industry has to become globally competitive by adopting a modernization program. An important factor inhibiting technology up-gradation is the high cost of capital required for carrying out such a program. The Ministry has therefore, bunched a Technology up gradation Fund Scheme for easy access to capital on softer terms for technology up gradation, and a cluster development approach has been adopted in the handlooms through newly launched schemes called Deen Dayal Hathkargha Protsahan Yojana to provide basic inputs, products and marketing support. In spite of their activities, the Government should take some move measures to protect the traditional art of weaving.

3

ISSUES AND CONCERNS OF RURAL INDUSTRIALIZATION: THE CASE OF DAIRY INDUSTRY IN CHITTOOR DISTRICT OF ANDHRA PRADESH

P. Vasudeva Rao, P. Kothandarami Reddy, and N. Suguyya

The Case for Rural Industrialization

Despite rapid strides in modern industrialization and urbanization 54 per cent of the population in low income countries (with a per capita income of 780 or less) live in rural areas. Poverty of different varieties and dimensions is mostly concentrated in the rural sector especially among the economically deprived and socialy disadvantaged groups. The eradication of poverty and the elimination of hunger have long been recognized as among the most central challenges before human society. Yet today there are probably more human beings suffering from chronic deprivation than ever before in history.[1] The absolute number of those living on 1 per day or less continues to increase. The world-wide total rose from 1.2 billion in 1987 to 1.5 billion today and if recent trends persist will reach 1.9 billion by 2015 according to the World Bank.[2]

The majority of the poor in the Asia and pacific region live in rural areas. Except in a few countries nearly 80 per cent of the poor reside in the rural areas suggesting the overwhelming per cent.[3] Further the share of economically active population in agriculture in India as elsewhere in most South Asian Countries is 64 per cent while the share of agriculture in GDP in 1996 was only 28 per cent. The imbalance between the sector share of output and employment reflects a widening of the disparity between the income levels of the urban industrial sector and the rural agricultural sector. No wonder the rural urban disparity index (RUDI) computed for twelve CIRDAP member countries (CMCs) including India, brings into limelight several rural development concerns.[4] Against this backdrop an attempt is made in this paper to look into the issues and concerns of rural industrialization in India illustrating from the case of dairy industry in Chittoor District of A.P.

Structural Characteristics of Rural Industrialization

The concept of rural industrialization is rather elastic and cannot be easily defined. Traditional cottage and rural industries naturally fall in its domain. Modern small scale industries which are situated in the rural sector also form a subset of rural industry. However, modern large scale enterprises which do not have forward and backward linkages with rural economy are generally excluded even if they are situated in the rural belt. The structural characteristics and technical coefficients of urban industry differ significantly from rural industry. It may be of academic interest to set forth some of these features in a tabular form (Table 1). The list of attributes and characteristics of rural industry in relation to urban industry presented in Table 1 is not exhaustive, it is only selective and hypothetical because it is not possible to maintain the rural-urban dichotomy and its corresponding economic, social and technological dualism because of the convergence of market forces and the operation of rural-urban continuum. Nevertheless this statement helps us to have comparative picture of the nature and the role of urban industry as well as rural industry in a densely populated, agriculture dominated, poverty-ridden economy which has experimented with different development paradigms and industrialization strategies. In the 1990's after the advent of the new economic reforms rural poverty and unemployment have tended not only to persist but also have

TABLE 1
STRUCTURAL CHARACTERISTICS OF RURAL INDUSTRIALIZATION

Sl. No.	*Characteristics/ Coefficient*	*Urban Industry*	*Rural Industry*
1.	Size and Scale	Medium & large	Tiny and small
2.	Organizational form	Corporate	Non-corporate
3.	Linkage	Mostly forward except in the case of agro-based enterprises	Both forward and backward
4.	Capital	From money and capital market	Mostly from own and informal sector
5.	Labour	Skilled and know-ledge based	Un-skilled and semi-skilled
6.	Wages	High	Low
7.	Product quality	High	Low
8.	Market orientation	National and global	Mostly local rarely global
9.	Technology	Sophisticated and mostly modern	Traditional and rarely modern
10.	Management	Trends to be pro-fesssional under competition	Trends to be tradi-tional
11.	Management infor-mation systems	Based on IT	Non IT based
12.	Profitability		
	(a) In the private sector	High	Low
	(b) In the public sector	Low	Low
13.	Capital output ratio	High	Low
14.	Capital labour ratio	High	Low
15.	Import intensity	High	Low
16.	Export potential	High	Low
17.	Environmental effect	Adverse	Favorable
18.	Energy intensity	High	Low
19.	Vertical and hori-zontal integration	High	Low
20.	Fiscal effect	Favorable	Not favorable
21.	Distributional effect	Not favorable	Favorable
22.	Sources of entre-preneurship	Commercial and technical beck-ground	Agricultural and traditional back-ground.

Source: Computed

marginally risen. While in 1980s there was a sharp decline in the number of people below the poverty line as well as their ratio, during the reforms period, the proportion below the poverty line went up from 35.1 per cent to 37.2 per cent. In absolute terms, the number of the poor went up from 291 million in 1990-91 to 348 million in 1997. This consequence is being related to sluggish growth in employment as a result of decline in employment elasticity from 0.41 between 1983-91 to 0.1 between 1991-98 as well as rural stagnation.[5]

The Case for Fostering Rural Industrialization

The pattern of economic growth despite its acceleration has not resulted in employment generation at least equal to the rate of growth of labour force. The question of backlog unemployment is a wider and deeper issue with serious consequences for stability of the preservation of democratic governance and social fabric. This type of jobless, ruthless and voiceless growth cannot be sustained on grounds of equality. Even efficiently interpreted in a broader social prospective demands a new development paradigm which is pro-poor. The present market friendly regime benefits those who are qualified enough and socially well placed to take advantage of the opportunities of capital intensive and labour displacing global technologies in production processes. No labour surplus and capital deficient economy can afford to have high capital intensive production techniques often imported from developed countries, as is happening quite often in India.[6] Because of its technological suitability, inherited and acquire skills of local labour, favorable effects on employment generation and thereby poverty reduction, saving of foreign exchange due to limited or zero in import intensity, favourable environmental, distributional effects, contribution to reduction of rural-urban migration and several other positive externalities, despite its adverse effect on the fiscal deficit due to subsidy, rural industry needs to be fostered and enabled to become strong, healthy, efficient and sustainable in India as also in countries under similar situations.

The Case of Dairy Industry in Chittoor District

India holds the first rank in respect of live stock and is reaching that rank in milk production.[7] People often talk of the white revolution after the green revolution. Chittoor District of Andhra Pradesh has also recorded a substantial progress in dairy industry though the potential is yet to be exploited. Dairying on an organized basis was a cooperative enterprise and it is only recently that there has been a spurt in private enterprise in this sector. The Chittoor District cooperative milk union and its infrastructure are given in Table 2. On an average 1 lakh liters of milk per day (LPD) is being processed against the installed capacity of 2.5 lakh LPD. Due to low capacity utilization (40%) and other organizational deficiencies and operational bottlenecks the Chittoor dairy has been running into losses. Nearly 80% of the mili is converted into powder and thee everyday and there are long time lags between sale of these milk products and realization of sales revenues partly due to keen competition from dairy units adjoining the border in Tamil Nadu and Karnataka.[8]

TABLE 2
INFRASTRUCTURE OF CHITTOOR DAIRY—1999

MPCS functioning	448
MPAC functioning but not registered	778
Total	1222
Members enrolled	66290
No. of pourers	37840
Milk routes	47
Milk chilling centers	15
Milk plant	1
Capacity of the plant	2.5 Lakh LPD

Source: NABARD: Potential Linked Credit Plan, 2000-2001, Chittoor, p. 34.

Milk production in the district is estimated to be 8.4 lakh LPD and the dairies in the cooperative and private sector are handling only 3.5 lakh LPD (Table 3). Therefore there is a potential for the growth of dairy units in other parts of the district. The Kalahasti Cooperative Milk Supply

Society (KCMSS) is an instance of small being beautiful. It procures milk nearly to the tune of 5.5 thousand LPD from 27 surrounding villages. It has only one freezer and needs other essential equipment for running its business on hygienic lines. Srikalahasthi town is its market destination. They procure milk at 7.50 and sell at Rs. 8.50. The quantity sold is roughly 3.5 thousand LPD in the winter season. In the flush season the surplus milk is either sold to the chittoor dairy or milk products are made and sold. Low maintenance/operating cost, low overheads, simple operations and less staff contribute to its profitable working.[9] It can be easily replicated at Tirupathi, Madanapalle and other towns.

TABLE 3
PRIVATE DAIRIES

Sl. No.	*Name of the Plant*	*Processing capacity LPD*	*Expansion*	*Total*
1.	Heritage Units at Tirupati	1 lakh (no procurement from producers and collected milk form their other chilling/processing units)		
	Piler	37500	6500	44000
	Chittoor	37500	12500	50000 (already achieved)
	Madanapalle	37500	6000	43500
	Santhipuram	25000		
2.	Bangarupalem Dairy	40000		
3.	Siva Sakthi Dairy	5000		
4.	Vintage Dairy	5000		
5.	Ravi Leela	5000		
6.	Sai Krishna	5000		
7.	Mayuri	5000		
8.	Bala Murugan	20000		

Source: NABARD Potential Linked Credit Plan, 2000-2001, Chittoor, p. 35

Linkages, Resource Gaps and Prospects

Dairy industry in the district as in any other region has

backward and forward linkages. Production of milk is a function of the quality and number of milch yielding cattle. Milch cattle unit is the most preferred scheme under IRDP in the district and therefore there is scope for the maintenance and improvement of milch cattle stock. Fodder is as important as the feed. The fodder gap in the district is estimated to be 21.2 lakh tonnes. The credit gap for the milch cattle development is estimated to be at Rs. 3.00 crores.[10] Milk and milk products have a high income elasticity of demand and therefore, marketing may not be a major hurdle in dairy development. Fortunately Chittoor district has a natural advantage in terms of proximity to Chennai and Bangalore. Tirupati is a growing urban conglomeration and can absorb large quantities of milk. But the problem is procurement of milk from villages which are not endowed with pucca roads. Therefore, the development of pucca roads linking all villages will give a boost to the sustained development of dairy industry in the district.

Concluding Remarks

Rural industrialization is the most appropriate strategy of employment generation and poverty reduction on a sustainable basis. Rural industry itself is undergoing dynamic transformation, technological modernization, managerial transition and business acumen to suit the needs of changing consumer needs and preferences. However, it needs state support because of its structural deficiencies in relation to urban industry and its positive externalities. The case of dairy industry in Chittoor district is illustrative of the constraints and prospects. The urban centers depend upon the supply of milk from the rural areas and milk processing units are working well in the private sector. The cooperate dairy at Chittor has run into financial troubles and is slowly recovering. But the case KCMSS is a shining example of small being beautiful and can be easily replicated. We need not look for models from outside the country. There are plenty of such models provided, there is a motivation and entrepreneurship at the grass roots level. It is hoped that they be identified and promoted by the state initiative despite its limitations as a promotional agency.

REFERENCES

1. IFAD: Rural Poverty Report, 2001, Oxford Publishers, p. iii.
2. The World Bank: World Development Report—Attacking Poverty, 2000/2001, p. 3.
3. CIRDAP: Rural development Report 1999, Dhaka, p. 8.
4. *Ibid,* pp. 8-12.
5. Ruddar Datt: Market-led growth, The Hindu Business Line, Feb. 1, 2001.
6. *Ibid.*
7. NABARD: Annual Report, 1998-99, pp. 87-88.
8. Chittoor Dairy: Office Records.
9. KCMSS: Office Records.
10. NABARD: Potential Linked Credit Plan 2000-2001, Chittoor, pp. 34-45.

4

THE INDIANISATION OF MNCs : ISSUES AND CHALLENGES

NVR Jyoti Kumar

Many global players sensed tremendous marketing opportunity in India with the opening up of the economy since 1991. Any MNC's overall business strategy continuum ranges between the two extremes of pure localization and a rigid global template. The dilemma faced by an MNC is whether to extend the same internationally popular brand names to the Indian market or to acquire local brands. The experience of many post-liberalization MNCs proved that their survival and success in India essentially depends on their ability to understand and to adapt to the local conditions. The crucial question is how can a company remain a transitional in India and still be as flexible as the domestic companies? *Business Today's* recent study made an attempt to answer that question. The study examined the strategies employed by the 17,000 transnationals which have entered the country with a collective investment of more than $44.20 billion since the New Economic Policy of 1991, and sought second opinions from more than 20 management and strategy specialists. The present paper is intended to identify the strengths and weaknesses of the marketing strategies adopted by some of the post-liberalisation transnationals.

The following examples reveal the glaring differences in the marketing performance of MNCs in certain Indian markets:

- After five years in India, Kentucky Fried Chicken (KFC) is struggling, with four outlets, while McDonald's has already 16 in just three years.
- Lee has 35 per cent of market share in the premium jeans market, whereas Levi's, the original American Jeans, has been suffering from poor customer perceptions.
- Sony TV, beaming just one channel, took only two years to achieve a turnover of Rs. 220 crores while Rupert Murdoch's Star TV, with seven channels in its armoury only expected to achieve Rs. 300 crores in 1999, even after its existence in the country over seven years.
- Hyundai has sold 20,000 Santro cars by 1999 against 5,000-odd that Matiz from Daewoo has against its name, though both hit the market almost at the same time. It is interesting to note that the Matiz sells the Atoz (the Santro by another name) across the world.
- Motorola launched all seven of its cell phones, but did not find a market in India. But Nokia which entered with only two models achieved tremendous success.

The Entry Strategy

The dilemma faced by a MNC is whether to extend the same internationally popular brand names to the Indian market or not. The marketing concept holds that consumer needs vary and the marketing programmes will be more effective when they are tailored to each target market. This also applies to global markets where political, economic and cultural conditions vary significantly. In India, Kellog found it a challenging task to change the breakfast habits of local customers who tended to eat heavy food. In the first year, Kellog continued to sell its globally-developed cereals in India without bothering about the local palates and eating habits. Its high pricing strategy only helped the local competitors to cash in on the awareness it has created. MTV which had originally positioned as a medium for Western music has now shifted its prime-time viewing to Indian music. Coca-cola acquired four brands from the Parle (its popular brands: Thumps-up, Limca, Gold Spot and Citra) with a view to give boost to its Coke. Now the company revived all the four brands to improve its overall market share.

The multinationals, therefore, have to see themselves not as a transnational operating in India. They have to perceive themselves as an Indian Company, catering to the Indian needs, within the Indian environment. It is to be noted that serving the local needs and competing on global brand images are not mutually exclusive. It is possible for a brand to adapt to the local environment without diluting its global image.

Pricing

Bringing in global brands with dollar-pricing would amount to wrong positioning of the product. Many MNCs entered the Indian television market with premium pricing. But they realized later that their products were out of the reach of a large number of customers. They further realized that unlike their foreign counterparts, the Indian customers are slow in replacing their TV sets. Perhaps this prompted the MNCs to come out with the exchange offers. Some MNCs have evolved a strategy to exploit the vast rural market which is price-sensitive.

When it entered the Indian Jeans market in 1995, Levi Strauss had the advantage of being known as the American company that invented jeans. Its objective was to cater to the needs of the up end of the market by establishing the brand's premium positioning. But by mid-1998, the management realized that their 27 exclusive retail outlets could not attract teenagers who perceived Levi's was too expensive, that it has jeans only for Rs. 2,000 onwards. According to an estimate, 80 pe: cent of all jeans are purchased by those in the 15-24 age group and it seems the company ignored a factor that such people in India do not have incomes of their own. On the other hand, Levi's competitor Lee launched a range priced between Rs. 995

and Rs. 1,995 in the same year as Levi's. Lee, owned by VF Corp is made in India by Arvind Fashions, part of the Arvind Group. Arvind is the third largest producer of Denim in the world and sells brands like Newport and Ruf and Tuf which straddle the mid-price segment.

Channel Management

In the post-liberalisation era, in India, MNCs such as Hindusthan Lever, Colgate-Palmolive and Philips had made enormous investments to develop effective distribution systems throughout the breadth and depth of the country, understanding the buying practices of customers is fundamental for achieving distribution effectiveness in a multicultural society like India. Even within the country, the MNCs need to design different distribution networks for different places. A globally standardized strategy may not work well. The shoe companies Reebok and Nike, entered on the premise that their brand image demanded exclusive shops. But their assumption proved wrong as the Indian customers were not loyal to one brand or the other. Now these shoe companies are selling their products in all types of shoe-stores. Similarly, companies like Sony and Samsung have started Indianising their distribution network to cater to small towns. They have also lowered their products' prices without diluting the global image. Coca-cola has modified its trucks and distribution-crates to ensure safe delivery on Indian poor roads. Its sales gathered momentum only after the company realized that it had to learn all about rural distribution in India afresh.

Marketing Communication

Companies can run the same promotion campaigns used in the home market or change them for each local market, a process called *communication adaptation*. The advertising war between Coca-cola and Pepsi in India in a six-year period between 1993 and 1998 underline the need to innovate only-for-India communication strategy that is different from global strategy. During the 1996 World Cup when Coke was a big sponsor, it came out with a campaign that proclaimed the brand's Indianness. Though beautifully shot, the commercial was a little pompous. Pepsi pricked Coke's pomposity with the delightfully irreverent 'Nothing Official About It' campaign that became a success. Coca-cola's initial failures with global advertising campaigns in Indian market underlines the need to innovate only-for-India communication strategy. Coca-cola in its advertisements has been depicting the Indian youngsters in situations. Reebok today uses Indian sports persons as celebrities. Likewise, LG Electronics composed anthems of good luck for the Indian cricket team, with the commercials featuring its Korean managers wearing the Indian tricolours. Similarly, Mercedes Benz has started using ads specially for Indian, appealing to Indian aspirations. These examples suggest the need to combine globally grown abilities with locally-acquired insights to create an only-for-India strategy.

5

INDIA'S INDUSTRIAL GROWTH

M.V. Rajyalakshmi

The Industrial Growth in India during the Different Periods of Planning

In India the rate of Industrial growth was not all uniform during different plan periods.

During the initial period of 15 years (1951-65) i.e., during the first three plan periods, Indian Industries experienced a steady growth of about 8 per cent. After that a fluctuating trend was observed in respect of Industrial growth. After experiencing a near stagnancy during 1966-68, Industrial sector experienced a high level of growth around 9.5 per cent during 1976-77. After that the country faced a negative growth rate of 1.4 per cent during 1979-80. Even in the sixties (1961-70) the average annual growth rate of industrial production was only 5.5 per cent per annum. During the seventies (1971-80) the average annual growth rate further came down to 4 per cent. Table 1 the annual growth rates of industrial production started with 9.3 per cent in 1981-82 after a significant fall of 3.2 per cent in 1982-83. If started to improve gradually from 6.7 per cent in 1983-84 to 9.2 per cent in 1986-87 and then fluctuated marginally and reached the level of 8.3 per cent in 1990-91 and then finally declined to 6.6 per cent in 1997-98. The annual average growth rate of industrial production during the eighties (1981-90) was maintained at a comparatively higher level of 7.9 per cent. But the year 1991-92 was disastrous for industrial sector, as the industrial production in 1991-92 was

TABLE 1
ANNUAL GROWTH RATES OF MAJOR SECTORS OF INDUSTRY

Year	*Mining (11.76)*	*Manufacturing (77.11)*	*Electricity (11.43)*	*General (100)*
1981-82	17.7	7.9	10.2	9.3
1982-83	12.4	1.3	5.7	3.2
1983-84	11.8	5.7	7.6	6.7
1984-85	8.8	8.0	12.0	8.6
1985-86	4.1	9.7	8.5	8.7
1986-87	6.2	9.4	10.3	9.2
1987-88	3.8	7.9	7.6	7.3
1988-89	7.9	8.7	9.5	8.7
1989-90	7.3	8.6	0.8	8.6
1990-91	4.5	8.9	7.8	8.3
1991-92	0.6	0.8	8.5	0.6
1992-93	0.5	2.2	5.0	2.3
1993-94	3.5	6.1	7.4	6.0
1994-95	7.6	8.5	8.5	8.4
1995-96	9.6	13.8	8.1	12.8
1996-97	–2.0	6.7	4.0	5.6
1997-98	5.9	6.6	6.6	6.6
1990-91	1.7	12.7	7.4	10.6
1991-92	–0.2	–2.5	9.7	–0.6
1992-93	–0.2	4.6	4.3	4.0
1993-94	3.4	3.9	7.6	4.4
1994-95	7.2	10.3	7.7	9.6
1995-96	10.3	13.7	8.9	12.8
1996-97	–1.2	8.3	3.8	6.9
1997-98	5.5	6.9	6.0	6.7
1998-99	–1.1	3.7	6.6	3.5

Source: Economic survey 1998-99, p. 95, cso (QE) 1998-99.

almost stagnant at the previous year's level with General Index of Industrial Production (IIP) showing a growth rate of 0.6 per cent. The stagnation in the industrial production was the result of poor performance of the mining and manufacturing sector. In 1996-97, industrial production registered a growth rate of 12.8 percent and the same rate further declined to 6.6 per cent in 1997-98.

The growth rate of mining sector which was as high as 17.7 per cent in 1990-91 and then increased to only 9.6 per cent in 1995-96 and finally declined to only 5.9 per cent in 1997-98. The manufacturing sector, the major segment in IIP, showed a growth rate of only 6.6 per cent in 1997-98 as compared to an annual average growth rate of 17.6 per cent between 1981-82 to 1990-91. But the electricity sector has maintained a steady growth rate 8.5 per cent in 1991-92 as against the annual average growth rate of 9.0 per cent between 1981-82 to 1990-91. In 1997-98, the annual growth rate of electricity sector was 6.6 per cent.

In 1995-96 (April-December) the annual growth rate of industrial production has showed an improvement of 12.8 per cent and the same rate declined to 6.7 per cent in 1997-98 (April-December) and then it further declined to 3.5 per cent in 1998-99 (April-December).

Causes for the Slowdown

The main factors which are mostly responsible for this industrial slow down during the period 1991-92 to 1997-98 were decline in the growth rate of exports, impact of tight monetary policy, liberalization on the industrial front, negative growth rate of 0.4 per cent of agricultural sector (1995-96), decline in government investment on infrastructure projects and so on. Thus, the period immediately, following the economic reforms was marked by low growth rates and even stagnation in major industrial sector. Complementary to industrial policy changes, significant transformation has been brought about in monetary, fiscal and external sector policies. The changes include transition to market-determined exchange rates and interest rates, removal of physical control on imports, rationalization and reduction of taxes and duties to enhance competitiveness of Indian Industries.

The growth rates quickly recovered and the index of industrial production (IIP) increased by 6.0 per cent and manufacturing sector by 6.1 per cent in 1993-94. Electricity generation has tended to maintain high growth rates throughout the period.

In 1995-96 capital goods registered a growth rate of 17.9 per cent and the consumer goods 14.3 per cent and that of intermediate goods and basic goods were 11.8 per cent and 8.3 per cent respectively.

Thus, it may be observed that since 1992-93, all the major sectors had responded to economic reforms with dynamism. However, during 1996-97 and April to February 1998, there has been a declaration of industrial growth rates due to poor performance by mining manufacturing and electricity generation.

Again during April to October 1997-98, over all growth of industrial production (IIP) registered a growth rate of only 5.0 per cent supported by a growth rate of only 4.7 per cent in manufacturing, 6.9 per cent in electricity and 5.3 per cent in mining such poor performance in industrial growth rates is mainly due to poor performance of by the manufacturing sector.

During more than last five decades of planning, industrial pattern in India had undergone perceptible changes like building basic infrastructure facilities like power, transport and communication along with the development of heavy engineering industries, rapid expansion of consumer durable industry chemicals, petro-chemicals and allied industries, massive expansion of public sector and so on.

The ninth plan (1997-2002) put adequate stress on the development of the industrial sector. But the overall growth in industrial production remains unsatisfactory.

From the very beginning the locational pattern of Indian industries was a large concentration of industrial activity in and around some big ports and commercial centers of India. This type of unbalanced industrial development is responsible for environmental congestion, inter-state disparity growth of urban slums, backward regions and so on.

The process of industrialisation over the plan periods failed to bring about satisfactory growth levels and the process involves many obstacles in the path. They are poor capital formation, poor performance of agricultural sector, lack of infrastructure facilities failure to reach targets fixed in the plans, poor performance of the public sector regional unbalances, industrial sickness etc.

The New Industrial policy initiatives and procedural reforms called for to encourage and assist Indian entrepreneuss to exploit and meet the merging domestic and global opportunities and challenges.

The attainment of technological dynamism and international competitiveness requires swift responses to meet the fast changing external conditions for the industrial world. This must be followed by Procedural transparency and fast processing of application must follow this by administration machinery.

The New Industrial policy aims at promoting foreign investments in India for the significant development of Indian economy in the areas of Technology transfer, marketing expertise, introduction of modern managerial techniques and new possibilities for the promotion of exports. This is particularly necessary in the changing global scenario of industrial and economic co-operation marked by mobility of capital.

As a step towards privatisation the key-sectors of the economy need to be diverted and diluted in public sector ownership. The public sector is endangered with a number of serious problems like inefficiency in productivity levels, poor human resource management, low rate of net return on capital, creating financial burden to the Government and so on.

The main focus of the economic reforms agenda (1991) is the public sector. A part from the liberalisation and globalisation, the performance of public sector needs to be assessed Ahluwalia Study (1994) indicates that while the public sector accounted for 55 per cent of the total investment, it contributes only 15 per cent of the output. This understanding led to the refocussing of public expenditure involving selective disinvestment of public sector.

Privatisation has become the keyword in the economic pastance and progressive disinvestment became the Government strategy. Dis-investment may take the form of dilution of government stake to a level that results in transfer of management or could also be liquited to such levels as would permit government to retain control over the organisation. Dis-investment beyond 50 per cent involves transfer of management whereas below 50 per cent would result in the government continuing to have a major role in the undertaking.

However the faith of success on delicensing of industries to attain high industrial growth faltered in a huge way. Dis-investment in the case of industrial enterprise in the public sector combined with invitation of foreign investment, liberalisation of foreign trade and exchange rate changes in collaboration with global flows of capital put as on the pedestal of hope in the growing of private sector especially multinational investment. The Government's initiative in lowering of customs and excise duties was really appreciated in having the way for healthy and efficient industrial environment. A cut indirect taxes on income and wealth of individuals and corporate bodies was intended to enlarge their investment resources.

After three years of recession Indian Industry failed to be revived. The previous financial year was estimated to have started with 12.1 per cent growth in industrial production in April 2000. But it slumped to 5.5 per cent in May, which was less than what, was recorded in that month in 1999.

There is slump in the capital goods industry as well as consumer goods industry. The industry review of the Confederation of India Industry (CII) predicts a gloomy picture of Indian Industry in the coming three years. The basic Industry the crude oil, cold rolled steel and pig iron are presented with negative growth rates. Consumer durable industry has growth by less than 10 per cent and the intermediate goods like castings, polyster filament yarn nylon have shown negative growth. Service sector covering construction, thermal, hydro and nuclear electric generation also growth trend is not encouraging small scale Industry is the worst hit under liberalisation and globalisation programme. The number of closures of production units in the sector runs into thousands with lifting of quantitative restrictions on the import of all consumer goods, the small-scale industry is faltering down. Of course, the government has closer to set up an interministerial group to make an assessment of the impact of phasing out of quantitative restrictions on all imports and devise adequate steps to ensure that Indian Industry including its small scale sector is given sufficient protection in the coming years.

Opening the doors of foreign investment wide open under the liberalisation programme, Indian Industry had to face tough competition in all its various segments. The cheap labour costs would not generate export surpluses due to slow technological developments. Many a time Indian Industry is import dependent for all major inputs like capital goods, components, and raw materials to survive. The economic reforms agenda failed to yield expected results. Dis-investment in the case of industrial enterprises in the public sector and liberalised foreign trade could not stimulated proper growth momentum in the industrial front.

In the final analysis it may be concluded that private sector in India has been competitive and instead of supplementing public sector has become a rival in the market. Private sector could emerge as a strong hold inover counter's economic development and the government has no other alternative but to go for dis-investment policy. Secondly the erosion or our Industrial progress took place by strong competition from external sector which is strong because of fast technological developments. Thirdly the competition from MNC's over the domestic corporate produces in the production of especially consumer durables is a blow to the industrial growth of India. The shortages in the domestic supply of power oil, petroleum products etc. acts as a hindrance to industrial production.

Finally, the world recession and slowdown in the

external trade of industrialised world acts as a blow to the Industrial growth of dependent economics like India and other Asian countries.

However, I would like to conclude with an optimistic note that the pace of recovery may be delayed but can never be denied.

6

SICKNESS IN SMALL ENTERPRISES

M. Munirami Reddy, B. Ramachandra Reddy, Madisetty Nagendra, G. Narasimhulu

Introduction

One of the most significant features of planned economic development in India has been the phenomenal growth of small scale industries. It has become an effective instrument of progress and development in terms of industrialization of rural areas and a measure of tackling the problems of unemployment plaguing the masses and the country. Development of Small-Scale sector has been necessary, because of its contribution and role played in the Indian economy. In the Indian context, small industry has become broad based by giving special recognition to the service sector in its developmental programme and it is currently referred to as the small enterprise sector, particularly in the context of generation of self employment opportunities.[1]

Sickness is not a new phenomenon, either in India or elsewhere. In the complex and diverse world of uncertainty, ignorance, inexperience, inefficiency, vast and rapid technological changes, changes in consumer preferences, monopolistic competition, growing labour power, and wise and unwise Government regulation of industry, sickness here and there should be expected. So long as sickness is sporadic, it need not cause much anxiety. However, if it were to assume large dimensions like an epidemic, it should be dealt with expeditiously and firmly.

Definition of Small Enterprises

A study group on development of small enterprise was

constituted by the Deputy Chairman of the Planning Commission in May 1999. While constituting the Study Group, representation was given to SSI entrepreneurs and secretaries of various departments like Ministry of small scale Industries and Agro and Rural Industries (SSI & ARI)), Reserve Bank of India, SIDBI, FICCI etc. The Study Group submitted its Interim Report on 6th July 2000. The term small-scale industry should be replaced by "Small Enterprises" which will consists of (i) Tiny industrial units, (ii) Small scale industrial units, and (iii) Service and business enterprises. As per the Report, the three tier definition of tiny, small and medium sector are:

- Tiny Units: Rs. 10 lakh investment in plant and machinery.
- SSI Units: Rs. 10 lakhs to Rs. 1 crore investment in plant and machinery.
- Medium Units: Rs. 1 crore to Rs. 10 crores investment in plant and machinery.

Definition of Sick Unit

The sick unit has been defined to be a company where the accumulated losses at the end of any financial year result in erosion of 50 per cent or more of its peak net worth during the immediately preceding five financial years. The net worth is the sum total of the paid-up capital and free-reserves. The free reserve means all reserves credited out of the profits and share premium account but does not include reserves credited out of revaluation of an asset, write back of depreciation provisions and amalgamation.[2]

Symptoms of Sickness

Sickness does not develop all of a sudden. It gives out warning signals. It is a gradual process with distinct stages. Thus there is a need for identification of various symptoms of sickness in small enterprises so that the concerned parties can check and maintained the health of units. The following points may give an idea of Symptoms of Sickness. They are:

- Continuous irregularity in cash credit Accounts.
- Low capacity utilization.

- Profit fluctuations, downward trend in sales and stagnation or fall in profits followed by contraction in the share of the market.
- Higher rate of rejection of goods manufactured.
- Reduction in credit summations—whenever the companies are in financial difficulty, they open a separate account with another bank and deposit all collections therein.
- Failure to pay statutory liabilities.
- Larger and larger outstanding in the bill accounts.
- Larger period of credit allowed on sale documents negotiated through the Bank and frequent returns by customers of the same.
- Non-Submission of periodical financial data, stock statement etc., in item.
- Decrease in working capital on account of increase in creditors, an increase in inventories which may include large number of slow or non-moving items.
- Existence of a large number of lawsuits against the company.
- Rapid expansion and too much diversification within a short-time.
- Diversion of funds for purposes other than running the units.
- Sudden or frequent changes in Management—whether professional or otherwise dominated by one man or few individuals.
- Any major change in the share holding.[3]

Position of Industrial Sickness

As per the Sick Industrial Companies (Special Provisions) Act of 1985, classify sick units into large, medium and small units, but later the classification was made more scientific and units were grouped under Non-SSI and SSI units. The following Table gives an idea of state-wise analysis of sick units in India upto 31st March, 2001.

TABLE 1
STATE-WISE ANALYSIS OF INDUSTRIAL SICKNESS IN INDIA

S. No.	*State*	*31-03-1997*		*31-03-2001*	
		Non-SSI Sick/Weak Units	*SSI Sick/Weak Units*	*Non-SSI Sick/Weak Units*	*SSI Sick/Weak Units*
1.	Maharashtra	399	19,360	611	8,056
2.	West Bengal	243	53,451	252	1,13,846
3.	Uttar Pradesh	202	23,286	233	23,117
4.	Andhra Pradesh	264	15,460	385	11,841
5.	Gujarat	213	6,510	328	5,408
6.	Tamil Nadu	175	9,809	317	9,959
7.	Karnataka	159	6,937	204	4,400
8.	Kerala	81	8,908	76	11,144
9.	Haryana	78	2,574	104	1,285
10.	Bihar	64	22,702	69	16,423
11.	Madhya Pradesh	111	12,070	161	6,614
12.	Orissa	62	3,408	59	6,668
13.	Rajasthan	84	14,561	102	6,395
14.	Punjab	62	2,466	91	1,832
15.	Assam	41	10,133	56	8,632
16.	Others	130	23,397	259	13,887
	Total	**2,368**	**2,35,032**	**3,307**	**2,49,511**

Source: 1. Ruddar Datt & K.I.M. Sundaram, Indian Economy, S. Chand & Co. Ltd., New Delhi, 2001, p. 668.
2. Business Line, 22nd Nov., 2001, p. 8.

It is an evident from the Table 1 that there has been an increase in the number of SSI sick units from 2,35,032 in March 1997 to 2,49,511 in March 2001. The percentage increase in sick units over a period of 4 years in only 6. The number of SSI sick units was highest in West Bengal followed by Uttar Pradesh, Bihar, Maharashtra and so on at the end of March 1997. Similar trend is observed in the year 2001 also. The number of SSI sick units tremendously increased in West Bengal state over a period of 4 years from 53,451 to 1,13,846 (112.99%). The number of SSI sick units are gradually decreased in all the states from 31st March, 1997 to 31st March, 2001, except West Bengal, Tamil Nadu, Kerala and Orissa. Out of 2,49,511 total SSI sick units, West

Bengal alone having the share of 45.6 per cent i.e., 1,13,846 units.

The total Bank Credit blocked in the sick units has increased from Rs. 13,787 crores (as on 31st March, 1997) to Rs. 19,464 crores (as on 31st March, 1999). The small scale sector has Rs. 4,314 crores i.e., 22.2 per cent blocked in its units while the Non-SSI sector has Rs. 15,150 crores (77.8 per cent).

Factors Responsible for Sickness of Small Enterprises

A review of the various studies* regarding small-scale units reveals the following:

1. Lock of management expertise is a very important factor. Young entrepreneurs start enterprises with romantic ideas. They keep high overhead costs, borrow at high rates of interest and do not care for making economics in costs, more especially during the period of infancy. Thus, inexperienced management of small units is one of the important causes of sickness.
2. Non-observance of the basic principles of business management is another major contributing factor to sickness. To start enterprises with a low equity base, to make no effort to build internal financial resources during good years, to maintain high inventories to total production, to invest short-term borrowings in medium-terms investments, etc., result in developing poor internal resilience to fight difficult times.
3. Under-utilisation of capacity caused by lack of working capital, lack of demand and non-availability to raw materials results in industrial sickness, leading to the death of small enterprises.
4. Easy approval of small-scale units by the state without proper screening of project proposals also

---

*Study Team Report of the State Bank of India, Entrepreneurial Development programme in Gujarat, Survey of mortality of small-scale units in South-India, Haryana's Study of Small-Scale Units and FICCI Survey on Sickness in SSI (1998).

resulted in sickness. This only under-scores the fact that assessment of viability of the projects is not made with adequate care, more especially with regard to financial viability.

5. The dead units depended mostly on their own funds i.e., on their individual savings rather than on borrowed funds. Among the dead small units, own funds accounted for 89 per cent of gross investments. For working capital requirements, these units depended on nationalized banks or co-operative banks.
6. Non-payment by the principal's to the ancillaries has been noted as an important cause of industrial sickness.[4]

Measures to Prevent Sickness in Small Enterprises

The problem of industrial sickness in small units has to be treated differently from the problem of sickness of the large units. It is basically the problem of increasing the competitive strength and viability of the small units. For this purpose, the following measures deserve consideration:

1. The Reserve Bank should issue guidelines for the operation of small units and thus make professional management expertise available for the guidance of small entrepreneurs. The management expertise should acquaint the small entrepreneur with the need for better equity base, prescribe norms for allocation of their surplus to depreciation, retained profits and expansion programmes so as a build their internal financial strength.
2. Since a majority of sick units die in the second or third year of their existence, a programme of monitoring and nursing them during infancy is very essential. In this way, the misuse of funds for purposes other than specified, and the factors leading to low capacity utilisation can be examined and quick remedial action taken.
3. The Government can accord priority in allocation of

scarce raw materials, extending marketing assistance and granting certain rebates and concessions to small units and more so to such units which show better record of performance.

4. Sickness of small units should be treated at par with scarcity/famine in agriculture and thus concessional rates of interest be charged at par with those loans, that are granted in scarcity/famine conditions in agriculture. The maximum rate of interest should be 7 per cent for small sick units to enable them to secure soft credit.
5. The Government should take penal action against the principals for non-payment for the delivery of goods by small units.

Conclusion

To help the marketing of SSI products, price performance policy of 10 per cent was made a permanent measure to project the interests SSI units. States have withdrawn this permanent preference measure. This has adversely effected the marketing of SSI products. This was uncalled for and the need of the hour is to receive this measure.

To help the growth and establishment of more and more SSI units, it is suggested that weighted deduction of 125 per cent of the salaries and wages paid by SSI units be allowed as deduction under the Income Tax Act.

A change of policies from protectionism to liberalisation has helped large Indian industry and multinationals to enter in areas reserved for SSIs. This extreme path should be avoided since this has done more harm than good. The country should more to a middle path and permit selective liberalisation with necessary safeguards.

The development of small scale industries will rebuild the rural India and accelerated the pace of economic growth and well being of the people. The government seeking quick ways to create more employment would do well to develop projects like small scale industries which are labour intensive, quick yielding, well dispersed and capable of bringing more jobs and more consumer goods to backward areas of the country. Finally, it is the prime responsibility of all the Financial Institutions, RBI and the Government to take corrective measures for the proper development of SSI units and ways and means should be devised in such a way that there should be proper co-ordination between all concerned to avoid delays and take correct decisions and implement them properly.

REFERENCES

1. Govt. of India, VIII Five-year plan, 1992-97, Vol. II, p. 132.
2. Ruddar Datt and K.P.M. Sundharam, Indian Economy, S. Chand & Co. Ltd., New Delhi, 2001, p. 676.
3. Vasanth Desai, Development of Samll Scale Industrial Units, Himalaya Publishing House, Mumbai, 2000.
4. Srivastava etc., Management and Monitoring of Industrial Sickness.
5. Sudharshan Lal, How to prevent Industrial sickness, 2000, p. 191.

7

INDIA'S INDUSTRIAL GROWTH : PERFORMANCE AND PROBLEMS

A.V. Naga Varma

For a predominantly agricultural country like India, development of industries is a must. And some industrial development in the country has, in fact, taken place. A look at the progress made and an assessment of the same is taken up in this seminar paper. However, as a preliminary to this, let us recapitulate major arguments in favour of industrialisation, as also from an idea of the present state of India industries.

Importance and Present Position

It is now an established fact that material riches and industries go together. This is amply demonstrated by the industrially advanced countries. Negatively it is proved by the less developed countries which lack industries, and whose people live poverty.

Role of Industrialisation

There is a strong case for the industrialisation of countries like India with vast manpower, large and varied resources, and continental dimensions. Main arguments put forward in this regard are as under:

Raising Income

The first and foremost reason is that industrial development above can provide a secure basis for a rapid growth of income. Industries produce products that are largely dependent upon man's hard work which is restricted by the limiting factor of nature. In the industrially developed countries, for example, the G.N.P. per capita is very high at $ 25,730. In the less developed countries it is very low at $ 410 for the low-income economies, and around $ 2,000 for the middle-income economies.

Meeting High Income Demands

Beyond certain limits, the demands of the people are usually for industrial products alone. After having met the need of food, incomes of the people are spent mostly upon non-food items. Till bellies are full and the variety in diet is met, the demand for agricultural products increases.

Overcoming Disparities in Export and Import Elasticities

An alternative to the development of industries is to concentrate on the products of primary goods, export them, and get industrial goods from industrially developed countries.

The disparities in elasticities, therefore, point to the difficulty of earning adequate foreign exchange. India is one of those underdeveloped countries, which cannot export to earn enough foreign exchange from the export of its primary products alone. Where this is so, says Jagdish Bhagwati, "Industrialisation is a rational consequence."

This situation, characterized by disparities in the elasticities of foreign trade can, therefore, be corrected only by industrialisation.

Absorbing Surplus Labour

Surplus labour and rapidly growing population characterize Indian economy. Add to this the labour that will become redundant as the process of technical improvement in agriculture proceeds. To absorb all this surplus labour, as also to provide work/jobs at a rate commensurate with the addition to the labour force, it is essential to industrialize the country too quickly.

Strengthening the Economy

Industrialisation of the Indian Economy can alone provide the necessary elements of strength to it. In this connection one may refer to four major things:

One: The development of industries producing capital goods i.e., machines equipment etc. enables a country to produce a variety of goods, in large quantities and at low costs.

Two: It makes possible the production of goods like railways, dams, etc., which are in any case non-importable.

Three: It is through the establishment of industries that one can impact elasticity to the system and overcome the historically given position of a primary producing country.

Four: The requirements for the development of agriculture can be met. For example, improved farm-implements, chemical fertilizers, storage and transport facilities, etc., appropriate to our own conditions (e.g., small farm size, abundant labor etc.).

Five: The industrial development imports to an economy dynamic element in the form of rapid growth and a diversified economic structure, which make it a progressive economy.

Growth and Structural Composition

Uptrend in Growth

The scenario as revealed by the growth of industrial production is one of a rising trend, with significant ups and downs spread over a number of years (Table 1).

Long-term Rise

Overall the growth rate of industrial production has been over 6 per cent since 1951. The first sub-trend lasted for 15 years since 1951 (i.e. from 1951 to 1965). During this period, the growth-rate has been higher than the long-term trend rate, and an accelerating one. Starting from growth rate of 6 per cent during 1976-81, it rose and remained high in the range of about 7 per cent and over 9 per cent during the 1980's, except for one year (1982-83) when it was low at

TABLE 1
ANNUAL GROWTH RATES IN MAJOR SECTORS OF INDUSTRY

Year (Weight)	*Mining 10.47 (11.46)*	*Manufacturing 79.36 (77.11)*	*Electricity 10.17 (11.43)*	*General (100.00)*
1981-82	17.7	7.9	10.2	9.3
1983-84	11.7	5.7	7.6	6.7
1984-85	8.9	8.0	12.0	8.6
1985-86	4.1	9.7	8.5	8.7
1986-87	6.2	9.4	10.3	9.1
1987-88	3.8	7.9	7.7	7.3
1988-89	7.9	8.7	9.5	8.7
1989-90	6.3	8.6	10.8	8.6
1990-91	4.5	9.0	7.8	8.2
1981-82	to			
1990-91	8.4	7.6	9.0	7.9
1991-92	0.6	–0.8	8.5	0.6
1992-93	0.5	2.2	5.0	2.3
1993-94	3.5	6.1	7.4	6.0
1994-95	9.8	9.1	8.5	9.1
1995-96	9.7	14.1	8.1	13.0
1996-97	–1.9	7.3	4.0	6.1
1997-98	6.9	6.7	6.6	6.7
1998-99	–0.8	4.4	6.5	4.1
1999-2000	1.0	7.1	6.6	6.6

Notes: 1. Growth rates from 1994-95 are as per Index of Industrial production with, Production with Base: 1993-94=100, and those for earlier years are for Index of Industrial, 1980-81=100.
2. Weights in brackets relate to Index of Industrial Production with base 1980-81 = 100

Source: Government of India Economic Survey 1996-97, 1997-98, 1998-99, 1999-2000, 2000-2001.

3.2 per cent. For the decade as a whole (1980-81 to 1990-91) the growth-rate has been 7.9 per cent. The rise in the growth curve continues to mark the 1990's with the growth rate at 6 per cent (1991-2000).

Unsatisfactory Performance

Taking together the achievements and shortcomings of Industrial growth, the picture of industrial development appears to be a mixed one. However, despite such an inference, the country is industrially stilled in a backward stage. The less developed nature of industrial scene is obvious also from the fact that the economy is still very far from the developed countries. In the developed countries, industry contributes around 40 per cent to the gross domestic product. No wonder as much as 67 per cent of the labour force is engaged in agriculture. In the industrially advanced countries, the proportion is much less at around 3 per cent. In this background, the existence of inefficient and sick firms, regional imbalances etc. pose very difficult problems. On balance, therefore, one is inclined to the view that the industrial development has been far from satisfactory.

Government Measures

A set of measures bare upon the reform of the economy to make it more competitive and efficient. The various steps taken in this regard include the following: reduction of custom duties; eliminating to a large extent quantitative curbs on imports and exports, making rupee convertible on current account; encouraging entry of foreign direct investment, abolition of several controls and delicensing of several industries etc.

To sum up, the problems of industrial sickness, which imposes huge costs on the economy, requires for its solution measures that make industries growth cum efficiency oriented.

REFERENCES

1. Jagdish Bhagwati, The Economics of Under Developed Countries.
2. Raul Prebisch, "Emphasis on Industry," Leading issues in Development Economics, Gerald M. Meier (Ed.).
3. S. Gupta, "Indian Plans, Retrospect and Prospects," The Indian Economic Journal, April-June, 1987.
4. C.P. Chandrasekhar, "Aspects of Growth and Structural Change in Indian Industry." Economic and Political Weekly, Special Number, November 1988.

5. The Eighth Five Year Plan, Vol. 1, p. 87.
6. Hoffmann, W.G., The Growth of Industrial Economics, Oxford, 1958.
7. United Nations, World Economic Survey, 1961.
8. K.N. Raj, "Growth and Stagnation in Industrial Development," Economic and Political Weekly, Annual Number (1975).
9. Planning Commission: Five-Year Plans.
10. Government of India Economic Survey, 1997-98, 1998-99.
11. Rosen, G., Industrial Change in India.
12. Isher J. Ahluwalia, Industrial Growth in India: Stagnation since the Mid-sixties (1984).
13. Annual Survey of Industries (1977-98).
14. Pronab Bardhan, The Political Economy of Development in India (1984).
15. M. Mehta, "Structure of Indian Industries." The Times of India Directory and Year Book.
16. Ministry of Industry, Report of the working group of central trade unions, performance of public sector undertakings (1978).
17. Sudarshan Lal, How to Prevent Industrial Sickness (1979).
18. Bagchi, Amiya and Banerjee, Nirmala (Editors), "Change and Choice in Industry" Center for Studies in Social Sciences, Calcutta, 1981.

8

SSE CLUSTERS—A BIG WAY FOR ECONOMIC DEVELOPMENT

R. Jayaprakash Reddy

Small scale sector plays an important role in the economic development of our country where the population is high and the incomes are low. It absorbs more men with low capital. Because of various other advantages possessed by this sector, it is inevitable to develop this sector. The Government of India identified the role of this sector in its Industrial policy 1956 and made it clear that *small scale industries provide immediate large scale employment, offer a method of ensuring a more equitable distribution of national income and facilitate an effective mobilisation of resources of capital and skill which might otherwise remain unutilised.*

The small scale sector has become the hub for many economic activities in India by virtue of its special features of capital sparing and labour intensiveness. Realising the role of this sector, the Government of India took several measures for the promotion and smooth functioning of this sector. The industrial policy pronouncements from 1948 to 1990, the progressive allocations made in the Five Year Plans, the creation of different promoting and supporting organisations both at central and state levels and the nationalisation of commercial banks reflect the spirit and effort of the Government towards the creation of a favourable climate for the growth and working of small scale sector. One of the important supports of the Government to this sector is widening of the investment limit. In 1966, a small scale unit was defined as an undertaking with a fixed investment of less than Rs. 7.5 lakhs. Government continuously increased the limit, and recently in 1997, on the recommendation of Abid Hussain committee, the Government has raised the investment limit to Rs. 3 crores from Rs. 60 lakhs. However, later it lowered the limit to Rs. 1 crore.

In fact, the progress and the performance achieved by this sector are the result of the various measures initiated by the Government for their growth and effective working.

Contribution of Small Scale Sector to Indian Economy

The small scale sector which plays a pivotal role in the Indian economy in terms of employment and growth has recorded a high rate of growth since independence because of the atmosphere created by the Government. It is now one of the fastest growing sectors in the country. It has made steady progress during recent years in spite of tough competition from large sector. The good performance of the small scale units is evident from their number, production, employment and foreign exchange earnings. The following table shows the growth and progress of small scale sector during the last three decades.

From the table it is clear that the growth of small scale sector in terms of units is commendable. There were only 4.16 lakh small scale units in 1973-74 which rose to 8.74 lakh units in 1980-81, 20.82 lakh units in 1991-92, 27.24 lakh units in 1995-96 and to 30.14 lakh units in 1997-98.

Contribution to Employment

The root cause for unemployment in India is overgrowing population which has outpaced the development of industry and agriculture. For a country like ours, with limited financial resources and huge reservoir of human resources, small scale sector is the only means for solving the unemployment problem. With its inherent nature of labour intensiveness, small scale sector has been providing employment at an increased rate which is evident from Table 1.

TABLE 1
GROWTH OF SMALL SCALE SECTOR

Year	*No. of units (lakhs)*	*Production (Rs. Crores)*	*Employment (lakhs)*	*Exports (Rs. Crores)*
1973-74	4.16	7,300	39.7	393
1980-81	8.74	28,060	71.0	1,643
1985-86	13.56	61,228	96.0	2,769
1990-91	17.00	1,55,340	125.3	9,100
1991-92	20.82	1,78,700	130.0	13,883
1992-93	22.46	2,09,300	134.0	17,785
1993-94	23.81	2,41,648	139.4	25,307
1994-95	25.71	2,93,990	146.6	29,068
1995-96	27.24	3,56,213	152.6	39,470
1996-97	28.57	4,12,636	160.0	39,249
1997-98	30.14	4,65,171	167.2	43,946

Sources: Small Industry Development Organisation
Hand book of Industrial Statistics, 1987
Economic Survey 1992-93 & 1999-2000.

It can be noticed from the table that during a period of 24 years (i.e. from 1973-74 to 1997-98), employment has grown from 39.7 lakhs to 167.2 lakhs i.e., more than four times.

Contribution to Output

Small scale sector has been contributing significantly to the Gross National Product of the country. Table 1 shows that the total production of this sector was Rs. 7300 crores in 1973-74 which rose to Rs. 2,41,648 crores in 1993-94 and to Rs. 4,65,171 crores in 1997-98.

Contribution to Exports

Small scale sector has registered a phenominal growth in the export field by contributing substantially to the total national earnings from exports. It has entered into hitherto untried markets of advanced countries against the stiff competition from the developing nations. The contribution of this sector to exports has substantially increased from Rs. 393 crores in 1973-74 to Rs. 25,307 crores in 1993-94 and to Rs. 43,946 crores in 1997-98. A very significant feature of exports from this sector is its share in non-traditional exports. The share of exports from this sector represents about 34 per cent of total exports in 1997-98.

Problems of Small Scale Sector

Inspite of various efforts put in by the Government of India and other agencies, the small scale sector is still seriously handicapped in comparison with large sector. Inequitable allocation system for scarce raw materials and imported components, lack of provision of credit and finance, low technical skill and managerial ability, and lack of marketing contracts are the problems. Because of these problems many of the small scale units are becoming sick. The report of the second *All-India census* of small scale industrial units revealed that 34.7 per cent of the small units are becoming sick due to financial problems, and 14.4 per cent due to marketing problems. Thus, it is clear that about 50 per cent of small units are becoming sick mainly due to financial and marketing problems. Table 2 shows the percentage of various problems that lead to sickness in small scale sector.

Industrial sickness has become the key economic problem of the day threatening the growth of Indian industry. It has assumed vast dimensions, particularly in the small scale sector in India in recent years. According to Economic Survey, 1989-90 growing incidence of sickness has been one of the persisting problems faced by the industrial sector of the country. Substantial amount of loanable funds of the financial institutions is locked up in sick industrial units causing not only wastage of resources.

According to RBI report on Currency and Finance, by the end of March 1997, there were 2,32,664 small scale sick units, where the bank credit was locked up to the extent of Rs. 3,609 crores which was 26.2 per cent in the total credit locked up in all the industrial units put together.

Steps Taken by the Government

To reduce the sickness in small scale sector on one hand

and to help the sector to grow faster on the other, Government of India have initiated several steps with the help of Small Industry Development Organisation (SIDO), Small Industry Development Bank of India (SIDBI), other financial, technical and service organisations. The Credit Guarantee Scheme evolved by RBI in 1960, the marketing assistance taken up by National Small Industry Corporation (NSIC) from February 1955, the supply of raw materials and import quota looked upon by the State Small Industries Development Corporations, the technical assistance given by Service Institutes and Extension Centres of SIDO, provision of infrastructure facilities through Industrial Estates and Industrial Development Areas by state Industrial Infrastructure Corporations, etc., are some of the key measures of the Government for the promotion of small scale sector. Further, the Government has been following a policy of reservation of items for exclusive development in the small scale sector. In addition, the commercial banks, State Finance Corporations and other financial agencies in the country have been supporting small scale sector for short-term and long term financial needs.

New Industrial Policy—New Challenges

As a part of liberalisation, the new Industrial Policy 1991 has taken a new diversion to deregulate and debureaucratize the samll scale sector, instead of protection, so as to remove all fetters on its growth potential. The new watchword, therefore, is competition and not reservation. This policy aims at strengthening the competitive capacity of small scale sector instead of concessions, subsidies, reservations and direct support. Some of the features of the policy are:

1. Shift from subsidised/cheap credit to adequate supply of credit.
2. Introduction of shareholding upto 24 per cent in small scale unit by some other undertaking, may be small or large, Indian or foreign.
3. Incorporation of law (Delayed Payments Act, 1993 has promulgated by the Govt.) to avoid delays in

payments to small scale units and avoid their sickness and closure.

To suggest measure to improve the growth of small scale sector the Government had appointed an expert committee under the chairmanship of Mr. Abid Hussain in December 1995. The committee submitted its report in January 1997. The main recommendations of the committee are:

1. Enlarging the concept of small scale industries to include small scale business and service enterprises.
2. Policy of protection to be replaced by the policy of promotion.
3. Setting up of support systems for small scale enterprises by developing clusters.
4. Development of small scale enterprises should be largely the responsibility of state Governments.
5. Abolishing reservations of products which can be exclusively manufactured by small scale enterprises only.
6. Raising of investment limit from Rs. 60 lakhs to Rs. 3 crores.
7. Encouraging bills culture and expanding factoring services as remedy for delay of payments to small scale enterprises.
8. 70 per cent priority lending for tiny sector from the small scale industry allocation.
9. Based on the recommendations of the committee, the Government increased the investment limit of small scale and tiny units, dereserved 15 items, reserved for manufacture by small scale sector, and wants to confine its role to policy formulation.

Present Scenario

There is no doubt that even today small scale sector is contributing nearly 34 per cent of our country's exports and a major contributor in employment generation and industrial production. Further, the small scale sector is competing in a large area with medium and large sector.

The Government, keeping the present global

environment in view, seems to be to confine its role to policy formulation, legal and institutional development, and throw the responsibility of development of small scale enterprises on the states.

At this juncture, it is very much doubtful whether the small scale sector continues to contribute well to the economic development of the country, come out of the serous problem of sickness and face competition from large and foreign organisations. Further, due to GATT and WTO, the crazy foreign products are flowing into the country leading to heavy competition to the products of small scale sector.

SSE Clusters—The Right Answer

It is evident from the above information and facts that in the near future the Government or any other organisation may not come into the rescue of small scale sector. Therefore, formation of SSE (small scale enterprises) clusters is only the available solution for the survive and grow.

The Abid Hussain Committee recommended that the state Governments should identify the existing SSE clusters and then promote new type of organisations which are joint ventures between the State Governments or local authorities and business associations in those clusters. The Cluster Small Enterprise Associations (CSEAs) should be autonomous and the Government should support them only if the local business associations are willing to provide some level of matching fund.

The proposal of SSE Clusters is good and if it comes into practice the competitive strength of the SSEs automatically increase. However, there appears some practical difficulties in its implementation. Keeping these in mind the author tries to show a new shape to the proposed SSE Clusters. In his opinion SSE Clusters should have the following features:

1. An SSE Cluster should be an association of small scale enterprises situated in an area producing similar type of product or service.

2. The members of enterprises in the Cluster contributing their share of fund on one hand, get the benefits like financial, technical, marketing etc. from the Cluster on the other.
3. A separate SSE Cluster should be formed for each product or service for each district, region, and state and the quality/quantity, price, brand and packing should also be almost same. In other words, a specific product/service produced from small scale sector in any part of the country should easily be identifiable in all its features.
4. SSE Clusters should continuously try to get all the financial, technical and marketing support from their respective states.
5. At the national level there should be an apex body (National SSE Association) for each product or service of small scale sector. It persues the policies of the Government towards the product/service, exports, imports of raw material, technical assistance etc.
6. The national level body with funds raised from its member associations and other resources should create an R&D division and tries to improve the quality of the products/services, and see that the products/services of the small scale sector are in no way less than that of any large scale organisation or any MNC.
7. The national level body should take all necessary steps to solve the problems of SSE Clusters and see that no small scale enterprise is closed because of sickness.
8. There should be a continuous communication among Clusters at different levels. As the product in all Clusters is same, advertisement, sales promotion activities can be done on a large scale and the expenses may be borne by member small scale enterprises.

Depending on the demand, the products/services may be transfered from one Cluster to the other. For good relations, and study the latest developments, brochures, magazines, reports may be published and circulated among all Clusters.

Often seminars and workshops may be conducted by the SSE Clusters at regional, state and central levels.

Conclusion

Based on the above mentioned idea of SSE Clusters for each product/service of small scale sector, there is no doubt, that the competitive strength of small scale sector increases a lot. S.S.E. Clusters can solve many problems of this sector. The changed policy of the government may not affect the speedy growth of the sector. Further, small scale sector in India continues to play a dominant role in the contribution to the Indian economy.

9

INDIAN INDUSTRY RETROSPECT AND PROSPECT—A CASE STUDY OF KHADI AND VILLAGE INDUSTRIES

P. Murali Krishna,
P. Venu Gopal & S. Sulochana

Introduction

The main objectives of this paper is to analyse the crucial role of Khadi and village industries in the process of economic development of a less developed economy like India. India is a typical example of poverty in the midst of plenty. Inspite of abundant human and physical resources, it is almost on the lowest rung of the ladder of economic development, as indicated by its vertically lowest per capita income. The various heavy industries started by the Governments during the post-independence period have produced only a ignorable marginal impact on the socio-economic picture of the country. The large scale industries based largely on mechanization have bought about neither the desired diversifications of the country's economic structure, nor paved the needed grounds for employment expansion. It is on this court that Gandhiji advocated the role of village and small scale, especially the Khadi and village industries in the Indian context.

The ideology of Khadi and village industries popularized by Mahatma Gandhi, caught imagination of our planners after Independence. Promotion of Khadi and village industries was specially mentioned in our construction as one of the Directive Principals of State Policy. It was recognized that these labour-intensive industries could mitigate unemployment and promote self-sufficiency. The First Five Year Plan, therefore, laid specially emphasis on Small Scale Industries including the Khadi and village industries with the objective of providing additional employment opportunities, mobilizing resources of capital and skill and providing a more equitable distribution of income and wealth.

The Mahalonobis model of economic growth adopted in our successive plans has belied our expectations particularly in relation to employment generation and poverty reduction. Of late its non-suitability is our conditions has been acknowledged. Development in situations such as ours demands a multi-dimensional and interdisciplinary approach, which in its operational sphere puts on a varied and complex character. A frontal attack on rural poverty is an objective of paramount importance in our development strategy. Unemployment visible as well as disguised, is the main cause of our poverty. We depended so far on developing Agriculture, Animal Husbandry, Horticulture, Fisheries, etc, comprising the primary sector of the generation of employment opportunities and growth of the economy in the rural areas. More than 60 per cent of our population is dependent on this sector. Naturally this sector offers little scope for further absorption of our additional man-power resources. Under the circumstances, we have to rely on Lewis-Nurkse model of unlimited labour supplies. Hence, the alternative lies in the promotion of the non-farm sector comprising Khadi and village Industries, ancillary industries and small business enterprises in our economy.

Need for the Study

Our experience during the last 50 years of planning for economic development has shown that the organized industrial sector by itself is not capable of solving the twin problems of poverty and unemployment in Rural Areas. According....... The only for hope solving the problems particularly of rural poverty and unemployment lies in the growth of the decentralized industrial sector giving maximum importance to Khadi and village Industries. Being labour intensive, they have great potential to provide gainful employment to the rural population.

Scope of the K.V.I.

The village industries include abroad spectrum of industries, including those commonly known as cottage and Household Industries such as processing of cereals and pulses, ghani oil, manufacturing of cane gur and Khandsari, palm gus making and other palm products, cottage match, manufacture of the fire works and agarbatties, cottage soap, collection of forest plants and fruits for medical purposes. Bamboo and cane works, hand made paper, bee keeping, village potters, manufacturing of manures, black smithy, carpentry etc. There are three types of Khadi: Cotton Khadi, Wollen Khadi and Silk Khadi. Each type has its own problems and features, which require special treatment. The most important type is cotton khadi, which accounts for more than nald of the entire Khadi production.

Role of K.V.I.

Khadi and village industries constitute that powerful engine which when extensively, effectively and intensively developed and placed on an ever-progressing self-reliant progress path have the potential of meeting the twin problems of unemployment and poverty in virtually all undeveloped and developing economics of the world which have choosen the process of sponsored growth ever since early fifties. It is so because most of these have from the contextual viewpoint common characteristics namely (i) explosively high growth rate of population, (ii) huge volume of unemployment and under-employment and high rates of unemployment, (iii) predominantly rural character of their economy, (iv) diversity and richness in local resources; and (v) in sufficiency or capital resources. Our own country is a leading example of these developing economics, and is one of the fittest cases whereas Khadi and village Industries have specifically important role to play.

Problems of the K.V.I.

History gives ample testimony to the great glory and popularity enjoyed by India's cottage and village industries since time immemorial right upto the setting in foot of British East India company. There after started the progress of their delay, which continued till the independence. In spite of the best measures taken by Government of India to solve the problems of Khadi and village industries after Independence, they have been suffering from a number of problems. The main problems confronting the Khadi and village industries in our country relate to inadequate supplies of raw materials, credit and other infrastructural facilities. Lack of adequate facilities, however, for development of new technology and modernization of technology also hindered the pace of development of these industries in the country. Similarly there was lack of enthusiasm for transmission of training and production centres. Inadequacy was also noticed in manufacture and supply of improved tools, in provision of equipment and machinery on decentralized basis, and in procurement and supply of critical and scarce raw materials, to articiams and entrepreneurs. Similarly desired success could not be achieved in the expansion of marketing and reorganization and decentralization of the administrative structure in this regard.

As compared to the position of Khadi and village industries during the pre-planning period, the concerned developments during the past few decades no doubt look impressive. But these had yet do wait for the future to attain their due importance.

Conclusion

Khadi and village industries are the most effective instruments of rural industrialisation, manpower absorption and Justice promotion in the country and for that matter more so in our own State where the percentage of rural population is highest among few states of the union. We have adopted multi-disciplinary and multi-agency approach for their promotion and development through the provision of integrated supplies of various types of developmental inputs in terms of production where withals and other infrastructural facilities. But the pond may be full yet the hore may refuse to drink if there is no will on its part to drink this necessitates all out efforts on the part of the various agencies including the State Board, DICs and the proposed Block level institutions with all their functionaries to so contact, reach and communicate with the beneficiaries at the other end in the provision of the needed facilities that thc will of the people at the grass-root is activised and continuously invested into improvement activities. The role of various mass media, education, demonstration and other devices for dissemination of information regarding the facilities available to the beneficiaries cannot be over-stated, because the functionaries in Khadi and village Industries sector have to deal with the people who are much less organized and have for long been victims of traditions and defeatism. To involve such a lot of and on such a scale in self-reliant improvement activities through the development of Khadi and village Industries in really and challenging task.

SESSION–3

THE PROSPECTS OF EXTERNAL SECTOR

1

SHIFTS IN DEVELOPMENT PARADIGMS AND POVERTY REDUCTION STRATEGIES WITH FOCUS ON INDIA AND PAKISTAN

G. Raghava Reddy

Introduction

Despite of the remarkable progress made on the social and economic front in the second half of the 20th century, poverty continues to be the greatest challenge. The contours and configurations of poverty as well as its nature and processes are subject to change but its absolute quantum is not reduced in most parts of the South Asia and Sub-Saharan Africa. Of the world's billion people 1.2 billion live on less than $1 a day, with 44% concentrated in South Asia, 23% in East Asia and Pacific and 24% in Sub-Saharan (World Bank 2000-2001). It is widely recognized that the income measure of poverty is utterly inadequate to capture the real picture of poverty. Besides income, education, health, nutrition and other indicators of human development are to be considered. Future demographic changes and depletion of natural resources are bound to add to the challenge of poverty almost everywhere in the third world. In this paper it is proposed to deal with the major shifts in development paradigms and poverty reduction strategies.

Shifts in Development Paradigms and Poverty Reduction Strategies

After the Second World War many countries of Asia and

Africa attained political independence from the colonial rulers. Political freedom without economic development and social progress was considered to be meaningless for the people of these countries, the so-called third world. Since most of these countries were caught in a low equilibrium trap and the vicious circles of poverty, a big push and a critical minimum effort were needed to put them on the path of accelerated growth. Harroddomar models of growth two-sector models of development such as that of Lewis dominated the field in the 1950s. Lewis recognised that "the central problem in the theory of economic development is to understand the process by which community which was previously saving and investing 4 or 5% of national income converts into an economy where voluntary saving is running about 12 to 15% of national income or more." Since saving are assumed to come largely from profits Lewis concluded that underdeveloped countries save little not because their incomes are low but because their capitalist sectors are small. Hence, a concrete policy measure is derived from the model to accelerate the growth of capitalist sector and the distribution of income in favour of the capitalist sector.

The importance attached to industrialisation by developing countries lies in the general association that appears to exist between industrialisation and real income per capita. Technical progress appears to be more rapid in industry and the scope of economies of scale greater, the practical importance of which is enhanced by the higher income elasticity of demand for industrial goods both domestically and internationally. The scope of productivity increase in industry appears greater over all. In fact, the greater the proportion of workers in manufacturing, the higher to be the level of manufacturing productivity (A.P. Thirlwall, p. 42).

In India the famous Mahalanobis model laid emphasis on the growth of heavy industry as a means of accelerating long run development of the economy as a whole. In other countries of Asia except China and Japan, a variant of this model which is borrowed from the USSR, was adopted and there was no explicit provision for safeguarding the interest of the poor. Community development programmes were initiated to mitigate the incidence of unemployment and poverty especially in the rural sector.

During the 1960s in most of the CMCs, green revolution physical and human capital development became the critical ingredients of the development paradigm. Agricultural growth based on new technology had shown promising results in terms of accelerating the rate of growth in the production of cereals. Since the technology was scale-neutral its was possible to extend it to all size-groups of farms. Since it is based on high pay-off inputs, it is not resource-neutral. Hence it has resulted in regional and social inequalities in the distribution of income accentuating the initial unequal distribution of assets and income. Human capital development approaches too have strengthened the inequality rather than reducing it leading to the failure of the Trickle down theory.

In the 1970s the issues of poverty and inequality began to surface and became critical for the survival of the systems—political, social and economic. Hence, growth with equity became slogan. The challenge of poverty could no longer be escaped. A direct attack on it became inevitable. A basic needs approach coupled with Integrated Rural Development Programmes (IRDPs) were formulated and implemented.

In the 1980s, structural adjustment policies and programmes entered the development horizon due to the debt overhang experienced by most of the non-oil exporting countries. The basic reasons commonly advanced for the economic crisis faced by most countries undergoing structural adjustments are: inward-looking, import-substituting development strategies and high degree of state intervention in and regulation of economic activities by governments. High protection of domestic industry, as an inevitable corollary of the import substituting strategy, is supposed to have led to inefficiency and misallocation of investable resources and loss of comparative advantage in international trade. Entry of governments in economic activities which could best be performed by private sector has resulted inefficiency and drain on budgetary resources. Regulation of private sector activity has meant unnecessary and undesirable curbs on the operations of economic activity resulting in slower growth of investment, misallocation of investment and encouragement to rent-seeking activities. The Fund-Bank initiatives in bringing about structural adjustments of the crisis ridden economies did not yield satisfactory results. A broad based, people oriented growth was sought to be achieved without much of a success. Social safety nets ran into rough weather in most cases due to the fiscal crisis in almost all countries. International financial flows became marginal or negative for the developing world. It is against this background of the persistence of absolute poverty at an unacceptable level that the UNDP's Human Development Reports among others have led to the human development paradigm in the 1990s. The World Bank's 1990 development report underlined the need for a two-part strategy: promoting labour-intensive growth through economic openness and investment in infrastructure and providing basic services to poor people in health and education. Targeted intervention and safety nets for the extreme poor and vulnerable were incorporated in the programme of poverty reduction.

These two-part strategies of development and poverty alleviation are further enlarged into a three-part strategy of development of the poor: 1. Promoting opportunity, 2. Facilitating empowerment and 3. Enhancing security (World Bank 2000-2001, p. 6). Overall economic growth is crucial for generating opportunity for the poor. So is the pattern or quality of growth which is pro-poor. Facilitating empowerment is a larger and complicated matter in traditional societies. Empowerment approach builds capacity, capability and willingness to take decisions by organising the community. The last point, namely organising the community, is the most crucial element because is envisages the removal of social and institutional barriers that result from distinctions of gender, ethnicity and social status. Enhancing security, reducing vulnerability to economic shocks, natural disasters, ill health, disability and personal violence. The three elements of the attack on poverty are deeply complementary. Each part of the strategy affects underlying causes of poverty addressed by the other two. The World Bank's development Report 2000-2001 rightly stresses that there is no simple, universal blueprint for implementing this three-part strategy. Developing countries need to prepare their own mix of policies to reduce poverty. The foregoing outline of shifts in development paradigms and poverty reduction strategies are summarised in what follows:

SHIFTS IN DEVELOPMENT PARADIGMS AND POVERTY REDUCTION STRATEGIES

Period	*Development Paradigm*	*Poverty Reduction Strategies*
1950s	Industrialisation	Community development
1960s	Green revolution Physical and human Capital development	Trickle down effect
1970s	Growth with justice	Basic needs approach & IRDP
1980s	Structural adjustments	Growth, HRD, safety nets and people's participation
1990s	Human development	Labour-intensive approach access to basic social services programme of targeted intervention; safety nets
2000s	Pattern and quality of growth	Opportunity, Empowerment and Security

Note: CMCs = CIRDAP member countries
(IRDAP means Centre on Integrated Rural Development for Asia and the Pacific).

Sourc: CIRDAP, Rural Development Report 1999.
World Bank, World Bank Report 2000/2001.

Prospects for Poverty Reduction in India and Pakistan

Since the disastrous events of September 11 in New York and Washington there is a spectacular change in the security environment of the world as a whole. The terrorist attacks of December 13 on the Indian parliament have escalated the Indo-Pakistan tensions across the border. These catastrophic occurrences have an adverse impact on sustaining the normal levels of economic activity and designing suitable strategies for growth with poverty reduction. Although the links between the political economy of terrorism and poverty cannot be directly established, there is no Chinese Wall separating them. On the face of it, it is religions or racial differences but issues of persistent poverty are at the root of intra as well as cross border terrorism. Since the conflict over Kashmir is bound to persist and plague the neighbourly relations between India and Pakistan and fourty-three per cent Pakistan's border is with India, it may be of some interest to look at different facets of human poverty in both these countries. It needs hardly to be emphasised that good neighbourly relations between any two countries will go a long way in reducing defence expenditure which can be utilized for the development of the poor. It may be noted that every Indian carries a foreign debt burden of $ 103 and every Pakistani of $ 350.

Trade between the two countries could be a far better route to foster the spirit of friendship and partnership. Unfortunately, Pakistan imports only 1.4 per cent of its requirements from India, while India imports even a lesser fraction, k at 0.2 per cent from Pakistan (N. Narashimhan, EPW).

Table 1 offers some of the relevant data.

The statistics of Table 1 are quite clear and they indicate that India has the lead in several dimensions of economic and human development. However in terms of human poverty index and income poverty as measured by the proportion of the poor Pakistan is better placed than India. This may be a matter of some solace for Pakistan. South-Asian Governments including India and Pakistan are committed to achieving the following goals by 2015 taking 1999 as the reference point:

1. Reduce income poverty by half.

TABLE 1
SELECT INDICATORS OF HUMAN POVERTY FOR INDIA AND PAKISTAN

S. No.	*Variable*	*India*	*Pakistan*
1.	Expectation of life at birth (years)	62.9	64.4
2.	Adult Literacy rate (5)	55.7	44.0
3.	Per capita GDP (PPP US $)	2077	1715
4.	Human Development Index	0.563	0522
5.	Infant Mortality Rate (Deaths per 1000 live births)	69	95
6.	Gross School Enrolment Rate (%)	54	43
7.	Proportion of the poor living on less than $ 1 a day	44.2	31.0
8.	Proportion of population as per national definitions	35 (1994)	28.7 (1993-94)
9.	Human Poverty Index	34.6	40.1
10.	Population without access to		
	(a) Safe Water (%)	19	21
	(b) Health Services (%)	25	15
	(c) Sanitation (%)	77	44
11.	Female literacy (%)	43.5	28.9

Sourc: Human Development Report 2000.
World Development Report 2000.

2. Reduce infant mortality rates by two-thirds.
3. Achieve universal primary education.

The challenge before the south Asian governments in general and India and Pakistan in particular is to convert their commitments into achievements by reducing tensions and designing suitable poverty reduction strategies coupled with development goals.

Outlook for Growth and Poverty Reduction

The economic outlook for the two big brothers of South Asia in the short-run looks uncertain the bleak. Economic growth for Pakistan and India is expected to be 3.5 and 5.4 per cent in 2000-2001. Pakistan economy is expected to grow at 4.0 per cent and Indian economy at 5.4 per cent in 2002 according to the report or RIS. During the 1990s the growth in GDP per capita in India has fluctuated between 2.6 per cent in 1993-94 to 5.4 per cent 1999-2000 as per the estimates of CMIE. While the stocks of food grains in India are piling up to unprecedented levels i.e., 60 million tonnes by 2001, the per capita availability of food grains has tended to marginally decline. This is the case of poverty amidst plenty. The country is self-sufficient and even tying to export, but the poor people have no purchasing power to buy adequate food for want of productive employment opportunities. The enlargement of productive employment opportunities for the masses by designing appropriate development paradigms involving the participatory methods of social mobilization is the major challenge before India and Pakistan, apart form resolving the cross-border terrorist problems and resolving other bilateral problems by diplomatic and other negotiating techniques.

REFERENCES

1. World Development Reports 1990 and 2000-2001, Oxford, New York.
2. A.P. Thirlwall, Growth and Development with special reference to developing countries, Macmillan & ELBS, 1982.
3. UNDP Human Development Reports, various issues, Oxford, New York.
4. UNOPS and UNDP Regional Progress Reports, various issues.
5. The Hindu (Chennai 14th Jan. 2002).
6. CMIE Monthly Review of Indian Economy, December 2001.
7. IFAD, Rural Poverty Report 2001, Oxford, New York.
8. Narayanan, Indo-Pakistan relations, EPW, Jan. 12, 2002, p. 172.

2

A REVOLUTION IN INTERNATIONAL TRADE—INDIA'S PERSPECTIVE

S. Saraswathi

Introduction

The traditional, paper based, Indian Economy is being transformed into digital Economy. This digital economy is reshaping international trade. The traditional trade in traditional goods and services adapt new technologies to cut and reposition their places and ranks in international markets. It is called as e-trade.

This e-trade opens new opportunities to export oriented firms especially small firms. It helps to eliminate intermediaries and reduces business transaction costs. Therefore the challenge is to acquire 'e-trade' capability at every stage of transaction. It requires a concerted response from entrepreneur, Govt., managers executives of trade support institutions like banks financial intermediaries, transporting concerns and tax authorities.

Internet

Internet has become an important tool for international trade. Buyers communicate with many suppliers simultaneously through internet, which saves costs, energy and time. Besides, it helps to bring together in one place information regarding all the participants of international trade-buyers, supplies, financiers, shippers, transporters and other allied services.

TABLE 1
INTERNET ADVANTAGES TO TRADE

1. Supply chain cost reduction	In terms of money, time and energy.
2. Process cost reduction	Lower transaction and communication costs.
3. Market efficiency	Abundant market information and choice of goods.
4. Increased revenues	Through new activities funded by cash released from reduced working capital.

There are nearly one thousand Internet Trading Exchanges in operation in various countries all over the world. The Internet allows service providers to go global by broadening market reach.

The following steps may be taken to harness internet to trade more effectively.

- Keep exporters and their suppliers informed about fast changing forces like e-commerce, communication can be through workshops, conferences, seminars and specialised journals on trade.
- Exporters to be trained in adapting business and manufacturing practices for digital economy.
- A new partnership among several trades promoting organisations and industries has come up. Exporters must work for access to such avenues.
- Export help firms' must be given practical training to convert paper information into digital format with less or no errors.
- Exporters must enhance buyers' confidence by providing 'up-to-date information.'
- Traditional paper services like certificate of origin quality standards, environmental friendly certificate etc., to be made on line (Internet).
- Local software to be developed in local language too.

New Business Opportunities

The new areas of export opportunities that emerged in

recent years can be broadly categorised into three-services: 'exporting, hardware and software.

Services exporting opportunities that exploit information and communication technology (ICT) are on hike as new changes are taking place in business practices, and intermediaries.

Hardware Market

According to ITC (International Trade Centre) demand for hardware is increasing at 10 to 12% per year. As new technologies stimulate broader and deeper demand for internet based services and devices, the world import market for ICT (Information Communication and Technology) equipment is expected to increase $ 1 Trillion by 2005. As a matter of fact ICT sector has become one of the major growth industries in foreign trade, exceeding world trade in agriculture, automobiles and textiles. The ICT market is dominated by MNCS. From the view of an exporter from developing countries like India, the market for ICT is featured by

- Formidable entry barriers to independent producers.
- Geographic and organisational separation or research and product development, production and marketing organisations.
- Focus is on components of the product rather than on complete product.
- Growing competition among task and component suppliers.
- Proximity to major markets and growth poles determine competitiveness.

The best strategy to enhance exports of hardware is to work with reputed MNCS, or with well established firms in the ICT hardware market.

Software Market

My paper concentrates on trade opportunities, trends and role and place of Indian Software industry in international trade.

India's Software Industry is growing at 50% per annum over the past few years, is a highly export oriented. It has established India as an exporter of knowledge intensive services.

The computers software industry of India is in its 'teens'. It has caught the attention of the world market and India is being identified as the major 'Power House' for the development of computer software.

As many as 212 Indian software companies have setups 509 overseas offices or subsidiaries, of which 266 are in North America, 122 in Europe, 59 in Asia excluding India, 25 in Australia, 25 in Africa and 12 in Latin America. A few leading companies have established extensive networks all over the world to tap opportunities in different markets. These companies are TCS, HCl Technologies, NIIT and Infosys. Four Indian companies got themselves accepted on U.S. stock exchange. It is all because Indian software industry maintains its international quality.

Quality Accreditation

250 Indian companies of software industry obtained ISO 9000 (International Standard Organisation) certification by March 2001. 38 companies from India have obtained SEI-CMM (Software Engineering Institute, U.S.A.'s Capability Maturity Model) certification at level 3.29 Software companies out of 31 non-U.S. companies, that are certified as 'high maturity levels' of 4 and 5 in terms of SEI-CMM are Indian. 16 companies out of 31 that are certified at level 5 are Indian. Level 5 represents optimizing level of process Maturity and is the highest stage to be reached. It indicates that India occupies No. 1 place in software quality in the world software industry.

Direction and Composition of Software Exports from India

Indian software services are exported to several countries. The geographical distribution of Indian software exports shown in Table 2.

Indian companies have developed expertisation in

various areas, and are able to undertake variety of tasks. It is represented in Table 3.

TABLE 2
DIRECTION OF INDIAN SOFTWARE EXPORTS

Region	*Share of India's Software Exports*
1. North America	62.0%
2. Europe	24.0%
3. Japan	04.0%
4. South-East Asia	03.5%
5. Australia and Newzealand	01.5%
6. West Asia	01.5%
7. Rest of the World	03.5%

Source: Nagesh Kumar: EPW 10.11.2001, p. 4281.

TABLE 3
AREAS OF SPECIALISATION OF INDIAN SOFTWARE COMPANIES

Areas	*No. of companies offering expertisation*
Banking insurance, stock exchange and financial accounting	247
Manufacturing, retail, trading and distribution	331
Transport/airlines/ports/railways	157
Web application/online information services	295
Engineering, electronics, design, automation and robotics	224
Medical and Health	163
Education, training and entertainment	115
Telecommunications	174

Source: Ibid, p. 4282

The share of software exports in India's total exports has increased from negligible percentage in 1990 to 8% in 2000-2001. While was 5.89% and 4.41% during 1999-2000 and 1998-1999 respectively.

Though the share of software exports in total exports of India may be less, it made a phenomenal growth over the last decade as foreign exchange earner. It is shown in the following Table 4.

TABLE 4
REVENUES FROM DOMESTIC SECTOR AND EXPORTS OF INDIAN SOFTWARE INDUSTRY (in U.S. $ Million)

Year	*Domestic Sector*	*Exports*	*Total Revenue*
1989-90	97	100	197
1994-95	350	485	835
1995-96	490	734	1224
1996-97	670	1085	1755
1997-98	950	1750	2700
1998-99	1250	2650	3900
1999-00	1700	4000	5700
2000-01	1960	6300	8260
2001-02E	2700	8500	11200

Note: E—Estimated.
Source: Ibid, p. 4279.

Factors Contributing for the Growth of Software Exports from India

Comparative cost advantage. The wages of software professionals in India are lower than their counterparts abroad. Now this gap is being narrowed. This comparative costs are represented in Table 5.

- Indian software engineers have carved out an inviable reputation in the world market for providing an undeeatable combination of quality software at a low cast. Indian software developers offer a cost advantage of 40 to 60% over their American counterparts.
- Continuous development of new software for P.Cs plays an important role in its growth of exports.
- Rapidly improving communications infrastructure has played a key role in creating confidence among importers of Indian software products and related services.
- According to UNCTAD, a traditional bank to bank/ branch transaction costs approximately U.S. $1, while, automatic teller machine costs to U.S. $20 and on line transaction brings it down to U.S. $0.01. It is cost effective and secure settlement of transaction.

TABLE 5
COST/WAGE COMPARISONS FOR SOFTWARE PROFESSIONALS (U.S. $ per year)

Type of labour	*Switzerland*	*U.S.*	*Canada*	*U.K.*	*Greece*	*India*
Project Leader	74000	54000	39000	39000	24000	23000
Business Analyst	74000	38000	36000	37000	28000	21000
Systems Analyst	74000	48000	32000	34000	15000	14000
System Designer	67000	55000	36000	34000	15000	11000
Development Programmer	56000	41000	29000	29000	13000	8000
Support Programmer	56000	37000	26000	25000	15000	8000
Network Analyst	67000	49000	32000	31000	15000	14000
Quality Assurance Specialist	71000	50000	28000	33000	15000	14000
Data Base Analyst	67000	50000	32000	22000	24000	17000
Metics/process specialist	74000	48000	29000	31000	15000	17000
Documentation/ Training Staff	59000	36000	26000	21000	15000	8000
Test Engineer	59000	47000	25000	24000	13000	8000

Note: Figures are average (approximately) for 1995
Source: Ibid., p. 4288.

Spillover Effects of Software Industry

The rapid rate of growth in software industry reversed braindrain to some extent, as it is providing rewarding Job opportunities in India itself. According to IIT Delhi Alumni Association the rate of braindrain has declined from 21% in 1990-92 to 18% during 1997-98. Besides a number of NRIs are returning to India to start software ventures. It has increased from 2% in 1991 to 8 to 10% by late 90's. At Hyderabad alone 100 companies were setup by returned NRI.

Software industry also contributed for brain in the course of executing projecting onsite or through "body shopping." A number of software personnel who went to other countries for assignments of their employers have stayed on. According to 1997 statistics 10% of software professionals are Indians in Australia, who stayed thereafter completing their assignments. This type of braindrain creates shortage of software professionals.

- NRI's of software industry in the U.S. have invested back home in subsidiaries that develop software for their U.S. operations.
- It enhanced bilateral relationships with other countries especially with U.S. Bill Clinton's visit to India in 2000, is an evidence for this. His agenda for his visit to India especially to Hyderabad is heavily loaded with I.T. related issues.
- The development of software industry has led to an increased inflow of capital to India from three angles:
  (a) FDI by MNCS into their subsidiaries and joint ventures in India.
  (b) Investments by foreign institutions in the stocks of software companies in India.
  (c) Capital raised by Indian software companies abroad.
- The growth of exports of software from India is by over 51% compound annual rate, has prompted policy makers of India to consider software industry as an "engine of growth."

Conclusion

The performance of this industry over the past few years has prompted the Government and industry to set up ambitious target of making annual export earnings from this industry, of U.S. $ 50 billion by 2008. But realization of this target is a big challenge because of:

(a) raising scarcity of trained manpower due to brain-drain,
(b) eroding labour cost advantage, as employers are rising salaries and other incentives to retain the trained professionals in India.
(c) emerging competition from other countries like U.S. based firms, Singapore, Israel, Ireland, Philippines, Russia and Eastern Europe. Even firms in India are competing with each other to capture foreign

markets. According to Carnegie Mellon University Survey, 82% of competitors of Indian software firms were located in India itself.

(d) Infrastructural bottlenecks like bankwidth for data transfer.

(e) The recent slowdown in U.S. economy and industry and war against Afganisthan have considerable impact on Indian software exports.

I would like to conclude that Indian software industry is a bright star among other glittering stars like other industries, in the sky like export basket.

Ref: 'Facts for you'—2001 issues.

Economic and political weekly—10-16 November, 2001.

3

TRENDS IN INDIA'S EXTERNAL SECTOR ISSUES, CONCERNS AND COMMENTS

G. Raghava Reddy and
P.V. Sesha Reddy

Introduction

The nation state is increasingly drawn into a situation of growing interdependence in the modern world. There are multiplicity of factors contributing to this tendency including information technology. The globalisation of national economies is manifested on several fronts. Trade flows across nations have been the earliest of international interdependence. The classical as well as the neo-classical theory of trade has been formulated on the assumption of immobility of factory of production. On account of the capital flows as well as labour flows though selectively across nations, the foundations of the theory of trade are rudely shaken. Besides trade in merchandise, trade in services, capital and labour movements as also the transmission of technology have contributed to the emergence of the so-called global village in our times. Therefore, globalisation is no more a slogan. It is a reality that is going to dominate and shape the future destiny of mankind. In this context, we propose to highlight the developments in he external sector of Indian economy and analyse the emerging issues and concerns of globalisation on the masses of India and make some comments that are warranted.

The Rise of Globalisation

It may be noted that globalisation is not a new phenomenon. It has been there since the days of the mercantilists. The classical economists were staunch advocates of private enterprise and free trade because their era roughly coincided with the dawn of the industrial revolution. The European nations were in search international markets for their industrial manufactures. The gold standard mechanism facilitated the basis for the growth and development of trade until its collapse in the initial phase of the 20th century. The great depression of the 1930s led to the resurgence of protectionism and beggar thy neighbour policy. Competitive exchange depreciation became the order of the day, that eventually led to the collapse of trade and payments systems.

The outbreak of the hostilities of World War II led to the revival of the economies as well as the destruction of some of the war torn economies. In the post-war era, the dawn of political independence in several parts of the globe led to rising expectations of the role of the state in accelerating the pace of development and reduction of mass poverty. Development planning was the chose instrument in many parts of the developing world because of the tremendous achievements of socialist development planning in the U.S.S.R. After the collapse of the U.S.S.R. and East European socialist regimes, the nations of the world are placed in a uni-modal capitalist growth path. The steering wheel of this machine is in the hand of the U.S.A. In the name of the United Nation, a vast array of multilateral organisations have been established at the global and regional level to promote international intercourse and development. Regional groupings and unions have emerged in almost all parts of the globe. Multinational corporations have become powerful not only in the transfer of capital, technology and management but also the transfer of political power in the host nations. International trade has grown twice as fast as worldwide income during the past two decades. Spurred by advances in information technology, a growing share of this trade is in the services rather than merchandise especially among rich countries. International direct and portfolio equity investment has also surged tremendously during this period. Apart from the OECD member countries and the East Asian Tigers, India is one of the 24 post-1980 globalisers along with China.[1]

Factors Behind Globalisation of Indian Economy

The initiation of the process of development planning in India in 151 was guided by the objectives of rapid growth, social justice, self-reliance, alleviation of poverty, modernisation and improvement in productivity.[2] Accordingly a development strategy was designed based on import substituting model of growth. It was justified on the ground of export pessimism on the one hand and the soviet model on the other. India could manage to withstand the foreign exchange gap and the resulting crisis until the 1980s. The year 1991 is an important landmark in the post-independent economic history of India. The country faced a severe economic crisis, triggered in part by a serious balance of payment situation. The crisis was converted into an opportunity to effect some fundamental changes in the content and approach to economic policy.[3] Under the leadership of Rao and Singh the inward-looking strategy of development was transformed into an outward-looking export-led strategy of growth on the model of East Asian Tigers. The static and dynamic gains of trade were sought to be achieved. The 'vent for surplus',[4] an important potential gain from trade which provides an outlet for country's surplus commodities which would otherwise go unsold and represent a waste of resources was sought to be realised. A series of liberalisation measures were initiated and executed on the domestic and external front of the economy. As a result of the economic reforms the growth path of the economy has been pushed to a higher plane compared with the past. The external sector of the economy, despite the persistence of the chronic, fundamental disequilibrium in trade and payments, has shown a marked improvement. We set out a few

TABLE 1
GLOBALISATION OF INDIAN ECONOMY IN THE 1990s

Years	*ITEMS*							
	India's Exports As % of World's Exports	*India's Exports As % of Imports*	*India's (US$ Million) (Growth Rate)*	*Exports (US$ Million) (Growth Rate)*	*Import (US$ Million) (Growth Rate)*	*Foreign Exchange Reserves (US$ Million)*	*Current A/C Deficit (as % of GDP)*	*Foreign Investment (as % GDP)*
1990-91	0.58	75.4	6.2	9.2	13.5	5834	–3.1	0
1991-92	0.56	92.0	8.1	–1.5	19.4	9220	–0.3	0.1
1992-93	0.56	84.7	7.8	3.8	12.7	9832	–1.7	0.2
1993-94	0.62	95.4	8.8	20	6.5	19254	–0.4	1.5
1994-95	0.65	91.9	8.8	18.4	22.9	25186	–1.0	1.5
1995-96	0.64	86.7	9.7	20.8	28.0	21687	–1.7	1.4
1996-97	0.65	85.9	9.5	5.3	6.7	26423	–1.2	1.6
1997-98	0.62	83.3	9.1	4.6	6.0	29367	–1.4	1.3
1998-99	0.61	72.2	8.0	–5.1	2.2	32490	–1.0	0.6
1999-2000	0.80	79.6	8.4	13.2	11.4	38036	–1.9	1.2
Average 1999-2000	0.63	84.7	8.4	8.9	12.9	21732.9	–1.3	0.9
Average 1992-2000	0.64	84.9	8.8	10.1	12.1	25284.4	–1.2	1.2

Source: RBI, Handbook on statistics of Indian Economy, 2000.

indicators of the openness of the economy in the 1990s which throw some light on the trend towards globalisation.

Globalisation of India

At the dawn of independence India's share in world's trade was around 2 per cent in 1950 and fell down to 0.5 per cent in the nineties; it is hovering around 0.6 per cent (Table 1). However, India's exports as a proportion of its imports has shown a modest improvement thereby reducing the trade gap. There is a striking rise in India's exports and imports is moderately falling. It is partly reflected in the steady rise of foreign exchange reserves. Current account deficit has been reduced from around 3 per cent of GDP to around 1 per cent to 1.2 per cent of GDP by the turn of the century. All the indicators of Table 1 demonstrate the growing openness of the economy. We present a comparative picture of opens of Indian economy vis-a-vis Chinese economy.

TABLE 2
INDIA AND CHINA: COMPARISON OF EXTERNAL SECTOR: 1996-99

Item	*Unit*	*India*	*China*
Exports	($ Bn)	33.6	183.8
As % of world Exports	(%)	0.6	3.5
Exports of Commercial Services	($ Bn)	11.1	24
Imports	($ Bn)	42.7	140.2
Current account Surplus/deficit	($ Bn)	–4.9	29.3
Forex reserves	($ Bn)	35.5	157.4
Exchange rate	(Rs./Renminbi per US dollar)*	46.8	8.3
FDI Inflows	($ Bn)	2.2	40.4
Total Debt outstanding	($ Bn)	98.2	154.6
Debt Service ratio	(%)	20.6	8.6

* Pertains to November 1, 1999.
Source: TATA, Statistical Outline of India, 2000-2001, pp. 138-139.

A comparison of the external sector of India and China reveals the lagging position of India in terms of all the indicators in relation to China. The picture is more glaring in the case of FDI inflows than in the case of trade flows and debt stock. Foreign exchange reserves of China are slightly more than four times to that of India. The incidence of poverty (not shown in Table 2) is 35 per cent in India and only 5 per cent in China. Therefore, there are several lessons to be drawn for India from the China's model of development. Recent studies[5] show that globalisation has a positive impact on poverty reduction. Therefore globalization is not only growth augmenting but also poverty reducing the state follows pro-poor social development and gender empowerment policies.

Concluding Remarks

Globalisation has a long history. The pace and pattern of globalisation have varied over time and space. Like business cycles, there have been phases of rise and fall in globalisation. The overpopulated developing countries had many reservations about the gains from foreign trade and investment. The experience of Europe, America and the East Asian Tigers has fostered confidence among nations about the strategy of export-led growth. Indian economy has been making rapid strides on its external front. Foreign exchange reserves are booming. The volume of trade: investment and allied flows have shown a spectacular improvement in the 1990s. However compared with China, India is lagging far behind not only on the external front but also in poverty reduction. There is a strong case for learning from Chinese development experience.

REFERENCES

1. David Dollar and Apart Kraay, Trade, Growth and Poverty, Finance & Development, September, 2001, 9-16.
2. RBI, Report of the Committee to Review the Working of the Monetary System, Bombay 1985, p. 4.
3. C. Rangarajan, Economic Reforms: An assessment, The Indian Economic Journal, Volume 49, No. 1, p. 2.
4. A.P. Thirlwall, Growth and Development, ELBS and McMillan, 1982, p. 337.
5. David Dollar *et. al. Ibid*, pp. 16-19.

4

IMPACT OF ECONOMIC REFORMS ON INDIA'S BALANCE OF PAYMENTS*

M. Sundara Rao and
A. Sailaja Devi

Introduction

The Balance of Payments (BoP) is an economic parameter, which shows the international financial position and indicates the changing international economic position of a country. It is a record of official estimate of all international transactions during a year. The balance of payments comprises all external transactions getting up from import and export goods, export and import services as insurance, shipping, tourism, investment, income and transfers such as remittances and capital inflows and outflows.

As a developing economy, India has, by and large, the similar constraints on her way to development and sound BoPs position as other DCs have. The persistent balance of payment difficulties in developing countries is the outcome of rising demand for imports and a relatively lower rate of increase in export earnings. While the rising demand for imports are generated by accelerated development efforts, rapid population growth and a thrust for rapid industrialization, the falling rates of export earnings are owing to, on the one hand, the lower foreign demand for

*Paper submitted for presentation in the UGC sponsored National seminar on "Indian Economy—Retrospect and Prospects," conducted by Department of Economics, Hindu College, Guntur.

domestic products and domestic supply constraints, on the other, leading to an inadequate foreign exchange receipts which in turn, may constitute effective structural constraints upon the growth and development of the country.

Against this background an attempt is made in the present study to analyse the different dimensions of economic reforms effects on India's BoP. In the foregoing sections, broad trends in the India's BoP during the pre-reform period (section 1), brief review of the economic reforms on the external sector front (section 2), broad trends in the India's BoP during the post reform period (section 3) and recent trends in India's BoP are discussed in brief.

Trends in India's BoP during Pre-reform Period

India has been experiencing BoPs deficit right from 1951. Through, over the period of the First Year Plan, the pressure on balance of payments was not so grave. The India's balance of payments position proved adverse in 1951-52 to the extent of Rs. 162.6 crores. During the Second Five Year Plan, the unfavourable position of BoPs owns its origin to a programme of rapid industrialization, which augmented imports over exports. During the Third Plan, India's position of balance of payments became worse enhancing deficit on current account from Rs. 306.4 crores in 1961-62 to Rs. 489.8 crores in 1965-66. And this happened despite the measures of exchange control, rigid imports restrictions, maximum utilization of foreign aid, promotion of exports and imports substitution, heavy borrowing from IMF (through SDRs) etc., were adopted.

The BoPs crisis was persistent, rather turning to be chronic, during the three Annual Plans as a result of considerable trade deficit. The position took a more severe form with a high deficit of Rs. 612.9 crores in years 1966-67. The crisis was lessened to an extent in 1968-69 when the deficit amounted to Rs. 365.2 crores. But the position of BoPs continued to be panicky in the following years with 1972-73 and 1976-77, the years of exception when the economy had surpluses. However, after the price hike in

1973, price of crude oil increased only from $11.65 per barrel in 1974 to $13 per barrel in 1978, but was almost trebled to $35 per barrel in 1979. The remarkable performance of exports from 1972-73 to 1976-77 was due to the conjunction of several favourable factors, such as the commodity boom of the early seventies which continued till 1974, the opening up of a large market for Indian exports in the oil rich Gulf countries consequent on the first oil price hike and finally to an effective devaluation of the rupee because of its link with sterling until 1975.

The BoPs deficits were of Rs. 880 crores in years 1972-1980. And the balance of payments deficits were in 1980-81 occurred due mainly to the second oil price hike. However, there was a steady improvement in the balance of payments situation, especially onwards the third year of the Sixth Plan, i.e., from 1982-83. With the progressive improvement, the ratio of current account deficit to GDP came down from 1.5 per cent in 1981-82, 1.1 per cent in 1982-83 and 1.2 per cent in 1983-84. Thus, India's balance of payments in the 1980s seems to have been mostly governed by the prices of improved oil, workers remittances and import substitution in crude oil.

Economic Reforms on the Front of External Sector

Till March 1985 it was the practice with the government to announce its export-import policy on a year-to-year basis. The first three-year import-export policy covered the period April 1985-March 1986, while the second covered the period 1988-1991 and the third the period 1990-1993. On March 31, 1992, a five-year policy covering the period 1992-1997 was announced. During this period two significant changes took place. Global funds and trade volumes have become larger than ever before and India was joined the W.T.O. The Government has responded by formulating a new long-term exim policy for the period 1997-2002. This was announced on March 31, 1997. Further modifications in the policy were announced as the when warranted in response to the developing situation. The objectives of the present policy are: To accelerate the country's transition to a globally oriented vibrant economy to derive maximum benefits from expanding global market opportunities. To stimulate sustained economic growth by providing access to essential items required for augmenting production. To enhance the technological strength and efficiency of Indian agriculture, industry and services—thereby improving their competitiveness and to provide consumers with good quality products at reasonable prices. Toward these objectives the important reforms introduced in trade policy are: tariffs progressively brought down but are still at high levels. All quantitative restrictions on imports of capital and intermediate goods have been removed. Most consumer goods are still under quantitative restrictions automatic approval is granted for foreign investment up to certain equity in selected sectors, 100 per cent equity is also allowed in these and all other sectors, but requires case-by-case approved by the foreign investment promotion board.

Trade policy reforms and changes during 2000-01 included the following:

Peak rate of basic customs duty was reduced from 40 per cent to 35 per cent and the total number of slabs in customs duty rates was rationalized from five to four (i.e., 35, 25, 15 and 5 per cent). Duties on various items (mostly customer goods and agriculture products) on which quantitative restrictions have been lifted have been placed at peak rate (35 per cent plus surcharge) to accord adequate tariff protection to these items. Setting up of Special Economic Zones (SEZ) to encourage export production free from the plethora of rules and regulations governing imports and exports. Evolution of a scheme for granting assistance to Sates based on their export performance for development of export related infrastructure. Rationalization of existing exports promotion schemes including abolition of Special Import License (SIL) from April 1, 2001. Sector specific initiatives to accelerate exports announced for core areas. Permission to import second-hand capital goods, which are less than 10 years old without obtaining any license on surrender of SIL. Deemed export benefits rationalized by extending benefits uniformly to eligible categories and expanding the definition of capital goods. Dereservation of the garment sector from the purview of SSI reservation in the new textile policy to boost garment exports.

The reforms introduced on the capital account during 2000-01 are:

Foreign Direct Investment (FDI) up to 100 per cent has been permitted in e-commerce subject to specific conditions. The dividend balancing condition for FDI in twenty-two consumer goods industries has been removed. The existing upper limit of Rs. 1500 crore for FDI in projects involving electricity generation, transmission and distribution (other than atomic reactor plants) has been dispensed with. For facilitating greater inflow of foreign funds in the crucial oil-refining sector, ceiling for FDI under the automatic route in oil refining was increased to 100 per cent from the existing 49 per cent. FDI under the automatic route has been permitted up to 100 per cent for all manufacturing activities in Special Economic Zones (SEZs) except certain activities. Foreign Institutional Investors (FIIs) have been permitted greater leverage in the primary and secondary markets by allowing enhancement of the aggregate FII investment ceiling in the issued and paid up capital of Indian companies from the normal ceiling of 24 per cent to 40 per cent subject to specific conditions. Foreign equity participation up to 20 per cent in insurance sector is allowed under the automatic route subject to obtaining necessary license from the Insurance Regulatory and Development Authority. ECB guidelines have been liberalized. A series of policy liberalizations have been affected for facilitating the use of ECB as a window for resource mobilization. Policies pertaining to international offerings through ADR/GDR by Indian companies have been further liberalized. 100 per cent FDI has also been allowed (with certain conditions) in telecommunications sector, for Internet service providers not providing gateways, infrastructure providers providing dark fiber, electronic mail and voice mail.

On the front of exchange rates after a step devaluation of about 22 per cent vis a vis dollar in July 1991, the rupee has practically floated there were two rates: market determined rate and an official rate. This was followed by shift to market determined rate of rupee in March 1993. The net result was an effective devolution of the rupee by around 35 per cent in nominal terms and 25 per cent in real terms between July 1991 and March 1993.

On the whole besides liberalizing the domestic economy the new economic reforms opened up India external actor to a great extent. The basic objective of the opening up process was to integrate Indian economy with the world economy so as to enhance our export earnings by having liberal access to compete international flow of capital and technology. The external sector reforms towards this end comprise the rationalization and dilution of tariff structure, permission of majority control to foreign investor, convertibility of rupee on current account a speedy disposal of the proposals for technical and financial foreign collaborations.

However the areas still waiting for reforms on the external sector can be listed as follows easing rules for automatic clearness of foreign investment proposals making a negative list of areas apart from which a foreign company can invest anywhere, reducing the discretionary powers that customs department has for fixing duty rates, improving export refinance facilities and making the rupees convertible on the capital account. Apparently, there is still a large menu left unattended on a scale of 10 economic reforms have still reached around five only. The pace of reforms has slowed down after the initial enthusiasm died down.

Balance of Payments during the Post Reform Period

The reform of the 1990s facilitated India to move away from a closed economy framework towards a more open and liberal economy. The selected indicator of external sector presented in Tables 1 and 2 reveal that there have been significant improvements in the structure of the external sector during the reform period. The export cover of import rose sharply from an annual average of 62 per cent during pre-reform period to 74 per cent during reform period. The ratio of exports and imports to GDP rose from an annual average of 13.2 per cent during pre reform period to an average of 19.9 per cent during reform period. The current account deficit as percentage of GDP declined from an annual average of 7.9 per cent during pre-reform to a well manageable level of 1.2 per cent during reform period. The capital account of BOP has also undergone a major structural change in favour of non-debt creating foreign investment flows. Foreign exchange reserves were built to a very comfortable level of about 8 month of imports from a critical level of about two months of imports in June 1991. External debt and debt service indicators marked sustained improvements over the 1990. External debt as a per cent of GDP, declined gradually from 38.7 per cent at the end of March 1992 to 21.9 per cent at the end of March 2000. Also debt service payments on external debt as a per cent of current receipts declined gradually from 35.3 per cent in 1990-91 to 16.0 per cent in 1999-2000. The strength of the external sector has enabled India to with stand fairly well the Asian financial crisis contagion and the related adverse spillovers.

The Balance of payment summary presented in Table 3 indicate that during the reform period the current account deficit in 1999-2000 was contained to 0.9 per cent of GDP. After some set backs in 1998-99, mainly as a fall out of East Asian crisis and partly due to the economic sanctions on India, capital flows improved significantly in 1999-2000. The moderation in current account deficit and the sharp increase in net capital inflows resulted in a large accumulation of official foreign exchange reserves. On BoP basis they rise rate by a substantial 6.14 billion. Invisible flows continued to maintain an upward trend during reform period. Private remittances account for the bulk of private transfer receipts. Despite revival of world trade, exports of developing countries like India continue to be threatened by the emerging projectionist sentiments in some sectors in the sense of technical standards, environmental an social concerns. The turn around in exports in 1999-2000 was led sharp rise in exports of manufactured goods while enhancing their share in total exports to 81.6 per cent. The composition of imports whose wide variations in import growth across commodity groups result in a sharp jump in share of these imports in total imports to 32.8 of per cent in 2000-2001.

On the external front reforms have enhanced India's competitiveness in labor and skill intensive industries, reduced the dependence of competitive industries on inefficient domestic suppliers and infrastructure and enhanced domestic competitive conditions, exports have been growing at 20 per cent in dollar terms. What is more significant is that the share of manufactured goods in the exports basket has risen while that of primary products has fallen. A recent study covering the post reforms period brings out that the export intensity has increased, whereas imports intensity has decreased. Both trade deficits and BOP current account deficits have considerably narrowed down. Various BOP indicators bring out continued improvement in the external sector.

The achievements in the external sector appear to be more credible. This is perhaps because the measures taken have been coherent and were so far reaching. The best way to ensure continued stability and viability of the BOP is by increased foreign exchange earnings from the export of goods and services to a sufficient level to pay for the imports and all other external payments on the current account. This requires control of inflation to maintain appropriate real effective exchange rate vis-a-vis other competing nations.

Recent Trends in India's BOP

The recent trends in India's presented in Table 4 reveal the following inferences:

(a) Current account deficit

India's balance of payments situation remained comfortable in 1999-2000. The deficit on the current account increased only marginally from US $4 billion in 1998-99 to US $4.2 billion in 1999-2000, despite an unfavourable environment in international trade and finance and almost two-third hike in India's oil import bill, reflecting the sharp increase in international prices of crude oil. This was made possible because of a strong recovery of exports and a surge in net inflow of invisibles reflecting sharp increases in software exports and private transfers. Net inflow of invisibles at US $12.9 billion covered 76 per cent of the deficit on trade account in 1999-2000, leaving a financing gap of US $4.2 billion on the current account. As percentage of GDP, the current account deficit recorded a marginal decline from 1 per cent in 1998-99 to 0.9 per cent in 1999-2000.

With the continued increase in oil prices and further increase on India's oil import bill, the current account deficit is expected to widen to 1.5-1.7 per cent of GDP in 2000-2001. According to the latest quarterly estimates of BOP made by the Reserve Bank of India (RBI), current account deficit widened to nearly US $4 billion in April-September 2000 from US $2.9 billion in April-September 1999. While net invisibles increased by only US $0.5 billion from US $4.7 billion in April-September 1999 to US $5.2 billion in April-September 2000, trade deficit on BOP basis increased by US $1.7 billion from US $7.5 billion to US $1.7 billion from US $7.5 billion to US $9.2 billion during the same period.

(b) Trade deficit

The trade deficit on the BOP account widened to US $17.1 billion or 3.8 per cent of GDP in 1999-2000 from US $13.2 billion (3.2 per cent of GDP) in 1998-99. Exports made a welcome recovery from a negative growth of (–)3.9 per cent in 1998-99 to 11.6 per cent in 1999-2000. Total imports, on payment basis, also rose sharply by 16.5 per cent in 1999-2000 mainly due to a 63 per cent increase in the oil import bill.

According to the latest quarterly estimates of BOP by RBI, exports increased by 22.1 per cent and imports by 22.2 per cent, resulting in a widening of trade deficit by 22.3 per cent to US $9.2 billion in April-September 2000. Imports of crude and petroleum products showed a substantial increase from US $4.5 billion in April-September 1999 to US $8.3 billion in April-September 2000 due to continued pressure on international prices of oil.

Export growth has accelerated further in the current financial year. According to DGCI & S data, merchandised exports in US Dollar value in April-December 2000 have witnessed a strong growth of 20.4 per cent, much higher than 10.3 per cent in April-December 1999. Imports grow by 9.0 per cent in April-December 2000 compared to 10.7 percent in April-December, 1999. The rise in imports was primarily due to the continued surge in oil imports, which increased sharply by 78.2 per cent due to hardening of international oil prices. The spurt in POL imports has, however, been offset by non-POL imports, which have declined by 8.3 per cent, reflecting weak domestic demand and subdued industrial activity. The continued buoyancy in exports and the declining trend in non-POL has resulted in a substantial decline in customs trade deficit from US $8.2 billion in April-December 1999 to US $5.9 billion in April-December 2000.

(c) Invisible Account

Net inflow of invisible earnings reached an all time high of US $12.9 billion in 1999-2000 from US $9.2 billion in 1998-99. Gross invisible receipts increased by 17.7 per cent to US $30.3 billion in 1999-2000 as a result of the continued buoyancy in private transfers and software service exports. Private transfer receipts increased by 18.8 per cent to US $12.3 billion in 1999-2000. Software service exports had grown at an annual rate of over 50 per cent during the four years ended 1998-99. The growth momentum was sustained in 1999-2000, when they recorded a growth of 53 per cent and reached US $4.02 billion.

Gross invisible payments recorded a moderate increase of about 5.0 per cent in 1999-2000 to US $17.4 billion from US $16.6 in payments on account of interest and dividends, financial services, management services, advertising, royalties and license fees.

Invisible flows continued to be buoyant in 2000-01. As per the quarterly BOP estimates by RBI, net invisibles increased from US $4.7 billion in April-September 1999 to US $5.2 billion in April-September 2000, mainly due to an increase of private transfer from US $5.8 billion to US $6.7 billion during the same period.

(d) Capital account

Capital flows improved significantly in 1999-2000. Net inflows of capital on the capital account of BOP increased by US $2.4 billion from an aggregate of US $7.9 billion in 1998-99 to US $10.3 billion in 1999-2000. This improvement was mainly due to a sharp recovery in portfolio investments and continued buoyancy in non-resident deposits. Fresh inflow of funds by the Foreign Institutional Investors (FIIs) increased to US $2135 million in 1999-2000 in contrast to an outflow of US $390 million in 1998-99. Net inflows of non-resident deposits in 1999-2000 was US $2140 million. Gross disbursement of external assistance rose moderately by US $3074 million in 1999-2000 compared to US $2726 million in 1998-99. Gross borrowing on commercial terms at US $3187 million in 1999-2000 was only marginally higher than such borrowings (excluding borrowings through Resurgent India Bonds) at US $2995 billion in 1998-99. During the first half of 2000-01, net inflows of capital amounted to only US $2.5 billion compared to US $3.7 billion in April-September 1999. The fall in net capital inflows was due to net outflows on external assistance and external commercial borrowing accounts, although foreign investment and non-resident deposits performed. The capital flows were augmented by the funds raised by the SBI from NRIs/OCBs through India Millennium Deposits (IMD) amounting to US $ 5.51 billion in October-November 2000.

(e) Foreign exchange reserves

The foreign exchange reserves consist of foreign currency assets held by the RBI, gold holdings of the RBI and SDRs. The in current account deficit and the sharp increase in net capital inflows in 1999-2000 resulted in an increase of foreign exchange reserves by US $6.1 billion on top of an increase of US $3.8 billion in 1998-99.

During the first half of 2000-2001, foreign currency reserves showed declining trend due to excess demand for foreign currency caused by the huge import bill on oil. As per quarterly BOP estimates, foreign exchange reserves declined by US $1460 million in April-September 2000 compared with an increase of US $821 million in April-September 1999. Subsequently, as mentioned earlier, the issues of India Millennium Deposits by SBI helped to raise foreign currency assets amounting to US $5.51 billion, which were added to RBI's foreign currency reserves in November 2000. Total foreign exchange reserves (including gold and SDRs) at the end of January 2001 amounted to over US $41 billion, providing cover for eight months of projected imports in 2000-2001.

(f) Exchange rate

The exchange rate of the Rupee against the US Dollar continues to be broadly market determined. During 1999-2000, the exchange rate market displayed reasonable stability, with the Rupee depreciating by about 2.9 per cent. The year 2000-01 witnessed significant downward pressures on the Rupee-Dollar rate from mid-May 2000. The forex markets were affected by considerable uncertainty with the Rupee depreciating by 6.7 per cent between end-April and end-October 2000. Since November 2000, the situation has shown large improvement and the forex markets have been relatively stable and the exchange rate of Rupee against the US dollar has also recovered partially. At the end of January 2001, the exchange rate of the Rupee was Rs. 46.415 per US Dollar, showing a depreciation of 6.1 per cent, compared with the rate of Rs. 43. 605 at the end of March 2000.

(g) External debt

The external debt to GDP ratio has been declining continuously over the years. The rates improved from 23.6 per cent at the end of March 1999 to 21.9 per cent at the end-March 2000 and further to 20.7 per cent at end-September 2000. The absolute value of external debt rose marginally from US $97.68 billion at end-March 1999 to US $98.44 billion at end-March 2000 before decreasing to US $97.86 billion at the end of September 2000. The share of short-term debt to total debt was 4.6 per cent at end-September 2000 compared to 4.1 per cent at end-March 2000. The debt service ratio fell from 18 per cent in 1998-99 to 16.0 per cent in 1999-2000.

Conclusion

The above-mentioned trends on the front of India's BOP indicate that the external sector reform has not bestowed its much favorable influence on the Indian economy. The full benefits of external sector reforms are yet to be achieved. It may be due to slow pace of India's opening up. Trade growth, to India have yet to come in a big way. Also reforms are yet to influence the exchange rate regimes and external debt front on more favourable lines. This indicates that India's program of economic reforms has been a mixed bag of success and failure; a final judgment on it has to wait. The reduction in the multiplication of export promotion schemes and freeing of imports are positive features. Liberalization of trade regime, removal of import and exchange control and progress towards lower and less dispersed bands of tariffs indicate that the Government appears to be roughly on target in dismantling quantitative restrictions by 2002 as per WTO requirements.

A major outcome of India economic reforms in the 1990s has been the evolution of the external sector with considerable inner strength to meet the challenges of foreign as well as domestic shocks. This has been demonstrated at the time of Asian financial crisis and related contagions and adverse spillover effects from mid-1997 to mid-1999.

Economic sanctions on India by the major developed countries in May 1998 and the more recent international oil price shock since the early 1999. The adjustments to these shocks have been smooth but they also left scars. The situation shows that India can minimize or even avert as in the past, the adverse effects of such shocks in future by strengthening the country's economic fundamentals like strengthening of policy stances in areas of exports, POL imports and foreign investment flows. This will greatly help India to grow in an environment of a viable BOP, reasonably stable exchange rate, a sustainable external debt profile and an external sector with durable strength and vigour.

5

EXPORT POTENTIAL OF CHILLI TRADE

M. Vijaya Lakshmi

The Agricultural wealth of a country is the barometer to gauge the extent of economic development of a country. Developed countries of ester years and developing countries of the present era have been primarily agricultural. The manufacturing industry in a country mostly depends upon the agricultural, horticultural and to some extent the flora cultural prosperity of the country. The National income and per-capital income of a country directly depend upon the agricultural wealth of the country.

Chilli is an important spices amongst the 52 spices popular in the world. Chilli is hat uses wonder. It belongs to the family solanocea and is a native of central and South America. It is cultivated in all the states and Union Territories in India and the important chilli growing states are Andhra Pradesh, Maharashtra, Orissa, Karnataka, West Bengal, Rajasthan, Tamil Nadu and Madhya Pradesh.

Andhra Pradesh is the leading producer of Chilli Crop and accounts for 46 per cent of Chilli crop and accounts for 46 per cent of chilli production in India. According to the latest statistical data available India produced 8,00,100 tonnes of dry chilli from an area of 9,30,000 rectare. India out beates the rest of the world in the area of cultivation and production of utilities.

Chilli fruit appears in different sizes, shapes and colour. Some Chilli varieties look like a bird's eye or a small sized orange fruit. The outer skin of some varieties are smooth leathery and corrugated. The colour varies from Green, Orange, Red, Blue, Yellow, Violet Yeamy White, and Blackish Red.

Chilli is an essential ingredient of Indian Curry. Chilli is used as broken splits, paste, powdery from and also as a whole. India achieved a record export of 64.776 tonnes of dry Chilli during 1999-2000. Chilli, besides imparting pungency and red colour to the dishes, it is a rich source of vitamins A, C and E. Recently Russian Scientists level identified Vitamin P in Green Chillies, which is considered to be important as it protects from "Secondary radiation in fury." It is also prevents heart diseases by dilating blood vessels. Chillies stimulates saliva and gastric juices and helps digestion. It is used as a counter cruitent in prickly heat powders, cosmetics, skin ointment liniments and pain balms.

The great renowned Telugu poet-cum-Philosopher 'Vemana' aptly mentions about Chillis as "The Chillies" see innocently, looks reddish, but once crushed it shows its pungency and valour and well compares it with the spirit of a Noble Person.

Increased consumer awareness and the great concern of the Government of food safety aspects have made the importing countries stipulate stringent quality specifications for spices, which find use as food ingredients.

Survey on Quality of Chillis—Surveys were conducted during the harvesting season of Chillies in the major Chilli-producing areas of Tamil Nadu and Andhra Pradesh. The survey team visited the growers in the villages and collected information on cultural operations and field practices. Chilli samples were collected from the growers for laboratory evaluation. The local traders were conducted and the ways and means of post harvest operations and storage facilities were assessed. Samples were collected from traders and cold storage's also. The quality specifications were determined by the methods suggested for Chillies.

The Agmark grade specification for dry Chillies emphasizes on the appearance of dry Chillies as expressed by colour, lengths, presence of stalks and broken Chillies presence of loose seeds, damaged and discoloured pods etc. Maximum limits have been suggested for moisture also.

Marketing—Quality has been a tradition in the spice trade of India. Standardization and grading is a pre-requisite for development of marketing and grading both for internal and external.

There are about 320 regulated markets mostly located in Andhra Pradesh, Tamil Nadu, Karnataka, Maharashtra and Gujarat. There are very few co-operative marketing societies landing Chillies and these are mostly in Tamil Nadu. The quality of Chillies handled by them is very meager and forms only a small percentage of the marketable surplus available in the area under their jurisdiction. There were occasions in the past when the prices of Chillies crashed due to over production in states like Andhra Pradesh. Arrangements for marketing on such occasion were made through state marketing Federations, National Agricultural Marketing Federation, State Treading Corporation etc.

The present system of marketing is through regulated market committees. The Agricultural produce market committees are operating market yards in all the major markets in Andhra Pradesh and Karnataka. The grower sells the produce at auctions organized by the regulated market committees directly or through the commission agents. Open auctions are conducted by the regulated market committees on a cash and carry system, which ensures, ready payment to growers. Dealers and commission agents operating in different market yards are also licensed by the regulated market committees.

Price Trend

Price of both green and dry Chillies varies according to quality, crop condition in general, internal demand, supply position and export demand. Season of Cultivation, variety, cultural practices, occurrence of diseases and pests influence the quality of Chilli fruits.

Export of Chillies

Srilanka, U.S.A., Canada, UK, Saudi Arabia, Singapore, Malaysia and Germany are the important buyers of India Chillies. India faces competition from China, Pakistan and Bangladesh who offer Chillies at lower prices. Export of Chillies from India during the last 4 years shows encouraging trend inspite of fluctuations. Chillies are exported in different forms such as fresh Chillies, stalkless Chillies, green Chillies, Chilli powder and also oleoresins. The intrinsic quality of Indian Chillies is superior but contamination of any type would render the produce unacceptable to consumers. Pesticide, residues and aflatoxin are the major problems affecting export of Chillies from India.

Suggestions—

1. The high fluctuation in prices and sometimes unpredictable prices ruling in the market are against the interest's of the producer—seller. Throughout the marketing year we found no supporting price, as the price of the product is fixed by the Government. In this connection a supporting price fixed by the Govt. will definitely the distorting price trend.
2. State Government should encourage MARKFED to enter the field to market Chillies.
3. Measures like lesser use of chemical fertilizers and better farm practices were needed to ensure quality of the produce. These could be explained to farmers by the Agricultural Officials.
4. Research Center in the markets may guide the farmers to improve the quality of the produce and get good returns.
5. Increasing future demands in respect of Oils, Oleoresins and other Value added products and also to explore new markets.
6. Organizing Kissan Melas, Karshakas, Vignana Vedhikas, Rythu Sdhassulu and Farmer—Scientist interaction programmes.

SESSION–4

BANKING AND FINANCIAL SECTOR REFORMS

1

INDIAN ECONOMY RETROSPECT & PROSPECT

M.L. Kantha Rao

The purpose of this paper is to examine the current macro economic situation in India along with a survey of the factors that have led to the present position and the prospects for further growth on the premise that what has been will be. Since the decade of Nineteen Nineties is characterised by astounding changes in the Economic Policy of India, growth of Indian Economy between 1950 and 1990 may be viewed as a prelude.

Section-I

The average annual growth rate of Gross Domestic Product (G.D.P) and real per capita income in the pre-independence era that is prior to 1947, were around 0.9% and 0.1% respectively with in the geographical boundaries of the present day India.[1] The annual average growth rates of N.N.P at factor cost and per capita NNP at constant prices were as follows up to 1990.[2]

From the foregoing data it is clear that while the average annual growth rate between the first plan and the fourth plan was hovering between 3% to 4% growth during the 80's was at an annual average rate of 5.9%. This was higher than the world output growth rate of 3.3% and that of developing countries at 4.3% during the same period. The annual growth rate in per capita GDP in the Nineteen Eighties was over 3.5% in spite of the average population growth rate of 2.0% However the aim of doubling the per capita income in the country in 25 years of planning—i.e., by 1975, could be achieved only by the end of 1980's. Further the percentage of population that could not get an average intake of 2400 calories per day in rural areas and 2100 calories in urban areas remained at 38.9% even in 1987-88.[3]

GROWTH RATES

Period	*Growth rate of NNP*	*Per capita NNP growth rate*
First plan period (1951-56)	3.6	1.8
Second Plan period (1956-61)	4.1	2.0
Third Plan period (1961-66)	2.5	0.2
Annual Plan (1966-69)	3.8	1.5
Fourth Plan (1969-74)	3.3	1.0
Fifth Plan (1974-79)	5.0	2.7
Annual Plan (1980-85)	–6.0	–8.3
Sixth Plan (1980-85)	5.3	3.1
Seventh Plan (1985-90)	5.9	3.7

Thus if we examine the impact of 40 years of planning from 1950 to 1990, we find that the economy was at its best in 1980's. But even then there were structural imbalances. An important factor propelling growth during this period was the enormous rise in Govt. expenditure, which led to deficits even in the revenue budget. Public enterprises created with borrowed money also did not yield adequate returns. The high fiscal deficit also was reflected in the emergence of current account deficit in the external sector, which was around 3.2% of the GDP in 1991. Further external debt of short duration on commercial terms also increased. The high growth of 1980s that was largely financed by internal and external debt shook the confidence of the creditors. The gulf crisis and a severe balance of payments problem ultimately led to a mortgage of Gold reserves abroad and an overall *gloom on the prospect of the Indian economy*. In 1991 exports were valued at Rs. 32553 crores as against imports of Rs. 43196 crores and foreign exchange reserves just Rs. 5541 crores in July 1990. The economy was in deep crisis along with weakening of international confidence. But this adversity had its own uses.

Section-II

All this made the Government of India review the policies followed in the preceding four decades, take a "U" turn and try to pull the economy from the brink of disaster and the verge of bankruptcy. In fact the growth rate of NNP (at factor cost in 93-94 price) in 1991-92 was just 0.5% and that of per capita NNP-1.5%. Dr. Man Mohan Singh presenting the Budget for 1991-92 asserted—there is no time to lose. Neither the Government nor the economy can live beyond its means year after year. The room for maneuver, to live on borrowed money or time does not exist any more. Macro economic stabilisation and fiscal adjustment alone cannot suffice. This must be followed by essential reforms in economic policy and economic management.[4]

The terms liberalisation, privatisation and globalisation (the new LPG) amply summarise the crucial aspects of the reforms started in 1991. The statement of the Union Finance Minister, made on the floor of the Parliament on 16/12/1991 highlighted the problems that confronted the Nation and the steps taken or to be taken by the Govt. of India. The Finance Minister claimed that the new Govt. moved swiftly, to the task of pulling the economy back from the brink of disaster and setting it once more on the path of rapid and sustainable growth.[5] Confidence of the creditors was restored and the fear of default was dispelled. The exchange rate was adjusted in July 1991 to a new level deemed credible. While ensuring competitiveness of exports without the need for large export subsidies trade policy witnessed major changes which included schemes for strengthening of incentives for exports and moving away from the system of import control. Export subsidies were abolished, fertiliser subsidy was reduced and defence expenditure was restrained. Monetary policy was also tightened reflecting the urgent need to control inflationary pressure in the economy.

The statement added that these measures of short-term economic management were accompanied by far reaching structural reforms in the area of industrial policy aimed at enhancing productivity and strengthening competitiveness in the industrial sector and *promoting an employment oriented pattern of industrialization*. The policy towards foreign investment was restricted to a*ttract foreign investment* especially in priority areas including critical infrastructure sectors such as power. Govt. also proposed to use supply management in critical commodities and accordingly state Govts. were allowed direct import of edible oils for supply to the public distribution system.

Regarding reforms in the field of Public Finances, the statement added—The burden of achieving reduction in fiscal deficit will fall heavily on the expenditure side. There is an urgent need to restructure and rationalise our tax system. Maintenance of *fiscal discipline* also means that plan expenditure cannot depend as heavily as in the past on ever increasing budget support. The budget cannot afford a continual drain on account of permanently loss making public sector units which are only preventing us from *investing our resources where they are most needed* such as in power, in agriculture, rural development, poverty alleviation, education, health and control of environmental degradation where acute scarcities are already evident.

The statement added that the decade of Nineteen Nineties would be a decade of scarce resources both domestically and externally—But we are determined to pursue with renewed vigour the goals of a *rapidly expanding economy, a socially just and technologically advanced self reliant society.* Scarcity of resources must be reflected in a *premium on efficiency* whether in the public or in the private sector. That must be the watchword of economic policy in the years ahead. There must be an all-round recognition that a higher standard of living can be ensured only on the basis of rising productivity and there are no short cuts to it. The fear of large-scale unemployment and closures resulting from these policies are wholly unfounded. On the country we envisage that these policies will lead to *greater dynamism and a larger growth in total employment*.

Presenting the Budget for 1991-92, the Union Finance Minister (July 1991) declared that employment creation and poverty eradication would continue to receive the highest priority. He also wanted the state Govts. to improve their fiscal performance and stream line the working of their public enterprises. Further in his foreword to the eighth five year plan (1992-97) which followed the launching of the new economic policy, the Prime Minister asserted that the strategy adopted in the plan was *not on of choice between market mechanism and planning but of dovetailing the two so that* they become complementary to each other. The Ninth plan documents (1997-2002) also reiterates that the reforms involve a major *reorientation of the state*. It will no longer be a pervasive controller of the private sector or a direct producer in many areas, but a *facilitator a path breaker and a promoter*. Thus a reorientation of the role of the Govt. as well as the process of planning was undertaken. The ninth five year plan document states that a vigorous private sector operating under the discipline of competition and free markets will encourage efficient use of scare resources and ensure rapid growth at least cost. Indian Industry must be unshackled from unnecessary bureaucratic and governmental control. It was also stated that a thorough *revamp of the controls and procedures* involved at the state govt. level could help to create a climate in which Indian industry can flourish. The *process of dis-investment* of government equity from public sector, enterprises, that however, envisaged the minimum of Govt. equity at 51% originally will be reduced to 26% as early as possible where national security is not involved. In respect of external trade the declared policy was one of *removing quantitative restrictions* on imports and phased *reduction of import tariff*. Globalisation also meant an explosion of *financial integration in world markets*. Further reforms in the real economy, need to be supported by an efficient financial sector capable of mobilising the savings of the community and allocating them to the most productive users. A *strong well functioning capital market* is an important part of the financial system and is an important source of funds for both the public and private sectors in future. The insurance and pension sector is particularly important for the financing of infrastructure which needs long term funds.

Regarding Agricultural sector, the Ninth plan document stated that Indian agriculture had always been based on individual farmers with a predominance of small and marginal farmers. So the development strategy must focus special attention on this sector which requires a unique combination of private sector and public support.

There was a general recognition of the fact that there can be mistakes and errors in public policy formulation and inefficiency in its implementation. Earlier the rationale for the dominant role of the government was the concept of "market failure" and inadequacies of the market mechanism. But subsequent experience exploded the Myth of the infallibility of governmental action and led to the recognition of the fact of the possibility of governmental failure. All this led to a greater appreciation of the respective roles of the public and private sectors in the pursuit of economic growth. Further more market does not mean less Govt. but only a different government with an eye on capabilities. The prime aim of these measures was to bring about increased competition, both domestically and externally and reduce rent-seeking activities. All these reforms had their own impact on the macro economic scenario of India and on the lives of the people at large. So, now let us examine the results of these multifarious reforms introduced since 1991 either because of choice or of necessity.

Section-III: Impact of Economic Reforms

Presenting the central Government's budget for the year, 2001-02, the Union Finance Minister on 28/02/2001 said, "It is now 10 years since economic reforms began in 1991. During this period the economy has grown at an average rate of 6.4% per year since 1992-93 compared to the 5.8%

recorded in the 1980s. Poverty has fallen from 36 per cent in 1993-94 to 26 per cent or less now. Summarising the impact of the decade old reforms, the Minister, asserted while economic reforms have placed the country on a much more secure and sustainable growth path, we still have some, serious concerns and can not afford to be complacent.[6]

Investment is the driving force of economic growth. When investment with in the country is not adequate to accelerate economic growth, foreign direct investment (FDI) has a crucial role to play. The cumulative F.D.I in flows since 1991 increased to $ 26.89 billion—Rs. 1,03,636 crores, while approvals were at $ 72.98 billion—Rs. 2,67,798 crores till August 2001.[7] This is one of the salutary effects of liberalisation and globalisation. Apart from Delhi, major recipients of FDI had been the states of Maharashtra, Gujarat, Karnataka, Andhra Pradesh and Tamil Nadu. However the flow of FDI at US $ 2.26 billion into India in 1998 was far lower than into countries like Singapore (US $ 7.22 billion) China ($ 45.5 billion) and Mexico ($ 7.24 billion). While foreign investment, as a percentage of GDP was almost zero in 1990-91 and 0.1% in 1991-92, its average during 1992-2000 was 1.2%.[8] The growth of the Indian Economy in the post reform era in several sectors in quantitative forms is shown in the table given below:

Savings and investment rates have remained more or less stable around 22/23 per cent. Further these rates are lower than the comparable rates in Singapore at 51.4% and 34.5% and in China at 42.5% and 38.8% respectively. Moreover the negative rate of savings in the Govt. sector because of revenue deficits is a matter of concern.

For the year 2000, in respect of current competitiveness index (prepared by the World Economic Forum) India's rank was 37 out of 58 countries, in respect of Growth Competitiveness Index (GCI) India was in the 49th position out of 59 countries, in respect of Emerging Market Index (that measures the market openness of a country) India's rank at 46 was higher than China. In the case of Globalisation Index (that measures integration with the rest of the world) the rate of integration during 1993-97 was about 2% per annum. The inference from all these measures is that India is a favourly stable economy.[9] Transport, power, telecommunication, water, sanitation etc., are the principal constituents of infrastructure, which is essential for sustained economic development. Indictors of development in this sector also are presented in the table give below:

TABLE
BASIC INDICATORS—BEFORE AND AFTER (REFORMS)

Variable	*1990-91*	*91-92*	*98-99*	*99-2000*	*2000-2001*
Growth rate of GDP	5.3	1.5	6.6	6.4	5.4
Employment in the organised sector (end of March) i.e., Public & Private Sector in Millions	19.06 07.68 26.74	19.21 7.85 27.06	19.54 8.85 28.39	–	–
Index No.	100	101	106	–	–
No. of persons on the live registers seeking employment—end of December in Millions	36.30	36.76	40.37	–	–
Index No.	100	101	111	–	–
Ratio of 5 to 3 per 100	136	136	142	–	–
Index No.	100	100	104	–	–
Growth rate of employ-ment in public sector	1.52 1.24	0.80 2.21	0.0 0.11	– –	– –
Gross Domestic Savings as % of GDP	23.1	22.0	–	22.3	
Gross fixed capital formation as % of GDP	22.9	22.0	–	22.3	
Total of Food Grains pro-duction Million tonnes	176.4	168.4	–	208.9	
Foreign Exchange Re-serves in Billions of US $	03.9	05.8	32.5	38.0	48.01 (21.12.2001)
India's external debt Rs. in crores	1,30,199	1,63,001	4,14,595	4,29,271	
Imports Rs. in crores	43,193	47,851	1,78,332	2,15,236	2,30,873
Exports Rs. in crores	32,558	44,042	1,39,753	1,59,561	2,03,571
Trade Balance	–10,635	–3,809	–38,579	–55,675	–27,302

Cont.

Variable	1990-91	91-92	98-99	99-2000	2000-2001
Index No. Industrial production	92	92	145	155	
Electricity generated (utilities only) Billion K.W.H.	264	287	449	481 (P)	
Cement (Million tonnes)	49	52	88	100	
Finished steel (million tonnes)	14	14	24	27	
Length of road—Total surface in thousand KM	1998	-	2466 (96-97)	-	
Wholesale price Index (93.94)-100	74	84	141	145	
Consumer price Index 1982 = 100	193	219	414	428	

Compiled from the Economic Survey 2000-01, G.O.I and Hand Book of Statistics—2000-R.B.I.

Section-IV: Assessment

The foregoing account indicates the success and failure (short fall) of the Indian Economy in achieving measurable progress in quantitative terms relating to macro economic variables. The question whether the progress is satisfactory or not, whether the prospects are rosy or gloomy for the Indian economy depend not only on quantitative factors, but also the qualitative factors/the imponderables that influence the work ethos of Indians themselves. For long, Indians have been largely described as those that work very hard every where excepting in India (with exceptions). Punctuality, abiding interest in the work assigned, dedication and sincerity have an important role to play in increasing productivity, particularly in the services sector.

Similarly the linkage between increase in productivity and increase in wages should never be under estimated. Possible pursuit of incomes policy about which we were talking in 1970s along with the recommended of Bhoothalingam Committee needs to be examined afresh. The query of the Eleventh Finance of Commission (EFC) whether periodic appointment of pay revision commission is warranted in view of the financial difficulties experienced by the union and state governments after the submission of the fifth pay commission, needs careful examination before such. Commissions are appointed in future. It should also be examined whether the "tyranny of the ten per cent" in the Indian Economy namely the work force in the organised sector that resists all changes unfavourable to it has been a stumbling block in the pace of economic reform and growth.

Another factor that reduces the utility and productivity of large investments in India is the extent of leakages and the so called all pervading corruption for which India got 46th rank among 54 countries in 1996 surveyed by the Transparency International and Gottingen University. It is this that made Rajeev Gandhi, the former Prime Minister, to draw attention to the abysmally low percentage of benefits that reach the targeted groups—beneficiaries, out of every rupee spent by the government. A number of persons of every description think that they are entitled to a share in the Governmental expenditure deprive the deserving of the benefits meant for then and rob the utility of public expenditure meant for development or reconstruction or social welfare. As a result the returns cannot be expected to be equal to the full value of the expenditures incurred by the Government while the objective of public expenditure is to make the governmental rupee go the farthest in terms of utility in practice in several cases it turned out to be futile and infructious expenditure.

Further limited government capacity and individual ingenuity in manipulating public programmes for private gain discredited the post war view that governments could directly replace the private sector to correct market distortions.[10] It has to be recognised that the governments in India are neither omnipotent nor vigorous (hard) in the pursuit of declared state policies. Having recognised the limits of markets and the limitations of the government, the strategy for accelerating economic development has to be worked out. In his address to the FICCI on 05/12/2001 the Union Finance Minister himself admitted that the government was not always the best and most efficient spender of national resources.[11]

It should also be noted that growth alone is not enough. It is not the be all and end all of all economic activity. Poverty anywhere in the world is a danger to prosperity everywhere. Over the past 40 years—(say between 1960 and 2000) the gap between the rich and the poor all lover the world has doubled—with incomes of the richest 20 countries now averaging 31 times, that in the poorest. In India the percentage share of income or consumption of the lowest 10 per cent was 3.5% in 1997 where as the share of the highest 10% was 33.5%.[12] The Gini index was 37.8 in 1997.

Good Governance matters very much for economic growth and poverty reduction. Good governance also means the absence of corruption, which can subvert the goals of policy and undermine the legitimacy of the public institutions that support market. Good governance in fact is broadly the ability of the state to provide those institutions that support growth and poverty reduction. Smart Govt. advocated in Andhra Pradesh may be taken as a concrete expression of good governance. Above all, public enthusiastic is the lubricating oil of planning and petrol for economic development. So how far the public at large is enthusiasm for participation in development activities initiated by the government is a moot question. Among the 162 counties listed in the Human Development Report 2001, India ranks 115 with Norway topping the list and Sierra Leone occupying the last rank.

India therefore has to develop its own strategy for planning and development. In the race for economic development every country has to keep running even to stand where it is, that is, even to protect its relative rank among the comity of nations. To improve the rank, naturally, hard work, right policies effective governance, sincere implementation of programmes, transparency and accountability are essential.

The Associated Chambers of Commerce and Industry (ASSOCHAM) in a recent paper says that what the country needs to day is good institutions to nurture its human capital. It has also warned that a sustained, accelerated economic growth will not be possible with out a significant improvement in the integrity and effectiveness of the governmental financial and other institutions on which the economy depends. It also emphasizes that governance is the key to India's future economic growth and lays emphasis on the need for strengthening the expenditure framework.[13] It is to be noted that even in 1999-2000 and 2000-01 about one per cent of GDP (1.32% & 1.04%) has been the estimated share of subsidies and more than 4.6% of the GDP was the estimated expenditure on interest payments in the central government's total expenditure of around 15.5% of GDP while total revenue expenditure was nearly 13% of the GDP. Plan expenditure, capital expenditure developmental expenditure. Expenditure on social and economic, infrastructure need to be increased significantly to achieve durable and sustainable growth.

It should be noted that in the post reform era, though the consumer has not become the "king" his importance has increased. He has a wide variety of goods, particularly consumer durables to choose among competing products at fairly competitive prices. In several cases the service attached to the products has also improved. The exhibitions and "melas" that are organised for most part of the year in several parts of the country is proof positive of the effort to woo the consumers, who were earlier confronted with a sellers market. But then the importance of sovereignty of the consumer depends on the quantum of the purchasing power he commands. While those who are fortunate to have a job to sustain themselves are in a fairly comfortable position, for those who expected to get a secure and stable government job of any description, life seems to have become a nightmare. On a rough estimate for every 100 persons that are employed in the organised sector, more than 142 persons are waiting to be employed without any guarantee that even when posts fall vacant (on account of retirement or other reasons) they would be filled because of the policy of the right sizing the government. Prolonged unemployment leads to unemployability and frustration and misery lead to hatred of the lucky ones, if not militancy. In a fast changing technological society where acquired skills become irrelevant and obsolete very soon, the challenge is to keep oneself ready to change and learn newer skills. Knowledge is power.

For producers, the days of complacency and sellers' markets seem to be disappearing. To produce properly and wisely, quality goods at competitive prices or to perish seem to be the choice open to them. The days of protectionism are almost over. Buyers are no longer passive and are more knowledgeable than at any time. Markets have become global. Trading environment, power and expectations of buyers have changed. So the producers and traders should be willing to take up the challenges or else will be pushed to the wall. As Dr. Y.V. Reddy wrote—tomorrow's problems cannot be solved with yesterday's strategies and can not be even understood with day before yesterday's knowledge. Hence the need for "Vivekavardhini" & "Vivekavyapti." "Sparadhaya Vardhate Vidya"—Cut throat competition and not all round altruism is the characteristic of business. If education is the basis for empowerment and prosperity it is necessary to discriminate between good and bad and take the right decisions at the right time ("Sadasadviveka Chathuratha" is Education) with the help of strong institutions. Honesty is the best policy is not only an ethical proposition, but a business proposition.

That the economy is poised for growth an is on the road to prosperity are not in doubt. How high the rate of growth will be, depends on all us—governance, people and proper exploitation of resources. Even for 2001-02 the GDP growth rate is expected to be around 5% in spite of the known constraints. Given political stability and peace it should not be difficult to achieve growth rate of 7 to 9 per cent in the next decade. But, Govt. should ensure (the old adage) that death and taxation are the only certainties in the world. Effective tax collection and expenditure management are the prerequisites for growth, among others.

In the context of the future of the Indian Economy we may recall what poet Shelley said namely that "we look before and after and pine for what is not." The imperative now is not to pine but try fine tune the economy think and implement vigorously an effective plan for the development of the country—Statesmen should think and act that they are trustees for the future not merely for the present or for themselves.

REFERENCES

1. RBI Bulletin—Dec. 2000.
2. G.O.I. Indian Economic Survey—2000-01, P.S. 4.
3. GOI. Ninth Five Year Plan 1997-2002, Vol. I.
4. Budget speech of the Union Finance Minister presenting the Budget for 1991-92, Part-A, 24.07.1001.
5. Statement of the Union Finance Minister on the floor of the Parliament, 16-12-1990.
6. Budget Speech of the Union Finance Minister, 28/02/2001, Part A, Para 1.
7. The Hindu of 18/12/2001.
8. RBI—Hand Book of Statistics on Indian Economy 2000.
9. RBI Bulletin—December 2000, p. 1298.
10. World Bank Policy and Research—Oct-Dec., 1997.
11. The Hindu, 6/12/2001.
12. World Development Report, 2001-02, p. 234.
13. The Hindu dated 18/12/2001.

2

REGIONAL RURAL BANKS IN INDIA, RETROSPECT AND PROSPECT

M. Tirupalaiah

Introduction

The percentage of population below poverty line in 1988-98 was at 35 per cent. This is a gigantic problem for a country of nearly 100 crore population. In recent years there has been a modest improvement in terms of human development index, gender development index, gender empowerment measure in India.[1] But compared with the situations in South Asian Counties, India's condition is pitiable. It needs to be improved by appropriate development India is located in the rural sector. One of the means of attacking rural poverty is through the provision of micro finance to the target groups. An attempt is made here to describe the progress and some aspects of performance of RRBs as instruments of micro finance to the rural poor in India.

The Focus of RRBs

The Government of India set up first six Regional Rural Banks (RRBs) in the last quarter of 1975, following the acceptance of the recommendations of the "Working group on Rural Banks".[2] According to the Group, this state sponsored and rural-oriented commercial banking institutions would combine the local feel and familiarity with the rural problems which the cooperatives possess and the degree of business acumen and organizational ability to mobilize deposits, access to central money markets and a modern outlook which commercial banks have. It would help to fill regional and functional credit gaps, help to develop the activities of the weaker sections of the rural society, take banking services to the door steps of the rural household, inculcating in them the habit of saving. The preamble of the RRB Act 1976 says, "With a view to developing the rural economy by providing for the purpose of development of agriculture, trade, commerce, industry and other productive activities in the rural areas, credit and other facilities particularly to the small and marginal farmers, agricultural labourers, artisans and small entrepreneurs and for matters connected therewith and incidental thereto". The motto of the RRB was to bring a change in the existing system to mass banking from class banking.[3]

Progress of RRBs in India

We have already noted that RRBs came into existence in 1975 in 12 districts with 17 branches. Since then there has been a rapid expansion of the number of RRBs, their branches and the districts covered until the end of the sixth five year plan. Roughly the first decade of the establishment of RRBs is a period of rapid growth. The second decade starting with 1986 to 1996 is a period of consolidation. We present the progress of banking activities of RRBs in Table 1.

As is well-known deposit mobilization and making advances are the primary functions of modern banking. RRBs are no exception to this rule. This is popularly known as financial intermediation between the saving units and spending units. Financial mobilization by offering a set of incentives and services and allocation on the basis of social priorities underline this activity CD ratio is a summary measure of banking activity of nay institution or the set of institutions or for any region or nation. We notice from Table-1 that except in the first two years of the establishment of RRBs the CD ratio was more than 100 upto 1986. Subsequently, it has tended to decline gradually. It means

TABLE 1
PROGRESS OF REGIONAL RURAL BANKS

(Rs. Crores)

Sl. No.	*As at the end of*	*No. of RRBs*	*Districts covered*	*No. of Branches*	*Deposits*	*Outstanding Advances*	*C.D. Ratio*
1.	Dec 1975	6	12	17	0.2	0.1	50
2.	Dec 1976	40	84	489	8	7	91
3.	Dec 1980	85	144	3279	200	243	122
4.	Dec 1985	188	333	12606	1286	1408	109
5.	Dec 1986	194	351	12838	1715	1785	104
6.	Sep 1990	196	380	14511	4268	3555	83
7.	Mar 1995	196	425	14509	11150	6291	56
8.	Mar 1996	196	427	14497	14188	7505	53
9.	Mar 1997	196	427	14461	18032	8718	48
10.	Mar 1998	196	448	14450	22189	9861	44

Source: NABARD, Statistics on Regional Rural Banks, various years.

that in the first phase not only the deposits mobilized by RRBs but also a part of the deposits of the sponsoring banks were drawn into the stream of advances. Since the advent of New Economic Policy a reverse situation is emerging. It implies that there has been an adverse effect on the clientele of RRBs who are generally poor. The post-reform era therefore has a deleterious effect on the rural banking scene and thereby on the rural poor.

Like the uneven development of industry, trade and commerce and agriculture banking sector including the RRBs exhibits an uneven pattern of growth across different regions of the country. For banking indicators the country is divided into six regions as shown in Table 2.

TABLE 2
REGION-WISE PROGRESS OF REGIONAL RURAL BANKS (END OF MARCH 1998)

Sl. No.	*Region*	*No. of RRBs*	*Districts covered*	*No. of Branches*	*Depo-sits*	*Outstanding Advances*	*C.D. Ratio*
1.	Northern	28	81	1947	2997	1157	39
2.	North-Eastern	11	54	653	896	343	38
3.	Eastern	40	102	3564	5320	1941	36
4.	Central	64	118	4579	8015	2646	33
5.	Western	19	34	1019	1200	625	52
6.	Southern	34	59	2688	3761	3149	84
	Total	**196**	**448**	**14450**	**22189**	**9861**	**44**

Source: MANARD. Statistics on Regional Rural Banks, March 1998, p.2

In terms of the number of RRBs districts covered and branches the central region occupies the first place followed by the eastern region. The north-eastern region which is comparatively less developed in all respects is also lagging behind in banking. Therefore, it is at the bottom. The other regions are in between. However, in terms of branches per RRB southern region takes lead followed by central region. North-eastern region is at the bottom. In respect of CD ratio the southern region's situation is significantly higher than the rest of the regions. Central region is having the lowest CD ratio.

Agricultural Advances and Overdues

On of the basic purposes for the establishment of the RRBs is to provide credit in the unbanked areas and the rural poverty groups such as small and marginal farmer, agricultural laborers, artisans and those engaged in animal husbandry and the petty trade. These segments of society have been altogether neglected by the cooperatives as well as commercial banks because they do not have collateral acceptable to these institutions. But RRBs are designed to sub serve the needs of the targeted groups of the rural society. In Table 3 we incorporate a few a few details of agricultural advances and the corresponding overdues.

TABLE 3
YEAR -WISE AGRICULTURAL ADVANCES AND OVERDUES ƆF RRBs

(Rs. Crores)

	Agricultural Advances		*Agricultural Overdues*	
Years	*Amount*	*% of Total*	*Amount*	*% of Total*
Jun 1977	12	58	–	–
Jun 1978	40	61	–	–
Dec 1986	1004	56	–	–
Sep 1990	1840	52	701	42
Sep 1991	1850	46	655	44
Mar 1992	1985	48	665	45
Mar 1993	2274	49	804	50
Mar 1994	2560	49	868	47
Mar 1995	3009	48	864	48
Mar 1996	3467	49	956	53
Mar 1997	4044	46	1596	80
Mar 1998	4695	48	1404	59

Source: NABARD, Statistics on Regional Rural Banks, various years.

We notice from Table 3 that there has been a slow expansion of agricultural advances in the initial stage by 1986 agricultural advances exceeded Rs. 1000 crores. By 1995 the figure has tripled compared to 1986. By 1998 the figure went up to Rs. 4695 crores. However, the proportion of agricultural advances has slowly declined from 58 per cent in 1977 to 48 per cent in 1998. This is due to diversification of the portfolio the RRBs for catering to the needs of the non-farm sector activities of the RRBs. This is justifiable not only from the point of view of the RRBs but also the vulnerable sections of the rural society who are engaged in a multiplicity of the activities in order to sustain their livelihood systems at the margin of the subsistence and are either in the ranks of the ultra poor or slip into that bottom most segment.

The persistence of a high level overdues is a striking feature of formal rural financial institutions and RRBs are no exception. There are a wide range of factors contributing to the overdues syndrome. They are classified in different ways based on economic, political, social and psychological status of defaulters.

We have shown the data pertaining to agricultural overdues since 1990 in Table 3. We find that overdues during the 9 year period have doubled. These proportions has gone up from 42 per cent in 1990 to 59 per cent in 1998. In 1997 it had reached the peak of 80 per cent. The rise in agricultural overdues of RRBs in the era of economic reforms in general and banking reforms in particular is somewhat disturbing and the needs to be controlled and reduced to facilitate a better recycling of funds for the rural poor.

In Table 4 we present region-wise distribution of agricultural overdues for the year 1998.

From Table 4 we observe that southern and central regions put together account for 76 per cent of overdues under crop loans, 39 per cent under agricultural investment and 34 per cent under allied activities. North-Eastern and western regions account for 9, 15 and 13 per cent of the overdues of the three categories of the loans listed in Table 4. Northern and western regions account for the balance of overdues.

TABLE 4
REGION-WISE AGRICULTURAL OVERDUES OF RRBs AT THE END OF MARCH 1998

			Term-Loans			
	Short Term (Crop Loans)		*Agricultural Investment*		*Allied Activities*	
Region	*Amount*	*% of Total*	*Amount*	*% of Total*	*Amount*	*% of Total*
Northern	14	3	118	30	152	33
North-Eastern	7	1	25	6	35	8
Eastern	57	12	63	16	93	20
Central	95	20	89	23	111	24
Western	38	8	34	9	25	5
Southern	271	56	63	16	48	10
Total	482	100	392	100	646	100

Source: NABARD, Statistics on Regional Rural Banks, March 1998, pp. 160-165.

Financial Ratios of RRBS

Table 5 shows the financial ratios of RRBs for the recent period in the post reform era the financial situation of the RRBs remains more or less the same and there no dramatic changes. However there is modest improvement in terms of financial return, financial cost and financial margin. In respect of cost of management, administration cost, transaction cost there is a moderate improvement and therefore, there is a reduction in the operating margin. Risk cost has tended to increase with exception of the year 1997-98. Miscellaneous Income has shown a humble rise, net margin has tended to persist negatively at a lower level except in the year 1997-98 when it has tended positive. If the management system can be further strengthened the financial health of the RRBs can be improved.

The Emergence of SHGs and Their Interlinkage

Group formation and group lending on the basis of its maturity, homogeneity and cohesiveness are the basic features of Grameen Bank Model. Pear monitoring is an important element of recovery process. First, the group is the

TABLE 5
THE FINANCIAL RATIOS OF RRBs FROM 1993-94 TO 1997-98 ARE AS SHOWN BELOW

Ratios	*1993-94*	*1994-95*	*1995-96*	*1996-97*	*1997-98*
Financial Returns	8.22	7.75	8.59	9.73	10.50
Financial Cost	6.24	5.70	6.41	6.88	7.10
Financial Margin	1.99	2.05	2.18	2.85	3.40
Cost of Management	3.60	3.44	3.67	3.21	2.95
Admn Cost	1.07	0.95	0.68	0.54	0.44
Transaction Cost	4.67	4.40	4.35	3.75	3.39
Operating Margin	–2.68	–2.34	–2.17	–0.90	0.01
Risk Cost	0.74	0.78	0.95	3.47	0.30
Misc Income	0.37	0.48	0.55	0.52	0.59
Net Margin	–3.05	–2.64	–2.57	–3.86	0.30

In 1993-94 & 1994-95 the total asset is taken as average working funds
Source: NABARD, Statistics on Regional Rural Banks, Highlights, March 1998.

guarantor for the repayment of loan. The weekly meeting is the time of weekly repayment, deposits to savings accounts, discussion of new loan requests or any other matter of interest to members. However, participation and empowerment do not just happen. There has to be a strategy and a set actions to allow them to develop.[4] This is the basis for the emergence of Self-Help Groups (SHGs) in the context of rural development initiatives and strategies in India. The NABARD is coordinating the interlink age of SHGs with the Rural Financial Institutions (RFIs) and the process is beneficial to the banking institutions and the SHGs. RRBs may also move in this direction to improve their recovery performance and the quality of credit management. This is the strategy of rural development that has proved to be successful in Bangladesh and Indonesia. The similarities are more explicit between India and the two countries where this experiment has proved to be successful.[5] There are therefore attempts to replicate the Bangladesh Grameen Bank's experience in North-East India on an experimental basis under the overall guidance and leadership of NABARD.[6] Out of total 1996 RRBs in the country 177 participated SHG-bank linkage programme (i.e. more than 90%). RRBs share in the total cumulative achievement has shown an increase in terms of SHGs linked, bank loan disbursed and refinance availed from NABARD. During the year, maximum number of SHGs have been linked by Shri Visakha Grameena Bank in Andhra Pradesh (7,339), followed by Nagarjuna Grameena Bank (4,802) in AP, Pandiyan Grameena Bank in Tamil Nadu (4,155) and Manjira Grameena Bank (2,189) in AP. The other RRBs showing significant achievement are Kalahandi Grameena Bank in Orissa, Vallalar Grameena Bank in Tamil Nadu, Cauvery and Sahyadri Grameena Banks in Karnataka, North and South Malabar, Grammena Banks in Kerala, Kanpur and Raebareli, Grameena Banks in UP.[7]

Concluding Remarks

The rural poor are severely constrained to have access to the formal financial market in many countries. Experience of institutions like the Grameen Bank of Bangladesh has been an eye opener to the credit worthiness and bank ability of the rural poor and especially of women. Therefore, the traditional urban and gender bias in banking has been questioned and is being reversed. The emergence of RRBs in India is an institutional innovation in rural banking combining the virtues of the cooperatives and commercial banks. However, because of their location, target groups, thin margins and inadequate motivation, they have encountered a host of problems regarding loaning, recovery, asset management and financial performance. If they can follow the group approach to lending and recovery. Their prospects are bound to be better than earlier as it is being proved by the experiments not only in Bangladesh and Indonesia but also in some parts of India where the SHG and bank linkage has proved to be a success beyond doubt.

REFERENCES

1. Tata Services Limited; Statistical Outline of India 2000-2001, pp. 271-272.
2. Government of India; Working Group on Rural Banks, Narasimham Committee Report, 1974.
3. Shete, N.B: Regional Rural Banks - An Analysis, National Bank Review (Sept, 1990), p. 32.
4. NABARD; Annual Report, 1988-99.
5. Centre on Integrated Rural Development for Asia and the Pacific (CIRDAP): Fighting poverty with Microfinance, March 1999, Dhaka, pp. 160-194.
6. NABARD : Annual Report 1998-1999.
7. NABARD : NABARD and Microfinance, 2000-2001, p. 8.

3

BANKING SECTOR REFORMS IN INDIA—A REVIEW

B. Ramachandra Reddy,
S. Vijayulu Reddy & B. Sakunthala

Introduction

Commercial banking system in India comprises of the scheduled and non-scheduled commercial banks. The scheduled commercial banks are further classified as public sector and private sector banks. The public sector bank consists of State Bank of India and its seven Associate Banks and nineteen nationalised banks. Apart from the other Indian scheduled commercial banks, the foreign banks are also included in the private sector banks.

One of the objectives of nationalisation of the banks in 1969 was to extend the reach of banking services to all parts of the country and to mainstream the neglected sectors of society. Since 1969 there has been a major significant spread of the banking habit and the banks have been the major mobilisers of savings in the economy. Despite significant achievements by the banking industry, the operational efficiency was unsatisfactory and characterized by low profitability, ever growing non-performing assets and relatively low capital base.

Most of the nations around the world, irrespective of their economic framework and political ideology, initiated restructuring through liberalisation. The elaborate recommendations of a Committee on Financial System popularly known as Narasimham Committee made in November 1991 are of great significance in this connection.

It has placed great emphasis on the steps needed to improve the financial health of Indian Banks and to make them efficient, market oriented, vibrant, dynamic and globally competitive with the gradual implementation of financial sector reforms such as accounting practices and procedures of international standards, capital adequacy norms, asset classification, provisioning for bad debts, entry of private and foreign banks etc.

The winds of freedom and change sweeping across the financial sector due to reforms, have thrown open several challenges to the banks. The most important changes that have overtaken the nation's banking industry relates to the fact that the competitive forces are sought to be introduced consciously in the financial services sector in general and banking industry in particular through the policies of interest rate deregulation and more particularly through a new liberal policy move to open doors wider to facilitate the entry of foreign banks and new private sector banks.

First Stage of Reforms

In India, the first phase of reforms in the banking sector was initiated since the formal announcement in the Union Budget of 1991-92 based on the recommendations of Narasimham Committee Report. A considerable ground has been covered in putting a place in financial system which can be meet the requirements of a more competitive and open economy. From 1992 there was an accelerated programme of banking sector reforms. Firstly, a concerted effort was made to move to market related rates of interest. Secondly, the pre-emptions by way of the Cash Reserve Ratio (CRR) and the Statuory Liquidity Ratio (SLR) were reduced. Thirdly, there was a total freeing of deposit and lending rates with only very limited controls. Fourthly, following the Basic Committee standards prudential norms were prescribed for capital adequacy, income recognition and provisioning. Fifthly, the banks were required to observe stricter disclosure norms. Sixthly, the regulatory/supervisory system was strengthened by the setting up of a Board for

Financial supervision. Lastly, institutional strengthening was undertaken to ensure the progressive development and integration of the securities, money and forex markets.

In India, by and large the financial reforms have proceeded in four major directions. First, setting the policy conditions right and removing the operational constraints of the financial system. The second directional change sector through reform measures such as relaxation of entry and exit norms, reform has been the strengthening of market institutions and allowing greater freedom to financial intermediaries. The fourth element of reform concerns the safety aspect of financial system.

In this paper an attempt has been made to analyse the response of the banking sector to the changes unleashed in the country as a part of economic reform process in general and financial sector reform in particular. The structures and systematic changes that are strategically being brought about by RBI and Government in terms of the Narasimham Committee's recommendations played significant role in smooth transition of banking sector to the reform process, one has to keep in mind that the banking system consists of a few distinct response groups—namely the government and the regulatory authority Reserve Bank of India, the managements of bank employees and above all the customers.

Measures Taken by Government

The Government of India has initiated the reforms process by appointing the Narasimham Committee whose report became the magnacarta of he financial sector reforms. The Government can claim due credit for (a) dismantling the iron gates of entry of new banks both domestic and foreign especially in the private sector, (b) its willingness to dilute its overall equity stake in the nationalised banks upto 33 per cent, (c) establishing the over the country, (d) merger of a weaker and non-viable banks whether in public sector or private sector (New Bank of India wasmerged with Punjab National Bank) and (e) introducing bank Ombudsman Scheme for redressing the grievances of customers.

Reserve Bank of India Measures

RBI also took major steps like market based interest rate structure both for deposits and advances, phased reduction of statutory pre-emptions like CRR and SLR, introducing internationally acceptable accounting norms for arriving at the bank's income and quality of assets, notably the income recognition, asset classification and provisioning norms.

(a) *SLR*—The Statutory Liquidity Ratio has been brought down in a phased manner to 25 per cent.

(b) *CRR*—The Cash Reserve Ratio has reduced to 8 per cent with effect from 1st April 2000 which is significant step taken by RBI.

(c) *Prudential norms*—

(i) As per the RBI guidelines, the minimum capital Adequacy Ratio of 9 per cent should be maintained by the Indian banks since March, 2000 according to Basle Committee recommendations. Most of the PSBs have achieved the minimum capital adequacy norm of 9 per cent.

(ii) Income recognition norms are primarily based on the principle of record of recovery rather than any subjective consideration. The income from NPA's is not recognised on accrual basis but is booked as income only when it is actually received.

(iii) In the light of the Narasimham Committee recommendations, the RBI has redefined the NPAs and advised the banks to classify their advances into fourbroad groups viz., standard, sub-standard

(d) NPAS—It should be defined as a credit facility or an advance as on the date of balance sheet, in respect of which interest has remained unpaid for a period of two quarters during the year ending March 31, 1995 and onwards. With a view to moving towards international best practices and to ensure greater transparency, RBI has decided to adopt the new income recognition norm of one quarter instead of existing two quarters from the year ending March 31st , 2004. RBI has suggested that the Net NPAs of banks should be below 5 per cent. The Goss NPAs of PSBs were reduced to 14.02 per cent and the net NPAs to 7.4 per cent by the end of March 2000.

Response of Banks and Employees

Coming to the response of bank managements, results for the financial year 1994-95 encouragingly indicate that all public sector banks except one have show operating profits as against a very gloomy picture of 1992-93 and 1993-94. This is all the more creditable as the profits are worked after adopting the international accounting norms for income recognition, asset classification and provisioning.

In the case of most public sector banks business per employee and profit per employee have shown improvement in the profit per employee have shown improvement in the recent period. The change in the attitude and helpful moves taken by the trade unions in facilitating to bring in higher productivity especially technology adoption etc., is perhaps significant in this context. The branches of PSBs are fastly computerizing and adopting e-banking, e-commerce techniques. The balance sheets of banks in India are to some extent transparent and further steps are talking to expose more transparency in them. Few banks urging the RBI to reduce their sake of more than 51 per cent capital with them.

Narasimham Committee II

The committee on Banking Sector Reforms popularly known as Narasimham Committee II submitted its report in March, 1998. Its mandate was to review the record of financial sector reforms since 1991, implemented on the basis of the recommendations of the committee on financial system 1991 and to suggest measures of strengthening the banking system.

Second Generation Reforms

The imperatives for the second generation reforms would

fall under five broad categories. Firstly, financial market integration had to be accorded top priority. Secondly, banks would have to seriously undertake the asset liability management function for better performance as they should have to work in an increasingly deregulated and largely off-sited supervisory system. Thirdly, as the credit risk coverage of the assets had to be broadened. Fourthly, systems and procedures in banks had to be designed pro-actively and innovatively with a view to effectively addressing the operational and legal issues that arise on to-day basis. Finally, the customer was going to rule the roost with advanced technical and product knowledge and therefore customer service could no longer be given a secondary importance. The second generation reforms in the banking sector are perhaps harder to implement but nonetheless we need to recognise that successful reforms would have their own rewards.

Conclusion

Saying of a renowned philosopher Jiddu Krishna Murthy "challenges are new but responses continue to be old"—aptly applies to the banking industry. Whatever may be the situation and the new challenges faced by the bank they are forced to attempt all these new things with the same old rigid structures and systems. What is required is more managerial and administrative freedom to the managements with commensurate and result oriented accountabilities. Surely the banks have to come out of the web of governmentalised banking and move towards professional banking with requisite freedom to operate freely in the market within the regulatory and prudential framework prescribed by the Reserve Bank of India.

4

"INDIAN BANKING IN THE NEW SCENARIO"

D. Nageswara Rao

The Indian economy opens up with the signing of WTO agreement. Now India has become a signatory to globalisation. The challenges of the open economy in the incisive WTO agreement is formidable for Indian Banking Organisation and service sectors. The license regime has ended with the entry of foreign players in Indian banking sector. This liberalised, privatised and globalised (LPG) Indian Economy throws mind-boggling process for existence and growth of the sector.

With the onset of 2001, the Indian financial sector has entered its 10th year of reforms and during this decade, the reforms have touched upon every segment of the Financial Sector. Nevertheless, it is the banking sector, which experienced major reforms and has come far away from the days of nationalisation. The Narasimham committee laid the foundation for the reforms in the Indian banking sector and thus paved way for enhancing the efficiency and viability of the banking sector with India becoming a member of WTO, the banking sector had to be opened for international players. In order to prepare the Indian banking industry for a vibrant global competition, a number of policy reforms were initiated by the Government. As the international standards become prevalent, banks had to unlearn their traditional operational methods of direct credit, direct investments and fixed interest rates. Nevertheless, increase in the number of banks, increase in the transparency of the banks balance sheets through the introduction of prudential norms and increase in the role of the market forces sue to the deregulated increase rates have all significantly affected the operational environment of the Indian Banking Sector. Further, the commitments made by India in the WTO Financial Service Agreement in December, 1997 have a significant impact on the banking industry. In this context, this paper attempts to examine the implications of General Agreement on Trade in Services (WTO) on the Indian Banking Sector.

GATS Commitments

The role of General Agreement on Trade in Services (GATS) on financial services liberalisation can be understood by considering the different types of government intervention that fall within the ambit of GATS.

1. Government intervention may be through a macro economic policy in general. For instance, when a central bank conducts open market operations, conditions in the financial sector could be affected through the impact of such interventions on the money supply, interest rates or exchange rates.
2. Government maintains prudential regulations in order to protect the financial services sector and ultimately the stability of the economy and the welfare of consumers.
3. Government may maintain other regulations, which are not prudential in nature, but which nevertheless can effect conditions of operations and competitions in a market.
4. The areas of policy intervention deals with trade liberalisation. Governments after impose of trade restrictions aimed at preventing or inhibiting the domestic establishment of foreign service suppliers or the foreign supply of services on a cross border basics. It is the reduction and elimination of these measures that constitute the primary focus of the

trade liberalisation efforts of the GATS. This is an important policy which will have an impact on the Indian financial services sector.

Sectoral Implications on the Banking Sector in India

The banking sector of India is expected to enjoy a number of opportunities in the WTO (e.g., latest technology, professionals, experts and competitive edge etc.) which it has posed a number of challenges to the sector. As per the Trade Related Investment Measures (TRIMs) agreement, member country will not impose any performance clause on a foreign investing company in relation to foreign exchange earnings, foreign equity participation and transfer of technology. The Indian banking sector has undergone phenomenal changes in the decade since economic liberalization resulting prismatic graduation from protected economy to open virtual market.

Vision of the Indian Banking

In the present scenario of WTO's developments, the Indian banks is in progress to achieve long-term gains as there are number of opportunities available in the present edge. India has already adopted the open market economic policy in this LPG era owing to the changes in the global financial sector, a profound transformation has been undergoing in the role of the banks in the process of financial intermediation. The primary sources of competitive banking are labeled as skills and the ability to changing face in ICE (information, communication and entertainment) age to determine the prospects of the prosperity and growth of the sector. In the present system the Indian commercial banks should claim to have significant presence in international financial markets.

Prospects of Indian Banking in the New Millennium

In India, till the eighties, the banks were operating a protective environment characterised by administered interest rates, high level of pre-emption in the forms of reserves requirements and direct credit. Banking sector reforms were initiated in India in 1992 against the backdrop of challenges faced by the Indian banks from with in and outside the banking system in the country as well as forces of globalisation operating worldwide. The accent of the reform process was to improve productivity and efficiency of the financial system and provide a competitive environment.

Despite liberalisation, government intervention in the financial sector is still apparent the RBI regulates the entry of foreign banks and all banking activities under the Banking Regulation Act of 1949 and Foreign Exchange Regulation Act of 1973. However, as part of India's commitments to the WTO under the new financial services agreement (1997), India has agreed to allow upto 12 licenses a year for foreign bank branches. In actual practice India has allowed foreign banks to open 15 branches in a year. In addition, off-site ATMs, which require a branch license, are outside this limit of 12. Therefore, the introduction of liberalisation measures in the banking sector and the emergence of new private sector and foreign banks (as a results of WTO commitments) equipped with latest technology led to an increase in competition in the banking sector.

Technology up-gradation is taking place in banking sector in a phased manner, computerisation is increasingly being in day-to-day deposits and loan operations, but the pace at which it has moved so far, has been somewhat limited. Moreover, there is a need for computerisation in a large number of areas of operations of banks, with customer service as the main focus. Technology has already enabled some of the banks, particularly the private sector banks, to introduce innovative products to their customers in the form of ATM (Automatic Teller Machine) facility, tele-banking, home banking, anytime and anywhere banking etc. Technology can also be harnessed in automatic and networking the branches that will ensure timely flow of information and aid decision-making process. The committee on technology upgradation in the banking sector, appointed by the Reserve Bank, in its report submitted in July 1999 has provided a medium-term road map for absorption of technology by banks and financial institutions. The banks that can adopt and absorb the new technology foster will have a competitive edge over their rivals.

Against the backdrop of preparedness towards technology upgradation, the Reserve Bank has made a pro-active effort in deciding to move towards a Real Time Gross Settlement (RTGS) system. In line with the announcements in the Monetary and Credit Policy for 1999-2000, the Reserve Bank has constituted a National Payments Council (Chairman: Shri S.P. Talwar) to focus on the broad policy parameters for designing and developing an integrated payments and settlements structure, with the proposed RTGS systems at the core of the system.

While the enabling policy framework and the operating environment provide a platform for improving the efficiency of the banking sector, its ultimate success depends on how individual banks respond to the competitive environment, identify their core competencies and reposition themselves effectively. These issues have been adequately addressed by the Second Narasimham Committee (1998) and accordingly the Committee recommendations form part of the agenda of the second generation of reforms in the banking sector. One of the major factors affecting efficiency is the organisational structure of the banks. With a view to reaping full benefits of WTO commitments and liberalisation phase, the organisational structures of the banks need to be studied carefully. In this context, the chain of command needs to be shortened with adequate authority delegated to the branches. This would also help to enhance efficiency. In addition to the organisational structure, adoption of proper internal systems and methods can greatly help in efficient functioning of the banks. Another issue that assumes importance in improving the efficiency of the banks is the human resource development. Recruiting the right people, training/retraining them on a continuous basis keeping in view the changing environment and increasing complexities, and having a remuneration/ incentive structure conducive to keep their morale high, are considered integral part of the process. Another significant factor determining the competitiveness is the customer service. The realisation that customer satisfaction is essential for survival and growth has dawned on all the banks. The banks that will emerge as the winners in the impending era will be truly customer-centric banks.

Conclusion

The Indian banking system has undergone transformation itself from domestic banking to the international banking. After a decade of reforms, the Indian banking sector is slowly emerging stronger. Regulations are forcing the banks to adopt better operational strategies and upgrade their skills. However, the system requires a combination of new technologies, well-guarded risk and credit appraisal, treasury management, product diversification, internal control, external regulations and professional as well as skilled human resources to achieve the heights of the international excellence to play its role critically in meeting the global challenges in WTO declarations.

REFERENCES

1. Mattoo, A. (1998), "Financial Services and the WTO: Liberalisation in the Developing and Transition Economics." WTO, Geneva, Switzerland.
2. The Role of GATS in Financial Services, WTO Publications, Geneva, Switzerland.
3. WTO Competitiveness-Challenges for Indian Business and Management Education: Edited by Prof. D. Panduranga Rao, President, AIMS, Excel Books Publications, 2001.
4. Kapila, Raj and Kapila Uma (eds), Ongoing Developments in Banking and Financial Sector Reforms, Vols. I & IV, RBI.
5. World Trade Organisation—Annual Report, 1999.
6. GATT Agreement—What it implies by P.J. Punambekar, IBA Bulletin, August 1994.
7. Business Today (F/N)—2001, January to October.
8. Front Line (F/N)—October-November 2001.
9. Economic Times & Business Line Daily Papers.

5

SOME ASPECTS OF FINANCIAL SECTOR REFORMS

B. Ramachandra Reddy,
V. Venkatesh & Yuvaraja Reddy

Need for Reforms

The need for financial reforms had arisen because the financial institutions and markets were in a bad shape. The banks were running either at a loss or on very low profits, and, consequently were unable to provide adequately for loan defaults, and build their capital. There had been organisational inadequacies, the weakening of management and control functions, the growth of restrictive practices, the erosion of work culture, and flaws in credit management. The strain on the performance of the banks had emanated partly from the imposition of high Cash Reserve Ratio (CRR), Statutory Liquidity Ratio (SLR), and directed credit programmes for the priority sectors—all at below market or confessional or subsidised interest rates. This, apart from affecting bank profitability adversely, had resulted in the low or repressed or depressed interest rates on deposits, and in higher interest rates on loans to the larger borrowers from business and industry. The phenomenon of cross-subsidisation had got built into the system where confessional rates provided to some sectors were compensated by higher rates charged to non-confessional borrowers.[1]

Further, the functioning of the financial system, and the credit delivery as well as recovery process had become politicised, which damaged the quality of lending and the culture of repaying loans. As the closure or across-the-board write-offs of the loans had seriously jeopardised the viability of banks. As the closure of sick industrial units was discouraged by the government, banks had to continue to finance non-viable sick units, which further compromised their own viability. The legal system was not of much help in recovering loans.

This was a lack of transparency in preparing statements of accounts by banks.

In other words, the reforms had become imperative on account of the facts that despite its impressive quantitative growth and achievements, the financial health, integrity, autonomy, flexibility, and vibrancy in the financial sector had deteriorated over the past many years. The allocation of resources had become severely distorted, the portfolio quality had deteriorated, and productivity, efficiency and profitability had been eroded in the system. Customer service was poor, work technology remained outdated, and transaction costs were high. The capital base of the system remained low, the accounting and disclosure practices were faulty, and the administrative expenses had greatly soared. The system suffered also from a lack of delegation of authority, inadequate internal controls, and poor housekeeping.

It was felt by many that all this the consequence of policy-induced rigidities; of excessive degree of centralized administrative direction of investments, credit allocations, and internal management of banks and financial institutions; massive branch expansion, overstaffing and union pressures; and excessive political intervention, interference, and pressures.

For a long time, an alarming increase of sickness in the Indian financial system had required urgent remedial measures of reforms which were ultimately introduced in 1991. The main and sub-objectives of these reforms have been as follows:

Prime Objectives of Reforms

(i) To develop a market-oriented, competitive, world-integrated, diversified, autonomous, transparent financial system.

(ii) To increase the allocative efficiency of available savings, and to promote accelerated growth of the real sector.

(iii) To increase or bring about the effectiveness, accountability, profitability, viability, vibrancy, balanced growth, operational economy and flexibility, professionalism and depoliticisation in financial sector.

(iv) To increase the rate of return on real investment.

(v) To promote competition by creating level-playing fields and facilitating free entry and exit for institutions and market players.

(vi) To ensure that the rationalisation of interest rates structure occurs, that interest rates are flexible, market-determined or market-related, and that the system offer to its users a reasonable level of positive real interest rates. In other words, the goal has been to dismantle the administered system of interest rates.

(vii) To reduce the levels of resource pre-emptions and to improve the effectiveness of directed credit programmes.

(viii) To build a financial infrastructure relating to supervision, audit, technology, and legal matters.

(ix) To modernise the instruments to monetary control so as to make them more suitable for the conduct of monetary policy in a market economy i.e., to increase the reliance on indirect or market-incentives based instruments rather than direct or physical instruments of monetary control.

The key words describing reforms have been liberalisation, deregulation, marketisation, privatisation, and globalisation, all of which convey reforms objectives in a succinct manner. The basic premise underlying the reforms has been that the state ownership and regulation have harmed the financial system, particularly the banks and the investors, and that such regulation is no longer relevant and adequate. To use the well-known academic terminology, the objective of financial reforms has been to correct and eliminate financial repression; and to transform a financially repressed system into a free system. At the same time, it has been held that the deregulation does not imply total absence of regulation; instead, it assumes sophisticated form of prodential, supervisory structure which would "Project the financial system without unnecessarily restraining it". The reforms are said to be directed towards "stringent prudential regulation" in a "deregulated environment".

Fields

Financial sector reforms have been broadly classified into 3 fields:

- The first and most important field concerns overall monetary policy including reserve requirements, interest rate refinance facility and activation of domestic debt management,
- The second field is capital adequacy and their prudential norms, and
- The third is concerned with amalgamation and entry of new banks in the private sector.

The reforms in financial sector have included the phasing in of prudential norms for income recognition and classification of assets and provision for bad debts in banks. In present globalisation scenario, financial sectors reforms included macro economic elements such as price reforms and exchange reforms. Financial sector would address issues in accounting legal and regulatory frame-work that support the sector policy. Financial sector policy covers some aspects such as interest rates, directed credit tax on financial institutions and credit subsidies. Financial sector reforms can explain with the following aspects:[2]

(a) Interest rate

Interest rate is equilibrium between the demand and supply of financial resources. Step rates of interest have chocked off a good part of demand for funds. The supply of funds being more than their demand automatically the interest rate comes down. In fact, the reference in economic advisory council report to stable real rates of interest does imply that depending on the inflation rates, the nominal interest rates would move up and down.

(b) Reduction in SLR and CRR

The reduction of Statutory Liquidity Ratio (SLR) and Cash Reserve Ratio (CRR) is designed to bring down level of pre-emption of resources by the government at below market rates. The Government has decide to SLR has been brought down to the statutory minimum i.e., below 3% and CRR to 10%. RBI reduces the SLR and CRR substantially to increase the lendable sources of Banks.

(c) Transparency

Transparency in statement of accounting was one of the first reform measure introduced in 1996. The major objectives behind transparency norms are:

(i) To eliminate the window dressing of the final accounts by Banks.

(ii) To facilitate more meaningful analysis of working of banks on the basis of extra data.

According to above norms income recognition is taken into account, the objective for income recognition is to improve recovery performance. For applying above concept the assets are classified into standard assets, sub-standard assets and loss assets.[3]

(d) Capital adequacy

Capital adequacy is the ratio of capital to risk weighted assets. The bank international settlement norm of capital adequacy is 8% of risk weighted assets. In adequacy of capital compared to the extent of risk exposures is a major problem affecting banks. RBI prescribed new capital adequacy norms banks having foreign operations were 8% and all other Indian Banks were 4%. Achievement of capital adequacy serves to strengthen the soundness and stability of banking system.

(e) Capital market

The following are the reforms regarding to capital market:

(i) In this context the abolishment of the office of the controller of capital issues in May, 1992.

(ii) Setting up of the Securities and Exchange Board of India (SEBI) with statutory powers and functions in February, 1992.

(iii) The next step in the reforms is setting up of the National Stock Exchange (NSE) and computerisation of Bombay Stock Exchange (BSE).

Recent Trends

In a competitive environment that is evolving in the financial sector, bank and other financial intermediaries are compelled to place cost and quality of delivery services at the fore front.

(a) RBI has progressed in the pursuit of the objective flexibility to the RBI to bring CRR and SLR even below 3%. In perusing this objective the RBI keeps inview not only the balance sheet of banks but also the need to move towards universal banking and diversifying financial intermediation.

(b) Several procedural initiatives of credit delivery systems have been taken. Two areas which needs immediate attention of credit delivery such as service sector and people sector (Agriculture sector).[4]

Conclusion

To sum up, financial sector reforms cover every sector of the economy. The years of reforms saw adoption of international capital adequacy and accounting standards, interest rates de-regulation and entry of private and foreign banks. It is essential to underline that the speed of financial sector reforms and sequencing of the reforms should take into account the realities of the Indian economy.

It must be recognised that key to financial sector reform is banking reform, key to banking sector reforms is public sector banking reforms, and key to public sector banking reforms is government initiation.

REFERENCES

1. L.M.Bhole, Financial Institution and Markets, TMH Publishers, New Delhi, 2000, p. 77.
2. Financial Sector reforms in times of Globalisation, Southern Economist, October, 1997, pp. 11-13.
3. Banking Reforms and New Challenges for Banks, Southern Economist, July, 1997.
4. R. Anjaneeyulu etc., Banking Theory and Financial Systems, 2000, Kalyani Publishers, pp. 104-108, Ludhiana.

6

DISINVESTMENT—A STRATEGIC APPROACH

A.G. Prasad

> *"Set the rules of the game"*
> *to maintain a fair playing field*
> *and vibrant competition*
>
> *Joseph Stiglitz*[1]

Almost 50 years ago, our country decided on a system of planning through a mixed-economy model to achieve our developmental objectives. Public enterprises are important instrument of public policy in general and planning in particular. Since then, there were a number of occasions when there was disenchantment with the performance of public enterprises. There were reviews of public enterprise policies by a host of Committees and we have been experimenting with holding—Company structures, Memoranda of Understanding etc. However, a review of the roll and functioning of public enterprises in the 90s has a qualitative difference. This is being done as part of economic reforms that we have undertaken. Economic reforms reflect a review of the role of the Government, or, more generally of the State vis-à-vis the market.

Let us examine the inherent strengths of public enterprises in many areas. These are often overlooked and more often inadequately exploited to the advantage of the enterprise. First, most private corporate sector is family oriented and surely Government as an honour cannot be less professional. Second, public enterprises as compared to private enterprises have large, very talented, qualified and experienced employees though they are often not adequately motivated, and poorly rewarded. Third, the public enterprises usually have physical assets which may not contribute directly to the income stream now, yet command high market value. Fourth, many public enterprises have reach and penetration in terms of technical collaborators, input-suppliers, market etc. and they can be actively explored for coping strategies. Finally, public enterprises can take initiative in foreign collaborations also. In brief, timely coping on the part of public enterprises by exploiting opportunities is possible and perhaps desirable, irrespective of decisions on the extent of ownership by Government.[2]

About the problems of public enterprises like pricing policy, under-utilization of capacity, problems related to planning and construction of projects, and problems relating to labour, personnel and management are at length discussed under various platforms, and further light on these issues are not desirable at this stage.

The new industrial policy announced by the Government in July 1991 emphasized the following four major measures to reform the public sector enterprises:

1. Reduction in a number of industries reserved for the public sectors from 17 to 6;
2. The disinvestment of shares of a selected set of public sector enterprises;
3. The policy towards the sick public sector enterprises to be the same as that for private sector; and
4. An improvement of performance through an MOU system by which managements are to be granted greater autonomy but held responsible for specified results.[3]

The new industrial policy 1991, provides that "In order to raise resources and to encourage wide participation a part of government share holding in the public sector would be offered to mutual funds, financial institutions, general public and workers".[4]

The major objectives of disinvestment can be stated as follows: (a) Revenue collection, (b) Improvement in efficiency, (c) Resource mobilization, (d) Direct participation by public, (e) Encourage employees' ownership; and (f) To reduce bureaucratic control.

The public sector which is supposed to occupy the commanding heights of the economy, has not been able to generate ingestible resources for expansion, modernization and diversification, and has instead become a drag on the economy. The total investment in 246 PSUs has amounted to Rs. 1,13,233.68 crores as on 31.03.1991. As against this, the profits earned by these PSUs during that period is Rs. 2,367.74 crores and the dividends paid is mere Rs. 364.86 crores. A large number of PSUs in non-core sector is either marginally profitable or loss making. Loss making PSUs will continue to be an increasing drain on the budget unless a viable policy of disinvestment is evolved and implemented for them. Hence, the Government has taken a decision to disinvestment the shares of public sector enterprises in phased manner. The Government of India has sold shares of PSUs in the past 9 years.

Details of the disinvestment programme from 1991-92 to 1999-2000 are presented in Table 1.

It is clear from the table, the actual realization from the disinvestments programme has been considerably below the target most of the time. Critics have pointed out that the Government carried out the whole exercise of disinvestments in a hasty, unplanned and hesitant way. It launched the programme without creating the required conditions for its take-off.

The department of Public Enterprises and the Finance Ministry adopted techniques and methods which resulted in far lower realization than justified.[5]

The average loss consequent upon the under-pricing comes to about 256 per cent. If we apply this percentage to the divestiture proceeds for 1991-92 and 1992-93 we find that the potential proceeds would have been Rs. 12,554 crores as against the actual realization of only Rs. 4,951 crores.[6]

TABLE 1
DISINVESTMENT OF EQUITY IN PUBLIC SECTOR ENTERPRISES

Rs. Crores

Year	*Target*	*Realization*	*Cumulative*
1991-92	2,500	3,038	3,038
1992-93	2,500	1,913	4,951
1993-94	3,500	0	4,951
1994-95	4,000	4,843	9,794
1995-96	7,000	362	10,156
1996-97	5,000	380	10,536
1997-98	4,800	902	11,438
1998-99	5,000	5,371	16,809
1999-2000	10,000	1,479	18,288

Source: Government of India, Economic Survey, 1999-2000 (Delhi 2000) Table 7.7, p. 119.

However, it has been estimated that given the then profitability of these high profile companies and their future prospects the shares offered for sale could easily be worth Rs. 8,000 crores. This shows that during the entire disinvestment programme, the public sector equity has been sold for a fraction of what it could actually fetch.[7]

Under the present scenario let us examine the following objectives:

(1) To what extent the disinvestment policy is desirable, and

(2) How to make this disinvestment policy a viable proposition.

By examining the actual practices of disinvestment the set targets and failure of realization from the above mentioned table, it is quite desirable to have a different perspective.

The following are the points worth considering at the time of disinvestments:

(1) Never begin with the premise that disinvestment is a political and not an economic exercise. In such cases the outcome is invariably all politics, no economics, and very little disinvestment.

(2) Don't try to achieve too many objectives. Stick to

fundamentals. What can one do to maximize corporate value, not only in the short run but also in medium term.

(3) If sub-optimal performance of a PSU is primarily due to inadequate management, then it is incorrect to privatize by broad base sale of equity to millions of small shareholders. This allows inefficient incumbent management to continue running the firm to the determent of future corporate value.

(4) Even where poor management is not the reason for under-performance the commission should always complement broad-based public issues with competitive private placement.

(5) Don't get tempted by a popular view that it is better to restructure PSUs before privatization. This is true only performs with competent management.

(6) While it is possible to privatize and yet limit the amount of labour redundancy, it does not come free. The number of workers in a firm effects cost. Beyond a point, a higher labour complement will necessarily lower the price of equity.

(7) State sponsored monopolies should be broken up into competing units before privatisation. This follows the principle that a profit-maximising private monopoly is worse than a social welfare maximizing public monopoly.[8]

(8) Finally for privatization to be credible, Government must ensure utmost transparency. The disinvestment commission should weigh all the related points and problems and then only appropriate decision should be taken.

The Government has decently managed to divest shares in three important companies—VSNL, Pardeep Phosphates and IBP. This follows the earlier disinvestment of CMC, Hindustan Teleprinters, Modern Food Industries and Balco. A few hotels have also changed ownerships. Both family owned enterprises and multinational companies have participated in the bidding process. The present structure of

Indian industry consists almost entirely of family run firms, public sector corporations and MNC controlled companies. Hence, if Government wishes to diverse then the choice falls on either family run corporations or MNCs. Indian opinion seems to have become divided into two camps; the privatisers say that "the Government has no business to be in the business", hence disinvestment is the only way out. The other camp holds the view that the Government should not hand over the family silver to crooks and charlatans who dominate Indian businesses, as these business houses are responsible the huge non-performing assets that the large Government owned institutions have piled up.[9]

Whatever the merits of the arguments, one cannot ignore either of these two opinions. The Governments have substantially failed to make a success of business and it is true of most economies and there is a global trend of Government getting out of business. On the other hand, a substantial portion of Indian industry in the private sector has flourished in the license permit raj, and is today facing the heat of global competition. Many units do not have the requisite managerial capacities, technical capabilities besides shortage of money to run and manage modern industry successfully. Most of them continue to depend on managerial capability within the family to run their business. Family members usually take key decisions even when external managerial staff is employed.

One can conclude that most of these business houses have no capabilities to take over the large units in the public sector and run them profitably over any length of time. When we look at even the MNCs in general have been rather luke-warm towards the privatization process. Of course when once the Government starts moving faster then these MNCs might act faster, then their interest may revive.

Instead of over emphasizing the need for disinvestment, can there be any alternative to strengthen the economy, to boost the moral of the public sector enterprises, and to create consciousness, confidence and commitment from the employees of this sector?

It is to be critically examined from the above mentioned issues.

- Make the PSUs on par with private sector enterprises by (a) giving full autonomy, (b) non-interference from bureaucrats, and (c) politicians.
- Introduce professional managers and assign them the task of managing the PSUs.
- On the advent of globalization it is the general phenomenon that small scale units and medium & large scale units with inefficient managements and other limitations cannot survive the global competition. It is already a known fact that most of the PSUs have under-capacity utilization and other greater inherent strengths. Therefore, those strengths should be garnered and nurtured and should be made globally competitive.
- By identifying some PSUs which can otherwise be good, except in the areas of the management. Competent and professional management experts should be drawn both national and international-wide, and these units must be handed over to them unconditionally. There are good number of turnaround managers who can undertake such challenging tasks.
- One should work towards a modern and competitive industrial structure, where different industrial ownerships and management patterns co-exists. One has to fill up critical gap in the corporate structure and that is the absence of professionally run companies whose shares are widely held. It is true, that most MNCs have this kind of ownership structure.
- In the Indian context, when disinvestment of a particular PSU shares takes place another PSU giant purchase the same (IBP shares have been purchased by IOC). In some other cases, the bidder will be other mutual fund or organizations like UTI, LIC, IDBI and SBI. These also happened to be other governmental extended arms (agents); it does not make any sense or

difference. Therefore, in the first incidence those organizations should be privatized.

- A team of management experts should be constituted and/or (like a think-tank) drawn from various fields (from industry, academics, and professional management experts etc.) and must be assigned the responsibility of running and managing these financial institutions on sound ethical business lines. There should be a steering committee and these professionals must guide these PSUs/FIs. These professionals should be independent and freedom to work in independent manner with market oriented salaries with incentives for better performance as well as disinsentives for non-performance.
- More transparency is desirable and all the parties concerned must be put fully in the picture. Public suggestions for the improvements of the performance of PSUs as well as disinvestment commissions is welcome.
- A pro-active role both from bureaucrats, politicians as well as the employees of the PSUs should be a welcoming sign. The synergy of these parties concerned must generate greater strength, especially in the context of globalization, where merit and only merit is the order of the day.
- Competition and comprehension of ever-changing scenario from national and international context should be examined. Quicker, positive and constructive suggestions to combat the critical situation should be emulated from the successful MNCs, proven entrepreneurs and professionals.
- Even for selling the loss-making PSUs, it is desirable, firstly, to make them a going on concern and a viable project by putting all the requisites and then considering divestiture. For this type of PSUs a search is needed to find out turn-around managers. Fortunately, talent in India is widespread, only the intention is missing.

- In case of profit making PSUs instead of thinking disinvestment it may be worked out a new strategy might be adopted to make them globally competitive and greater emphasis must be laid in this direction.

As a consequence of new economic environment the attitude of workers and management may be changed. The new reality is "enterprise" and not "public ownership". The public ownership is being diluted. Hence, the attitude of the management and workers will be oriented towards the survival and growth of each enterprise in order to maximize their own welfare.

This way the PSUs can be saved, targets of disinvestment can be achieved, and global challenges and competition can be meted out.

REFERENCES

1. Prof. Joseph Stiglitz, former Chairman of the Council of Economic Adviser to the then President of US—Clinton.
2. Venugopal Reddy Y, Deputy Governor, RBI, 'Public Enterprises & Economic Reforms', The Indian Journal of Commerce, Vol. 1, No. 190, Part 1, Mar 97, pp. 34-42.
3. Jagdish Prakash Rao Shukla—'Administration of Public Enterprises in India', Himalaya Publishing House, New Delhi.
4. Venugopal Rao, Ramaprasada Rao, 'Economic Reforms in India', Indian Economic Panorama, Vol. 9, No. 1, April 99, p. 9.
5. R.K. Mishra, R. Nandagopal, *et.al*, 'Sale of Public Enterprise Shares: Frittering Away Nation's Wealth', Economic & Political Weekly, Nov. 27, 1993, P.M. 168.
6. Sunil Mani, 'Economic Liberalization and the Industrial Sector', Economic and Political Weekly, May 27, 1995, pp. 41-42, 45.
7. S.P. Kothari, 'PSU Disinvestment: Underselling', The Economic Times, Nov. 17, 1994, P. 8.
8. Omkar Goswamy, 'Disinvestment: Ten Tenets', The Economic Times, Vol. 36, No. 150, Aug. 27, 1996, p. 4.
9. Abhijit Roy, 'Disinvestment by Rote', The Hindu, March 7, 2002, P. Bs-1.

7

REFORMS AND CAPITAL MARKET

C. Anil Kumar
Vijaya Sree K

Capital market evolution takes place through changes in market practices and conditions laid down by policies. What was considered to be a control/regulatory regime was expected to have transformed into an open, transparent and market regine, during the nineties of the last century. Several policy changes brought out by the Govt. in the name of liberalisation or reforms have totally changed the situation of the India Capital market.

The repealing of Capital Issues (Control) Act 1947 has put an end to regulatory pricing mechanism giving rise to free pricing based on the market conditions. Promulgation of Securities & Exchange Board of India Act paved away for investor protection through sufficient disclosure norms. Freedom to determine the offer price led to the popular use of book building mechanism. The replacement of floor-based system by electronic system resulted in more transparency, efficient pricing and reduction of transaction costs. Introduction of innovative financial instruments combining the features by both equity and debt to cater to the needs of investors widened the base of the capital market. Introduction of depository system led to the acceleration of scripless trading and rolling settlement shortened the settlement cycle. Introduction of circuit breakers/price brands slowed down the market momentum contained excess volatility and helped in maintaining investor confidence in the market. Presence of several disclosure norms, regulations governing substantial acquisition/ takeovers, prohibition of insider trading etc. have strengthened capital market.

Against this backdrop of changes affected and likely effect predicted by policy-makers, an attempt is made in this paper to evaluate the real impact of capital market reforms. Basically reforms are aimed at strengthening the capital market in the sense that the market must provide for the smooth flow of funds from the suppliers to the users of funds. This can be achieved when the investor's sentiment and confidence is in favour of various financial instruments issued by the users to raise required funds. Whether this has been achieved or not?

Domestic Household Savings in Financial Assets

Domestic savings in India account for more than 22 per cent of the Gross Domestic Product (GDP). Capital market in any country is expected to promote savings and channelise into desired forms. During the decade of implementation of reforms domestic savings as a per cent of GDP rose from 22% in 1991-92 to 25% in 1995-96 and fell back to the old level of 22% by 2000-2001 (as per Table 1). But household savings continuously increased from 17% to 20% during 1991-92 and 2000-2001. Economic growth requires increase in capital stock which is possible only if the savings are channelised into productive investment which means that savings should take the financial form (i.e., shares, debentures, bonds, deposits, etc.). Domestic Household savings in financial assets fell from 11.0% in 91-92 to 8.9% in 95-96 and rose to 10.5% by 2000-2001. It implies that the remaining savings are taking the form of gold, jewelry, real estate, bullion etc. The share of shares and debentures issued by private corporate sector is a meager per cent of 0.02% (of GDP).

The above analysis reveals that the market reforms have not yielded the desired effect of promoting more savings and channelising the savings into financial assets (corporate sector stock or debt).

TABLE 1
GROSS DOMESTIC SAVINGS AS PER CENT OF GROSS DOMESTIC PRODUCT

	GD Savings	*Household Savings*	*Financial Savings*	*Savings in shares and debentures*
1991-92	22.0	17.0	11.0	0.05
1995-96	25.0	18.0	8.9	0.03
2000-01	22.0	20.0	10.5	0.02

Source: Economic Survey, Central Statistics Organisation

Growing Importance of Financial Intermediaries

Capital market is made by the suppliers and users of funds. If the market is efficient and perfect the funds must directly flow from the suppliers to users. In any market when the expectations of the suppliers and those of the users differ, there will be no flow of funds. In a low-income country where the savings are low, the suppliers of funds/ savers look for the short-term maturity and immediate liquidity and whereas the user industry requires funds for long-term. This gap between the expectations of users and suppliers give rise to financial intermediation and the emergence of financial institutions. In India the government followed a deliberate policy of establishing financial institutions to fill the gap. Market reforms, to be effective, must result in bridging the gap not through FIs but through developing market sentiment and confidence, in favour of direct investment in corporate sector or industry. Indirect investment through FIs or financial intermediation is an imperfection. Capital market reforms attempted throughout a decade have not reduced the imperfection. On the other hand, the role of FIs has grown by leaps and bounds.

As per Table 2 during the post reforms period the amount of assistance sanctioned has increased from Rs. 19 thousand crores in 90-91 to Rs. 118 thousand crores in 2000-01, with a six fold rise and the amount of assistance disbursed rose from Rs. 13 thousand crores to Rs. 72 thousand crores. This substantial quantum jump the financial assistance by FIs clearly indicates the over dependence of the Indian industry on indirect financing. If ensuring the efficient use of capital should be the prime objective of any government, it is desirable that institutions are not give any preferential treatment over the capital market.

TABLE 2
ASSISTANCE SANCTIONED & DISBURSED BY FINANCIAL INSTITUTIONS

(Rs. in Crores)

Year	*Sanctioned*	*Disbursed*
80-81	927	1848
85-86	6533	4940
90-91	19202	12810
95-96	64163	38650
2000-01	117926	72188

Source: RBI Bulletin

Equity Versus Debt Issue

Capital market provides the channel to raise ownership capital (equity) and creditorship capital (debt). If the capital market is in position to accept debt issue against equity issue, it reflects lower investor's confidence and investor's risk aversion and weak investor's sentiment. After 1991 (period of post reforms) the investor's sentiment was in favour of subscribing to risk capital. The reforms have definitely helped in the direction of building investors confidence till 1995-96. During 9194-95 and 1995-96 alone around Rs. 30,000 crores equity capital was raised (Table 3). The share of equity as a per cent of resources mobilised by the industry rise from 30% in 90-91 to healthy level of 75% by 95-96. 1994-96 period was termed as boom period for equity. But it turned out to be a nightmare for the investors who entered the equity market during that period. Several companies, which came for a public issue during that period went into dark, several companies whereabouts were not known and the vulnerable investor had a prey to these fly-by-night fallen companies. This speaks about the total lack of or collapse of the regulatory mechanism in the India capital market.

TABLE 3
EQUITY AND CAPITAL RAISED FROM THE PRIMARY MARKET BY NON-GOVT. PUBLIC LTD. COS

(Rs. Crores)

	Equity		*Debenture*	
Year	*Amt.*	*(%)*	*Amt.*	*(%)*
90-91	1297	30%	3015	70%
91-92	1918	31%	4275	69%
92-93	9753	50%	9850	50%
93-94	9960	52%	9370	48%
94-95	17546	66%	8871	34%
95-96	12105	75%	3970	25%
96-97	6176	59%	4233	41%
97-98	1167	37%	1972	63%
98-99	2622	52%	2391	48%
99-00	2753	53%	2401	47%
2000-01	2789	57%	2140	43%

After this debacle, the share of equity fell back to its original level around 30%. Post 94-96 period witnessed total collapse of equity market and total absence of equity market. Though small amounts were raised, most of the issues were by the information technology/software industry. The manufacturing sector is conspicuous by its absence.

Dependence on Private Placement

The method of raising funds from the capital market through private placement has become popular and widely dominant after 94-96 Pseudo equity boom. Private placement is placing the equity issue privately rather than going for a public issue straight away.

It is clear from Table 4 that the dependence on private placement has gone up significantly. From a low per cent of 39 in 95-96 to high per cent 91 in 2000-01. The share of resources mobilized through private placement from the primary market has increased. It reflects the lack of confidence on the part of the industry to raise funds directly through the public issue.

TABLE 4
RESOURCES MOBILISED THROUGH PRIVATE PLACEMENT FROM THE PRIMARY MARKET

Year	*Per cent*
95-96	39.3
96-97	49.3
97-98	86.6
98-99	84.1
99-00	88.8
2000-01	91.3

New Versus Existing Companies

The capital market must provide a base for new companies to come into existence and thereby result in industrial growth. According to Table 5 around 35% of the funds were raised by new companies before the introduction of reforms. This percentage has fallen to a very low of just 1% in 98-99 indicating the strength of the market in providing proper base for the new companies.

TABLE 5
NEW CAPITAL ISSUED BY NEW EXISTING NON-GOVT. PUBLIC LTD. COMPANIES

(per cent)

Year	*New*	*Existing*
70-71	46%	64%
75-76	64%	36%
80-81	35%	65%
85-86	34%	64%
90-91	17%	83%
91-92	15%	85%
92-93	17%	83%
93-94	29%	71%
94-95	24%	76%
95-96	19%	81%
96-97	22%	78%
97-98	22%	78%
98-99	1%	99%

Popularity of Mutual Funds

While financial institutions provide financial intermediation, mutual funds provide investment intermediation. Mutual funds offer a wide variety of units based on the risk taking ability of the small investors. The increasing significance of mutual funds is reflected by the quantum of resources mobilised by the mutual funds. Table 6 shows that mutual funds at the private sector have come to play a dominant role in the Indian capital market. Mutual funds of UTI and financial institutions are slowly loosing the significance as they survived during a period when private sector was not allowed and there was no competition. Since 1993-94 resources mobilised by private sector mutual funds rose from Rs. 1560 crores to Rs. 17171 crores in 90-00. The growing significance of mutual funds indicates the increasing importance being given by the investing public to the secondary market operations against primary market dealings. Without an increase in number of companies and a growth in equity base, too many market players in the secondary market will only lead to too many fluctuations.

TABLE 6
MOBILISATION OF RESOURCES BY MUTUAL FUNDS

Year	*Total*	*Pvt. Sector*
92-93	13021	–
93-94	11243	1560
94-95	11275	1322
95-96	5833	133
96-97	2037	864
97-98	4064	749
98-99	3611	2519
99-2000	21972	17171

Premium Issue of Equity

If more premium issues hit the primary market and they are over subscribed, that indicate the overwhelming confidence of investing public in the equity issue. Indian capital market too witnessed such premium issues during the post liberalisation period. Supported by the free pricing mechanism introduced by the government through abolishing the Capital Issues act and regulatory mechanism, many companies entered the market. 1994-96, a period which was considered to be boom for the equity market has ultimately turned out to be pseudo boom. Though percentage-wise, the number of issues and amount raised through premium issues have shown an increasing trend (as per Table 7), the absolute figures speak volumes about the dwindling equity market. During the recent period excepting some IT/software companies, no noteworthy public issues came from manufacturing industry.

TABLE 7
PREMIUM ISSUE OF EQUITY SHARES

Year	*No. of Issues*	%	*Amt.*	%
91-92	56	15.3%	237	12.4%
92-93	324	37.4%	5184	5.9%
93-94	372	37.4%	5184	5.9%
94-95	628	40.6%	8420	48.4%
95-96	467	29%	4993	41.0%
97-98	29	33%	653.5	56%
98-99	19	58%	1326	52%
99-00	48	70%	2169	79%
2000-01	57	44%	1267	48%

The above analysis leads us to the conclusion that whether reforms have led to the growth of equity market or to the total collapse of equity markets.

Positive Impact of Reforms

Though the above analysis indicates the negative effect of capital market reforms, reforms are not devoid of positive impact. On the domestic front, though the reforms have not strengthened the capital market, on the international front they have some favourable effect.

(a) Foreign Investment flow

From Table 8 it can be observed that FI inflows have

increased from a negligible level of 103 US $ million 1990-91 to 6133 US $ million in 96-97. Later the total decreased to 2401 US $ million in 98-99 and rose to 5181 US $ million in 90-2000 and again fell to 3422 US $ million. These fluctuations were due to changes in portfolio investment. But direct investment has been above 2000 US $ million since 95-96, with slight fluctuations. Direct investment through acquisition of shares was absent till 94-95 and the amount rose to 500 US $ million by the end of the century.

TABLE 8
FOREIGN INVESTMENT INFLOWS

Year	*Direct Investment*	*Portfolio Investment*	*Out of which GDRs/ADRs*	*Total*
90-91	97	6	–	103
91-92	129	4	–	133
92-93	315	44	240	559
93-94	586	3567	1520	4153
94-95	1314	3824	2082	5138
95-96	2144	2748	683	4892
96-97	2821	3312	1366	6133
97-98	3557	1828	645	5385
98-99	2462	61	270	2401
99-00	2155	3026	768	5181
2000-01	2339	1083	831	3422

(b) GDR/ADR Issue

Indian industry raising capital abroad was never heard of piror to 91-92. After the liberalisation and several reforms, the issue of global depository receipts has become a reality. Success of many of the companies in GDR issue indicates the confidence of the international investors in the Indian companies. From a moderate beginning of 240 US $ million in 92-93 resources raised through GDRs rose to 2082 US $ million in 94-95.

March 1999, a milestone in the Indian capital market history when Infosys, ICICI, Satyam Infoway entered the American market through the issue of ADRs, later followed by Reliance, Zee telefilms, Dr. Reddy's Labs, HDFC bank etc.

The success of Indian industry in international markets is one of the very favourable impact of capital market reforms. Stock markets in India have been closely following the developments in the international stock market especially the NASDAQ. Opening of trading terminals abroad.

Conclusion

Indian capital market reflects a picture of confusion and chaos. Technological changes and regulatory framework have come a long away. But when it comes to the question of the existence of market itself there is a long way to go. The base of the capital market is very poor. Against which any attempts to mechanise or attempt to regulate will be futile exercise. Effective enforcement and supervision will check scams and unscrupulous companies thereby build investor's confidence.

SESSION–5

ECONOMIC SECTOR REFORMS—A FRESH LOOK

1

POWER SECTOR REFORMS IN ANDHRA PRADESH : RETROSPECT AND PROSPECTS

C. Suravinda

Power is a vital input for economic development. It is the most essential infrastructural requirement in today's growing economy. The state relies heavily on power for development in agricultural industrial or for that matter, overall economic development. In Andhra Pradesh, where agriculture is the primary occupation of about 70% of the population. Only 36% of the land is covered through flow irrigation. Hence, there is every need to promote pump irrigation by augmenting power supply. The expansion of electricity service for irrigation to far flung villages has made the farmers less dependent on the vagaries of monsoons and has made tackling drought easier.

Andhra Pradesh State Electricity Board (APSEB) was formed in the year 1959 and is responsible for all the three functions of the power sector, namely, generation, transmission and distribution of power. Besides generating power from its own power plants, APSEB procures power from central sector generating stations, other states, joint venture power plants and more recently from the private sector since 1995. The entry of private sector into power generation was facilitated by the central government under a liberalized policy announced in 1991.

APSEB witnessed stupendous growth during the last four decades. The present installed capacity is 7341 MW comprising of 5612 MW of its own capacity, 897 MW of share from central sector, 273 MW from joint sector and 560 MW from private sector. The peak demand met in 1998-99 was 6480 MW.

Despite the significant growth of the power system, APSEB has been finding it increasingly difficult to the growing demand for power in the state. It addition of 1791 MW of new generation capacity in the 8th plan, was the highest among all the states in the country Despite severe financial strain it was facing, the APSEB could commission the 2 × 250 MW of ktpsv record time. Similarly the two units of stage-II of AP Gas Power corporation Ltd. Were added in record time. The first two fast track plants in the country, the 216 MW Jegurupadu power plant of G.V.K. Industries and the other of 208 MW of spectrum power plant, Kakinada have come up in the state. Still the state is finding it difficult to eater to the unrestricted demand for power. Power shortages are experienced interms of energy and peak demand year after year. Power cuts mainly to HT industries had become necessary. Beside peak load restrictions, regulation of hours of supply to irrigations, regulation of hours of supply to irrigation pump sets had to be imposed in summer months. The unmetered flat rate tariff for supply of power to agricultural consumers is one of the main factors contribution got the difficulties of the power sector. The tariff causes acute financial loss to the State Electricity Board as it is way below the ever increasing cost of supply. Besides this it encourages profligate consumption, necessitating substantial power cuts on HT consumers, whose tariffs are well above the cost of supply. The growing agricultural consumption in the face of stagnant H.T. consumption has been causing sever two-fold financial difficulties to the Board. Agricultural demand side management has thus acquired great importance in balancing the need for equitable apportionment of available supply resources among the various classes of consumers vis a vis the pressing irrigation needs of farmers.

The APSEB has been making substantial investments in

upgrading and expanding its Network. During the period 1991-92 to 1996-97 the network of APSEB has been augmented by 26.4% hereby achieving the highest network expansion among SEBS in the country. The number of substations increased substantially from 1135 in 1990-91 to 1844 in 1998-99. The number of distribution transformers increased from 88000 to 171083. Despite an enormous and continuous growth over the years, the T & D system is still inadequate to convey the power to the consumers and is characterized by high T & D losses and poor voltages. The commercial losses are also quite high and cause concern. The unmetered agricultural tariff makes it difficult to segregate the commercial and technical losses.

The finances of APSEB have been under severe strain for the past few years as the cost of its operations have vastly outstreached the revenues from sales of energy. APSEB has been facing severe financial strain since 1989-90 and has been struggling to achieve the statutory rate of return steps like converting of governments loan to APSEB to equity, writing off of long term government loans have been resorted.

These daunting financial problems faced by APSEB, have made it difficult for it to mobilize the resources needed to bring in capacity additions in generation, transmission and distribution commensurate with the growth in demand. The credit worthiness of APSEB which is the sole buyer of IPP Power, has been making it difficult for the power sector to attract private investments.

Recognising the problems faced by the power sector, the government of Andhra Pradesh appointed a High level committee early as in 1995 to review the governments approach towards private participation in the power sector and suggest and suggest guidelines in the matters of restructing and privatization of power sector and on tariff policy. The committee was headed by a former member of the planning commission Sri Mitten Bhayya and comprised other three former chairmen of AP State Electricity Board and a former chairman of PFC.

The High level committee suggested a radical restructuring of the power sector on functional lines through unbundling of generation, transmission and distribution functions into advised setting up of a new regulatory environment for rational tariff fixation and for ensuing the balanced development of power sector. It also suggested steps to facilitate private investment in generation and distribution.

Consequently and keeping in view the persistent demand supply gap, the growing demand for electricity and severe shortages of electricity on the economic development of the state and the need to distance the state government from the power sector management and regulation, the government of Andhra Pradesh formulated its policy in February 1997 in regard to reforms of the power sector.

In accordance with reforms policy, the government of Andhra Pradesh enacted the AP Electricity Reform Act 1998 (Act No. 30 of 1998) and made it effective from 1-02-99. The main components of the Act are:

1. The creation of an independent regulatory commission to be called AP Electricity Regulatory Commission.
2. The facilitation of the reorganization of the Electricity supply industry on functional basis through creation of separate corporations for transmission and generation under the Indian Companies Act, 1956.
3. The defining of the respective roles of the various players in the power sector.

The Andhra Pradesh Electricity Regulatory Commission will be solely responsible the State to issue electricity transmission and supply licenses and regulate tariffs for transmission and supply of electricity. The commission will also fix and enforce standards of performance and quality of supply for the licenses duly taking into account the financial viability of the licenses and the legitimate interests of the consumers.

The reforms act seeks to restructure the power supply industry through incorporation of a transmission corporation to be termed the Transmission Corporation of Andhra

Pradesh Ltd (AP TRANSCO) under the Indian companies Act 1956. The APTRANSCO will engaging in the business of procurement, transmission and supply of electricity.

The financial problems of APTRANSCO surfaced as early as 1990-91 when subsidly from state government from state government was required. It was only from 1995-96 onwards that the government has actually provided relief to APSEB by writing off loans etc. During 2000-01 (up to 8-8-2000) govt. have extended cash support of Rs. 522.13 crores comprising of Rs. 325.25 crores subsidy to APTRANSCO and Rs. 198.99 crores as debt servicing on account of bonds as per the govt. of Andhra Pradesh Commitment to Regulatory Commission.

The annual deficits of APTRANSCO have been rising during the last few years. The main reasons for this are:

1. Changing Hydro-thermal Energy mix over time. Considerable hydel capacity. Hyder power accounted for about 50% of the total energy supply. But by 1999 the hydel thermal energy mix stands at 18:82. The pooled cost of power has therefore been rapidly rising due to the increase in the expensive thermal component in the Hydel-thermal mix.
2. Heavily subsidized supply of power to domestic and agricultural sectors.
3. Technical and non-technical losses. The technical losses are on account of power consumed by the system in Transmission and the non-technical losses are due to kept of power.

APTRANSCO has appointed Expert Consultants who made detailed supply of existing losses in the system. They have estimated that the Technical losses are around 22% while commercial losses are around 13%. The further break up of commercial losses are indicated to the about 4% due to unauthorized agricultural pumpsets and the balance 4% due to theft by other sectors.

The consultancy studies revealed for every 1% reduction of technical losses, an investment of around Rs. 890 crores is to be spent for T & D infrastructure improvement.

Theft of energy has become rampant and assumed alarming proportions threatening the very viability of power sector. Theft of energy also overloads the system and causes failures of transformers and equipments. It also causes weakening of lines due to repeated 'looking'. All this results in deterioration of quality and reliability of supply. Honest and law abiding electricity consumers have to hear additional burden in terms of increased tariff and also bear inconvenience due to poor quality of supply.

AP Ordinance No. 8 of 2000 amending the relevant clauses of the Indian Electricity Act 1910 dealing with pilferage of energy. The ordinance was promulgated on 31st July, 2000, with this the period of imprisonment raised to 5 years (from the existing 3 years). In addition to imprisonment penalty up to Rs. 50,000 with a minimum stipulation of Rs. 5000 is proposed.

A campaign for regularization of a unauthorized connections were taken up during 19-6-2000 to 25-6-2000. In one month about 1.8 million connections were regularized.

The bold initiative taken by the government of Andhra Pradesh in launching reforms has kindled investor interest and investors are eagerly coming forward to invest in the power sector in the state. The World Bank has agreed to lend up to Rs. 4500 crores for Transmission and Distribution improvements and augmentation of system ever a decade. This will be given as a series of loans under their Adaptable program lending. Department for International Development has sanctioned Rs. 346 crores as a grant to revamp the distribution system, and Rs. 196 crores as a technical assistance grant to the power sector.

The objective of the long-term program is to ensure that the energy need of the state are met by 2007 and that consumers are provided with a reliable, high quality, and cost effective electricity supply by credit worthy and commercially-operated power utilities functioning in a competitive and appropriately regulated power market with significant private involvement of the private sector.

The power sector reform program complements the ongoing bank-supported Andhra Pradesh Economic Restructuring program that provides resources to meet priority needs for nutrition, primary health, and primary education programs and in the maintenance of the economic assets affecting the rural poor namely irrigation, rural roads, and access roads. The investments are linked to a program of fiscal reforms aimed at bringing about a permanent shift in the states public spending and debt.

Taken together the Andhra Pradesh Economic Restructuring program and Power Restructuring program will make a major contribution to reshaping the state's finances and speeding up economic growth, human development and poverty alleviation.

2

GROWTH RATES OF INDIAN ECONOMY — AN ANALYSIS OF PRE- AND POST-REFORM PERIOD

G. Durga Prasad

An Overview

Today India is standing an the threshold of sweeping reforms. Since the Balance of Payments Crisis of 1990-91, economic recovery has been unexpectedly rapid and robust. India now has a record in the 1990s of successful policies of economic stabilisation and structural adjustment following the crisis in 1991. There is a significant change in our development strategy from a regulated economy to economic openness combined with economic growth. The government has quite liberalised the investment, trade, and foreign exchange regimes including the tax structure. In the process, a consensus has developed on the need to pursue and sustain a long-term programme of reforms. Until now, emphasis has been given to trade and industrial reforms.

The Indian economy has undergone gradual structural transformation during the Post-Independence period, the pace of such transformation, however, being relatively rapid since the 1980s. During this period, the performance of the Indian economy has accelerated to over 5.5 per cent per annum from a less than 2.8 per cent per annum in the 1970s. The rate had risen to 6.9 per cent per year during the following decade. Naturally, it was aimed at sustaining the 7 per cent rate in the coming 10 years. During the later part of the 1990s, i.e. 1990-2000, a rate of 5.9 per cent is expected to be achieved by the economy following the recovery of the industrial sector form the cyclical downturn during 1997-98 and 1998-99. All this positive trend in growth is because of following a major shift in macro-economic policy oriented towards 'L.P.G,' in the wake of 1991 crisis, the economy has once again been set on a high growth trajectory.

The overall growth performance has been accompanied by substantial inter-state variations in growth over the decades in spite of the focus in successive plan policies and programmes on the objectives of reducing the incidence of poverty and of achieving balanced regional development. For instance, Gujarat and Maharashtra achieved the best performance in its SDP growth, whereas U.P., Bihar and Orissa remained on the lowest rung of the ladder. Further, substantial structural change has also taken place that has altered the relative importance of various sectors in the economy transferring the economy from an agrarian emphasis to one of growing prominence of the industrial and service sectors.

Objectives of the Paper

The central importance in policy is now being given to the objective of achieving and sustaining a higher and overall growth rate in the Indian economy in the reform period of the 1990s and beyond. In the words of our Honourable Prime Minister, Sri A.B. Vajapaye, "a per cent per annum growth rate during the Tenth Plan is essential to meet the increasing requirements of our population at large and to place the economy on a higher trajectory." For this, high levels of foreign and domestic investment are needed to reach the growth target.

Therefore, it is proposed to study the structural transformation since the 1980s of the Indian economy by taking a 2-period classification, namely, (i) the pre-reform period, 1980-81 to 1990-91—Period I, and (ii) the post-reform period, 1992-93 to 1997-98—Period II.

The objectives are—(a) to examine the growth rates of 'Real G.D.P.'; (b) to consider the growth rates of Saving and

Investment; and (c) to analyse the inter-state variations in S.D.P.

All this exercise is based on 1981-88 Series for the entire period under study, 1980-81 to 1997-8.

Section I: Growth of Real Gross Domestic Product

The transformation of Indian economy from a stagnant to a vibrant economy over the decades is a consequence of the development process withnessed since the beginning of planning Era in 1951. This is reflected, inter alia, in the growth rate and in the changing sectoral composition or the Gross Domestic Product (GDP). With the Indian economy shifting to a high growth path during the 1980s i.e. during Period I, GDP has recorded a trend rate of 5.5 per cent which is slightly lower than average growth rate of 5.8 per cent (Table 1). On the other hand, for the entire period under study, the growth rate was 5.6 per cent. This is considered to be a success on the part of the policy-makers. However, there was considerable volatility in the annual growth rate and GDP originating in Agriculture in which a rate of 3.1 is recorded during Period I. But widening of Saving-Investment Gap and rising fiscal deficits, the high growth phenomenon of the 1980s could not be sustained particularly so due to the declining annual growth rate to a low of 0.8 per cent during the crisis year, 1991-92.[2]

During the post-reform period (Period II), the trend rate is placed at 6.9 per cent which was distinctly higher than 5.5 per cent rate of the 1980s. The performance of the economy is also better in Period II in terms of average growth rate which stands at 6.5 per cent, 5.8 per cent being the rate of the 1980s. This could be understood to have taken place with the opening of the economy. In addition, the industry and service sectors experienced high growth rates, whereas agriculture and allied activities registered a low rate as compared with the 1980s.

To go into the sectoral details, the growth rate of industrial production, the centre piece of economic development policy, was low despite high rates of protection during the 3 decades of our independence. From 1956-57 to 1981-82, it averaged only 4.3 per cent.[3] An acceleration took place in overall growth during the 1980s to an average of 7.2 per cent. This has been sustained in the 1990s following the recovery from the economic crisis in 1991 and the fact it is 8 per cent in the post-reform period. On the other hand, the trend rates are 7.6 and 9.3 per cent respectively during 1980s and 1990s. On the other hand, the service sector also achieved a high growth of 6.5 per cent in the 1980s and 8.4 per cent in the 1990s. This is due to the widening and deepening of the financial sector reforms.

Regarding the sector-wise growth rates, Agriculture sector was the poor performer of all the sectors during both periods understudy (Tables 1-4). The major contributor of industrial growth is manufacturing which records a trend of 7.4 per cent in the 1980s and it has risen to 10 per cent in the 1990s. The others such as Mining and Quarrying and Electricity, although registered a high growth during the 1980s, have in fact fallen drastically during the 1990s. On the other hand, in the Service sector category, trade, hotels, restaurants and Financing Insurance, etc have contributed a major share in the growth of service sector.

Composition of Real G.D.P.

In developed and mature economies, the industrial and service sectors contribute a major share in GDP with agriculture accounting for a relatively lower share. During the process of growth over the years, the Indian economy too experienced an improvement in the shares of industry and service sectors in overall GDP. For instance, the sectoral composition of real GDP shows that the share of agriculture sector in GDP gradually declined from 34.5 per cent in the 1980s to 27.5 per cent in the 1990s (Table 2). On the other hand, the shares of industry and service sectors increased from 23.2 per cent to 25.9 per cent and from 42.2 per cent to 46.6 per cent respectively during the same period. In industry, the major contributor once again is manufacturing sector. Within then service sector, it is also once again 'trade, hotels, restaurants and financing, insurance, etc.' There was a surge in the growth of service sector since the early 1980s. As per the recent experience, the service sector provided the necessary resilience to the economy particularly in times of adverse agricultural shocks.

Table 3 provides an account of year-wise trends in real GDP from 1991-92 to 1998-99. Apart from the crisis growth rate of 0.8 per cent in 1991-92, the economy grew from 5.3 per cent to 6.2 per cent from 1992-93 to 1993-94 at 1980-81 prices. Taking into account 1993-94 as base year, GDP growth rate increased at a constant, almost, rate of 7.8 per cent from 1994-95 to 1996-97. But in 1997-98, GDP grew by 5 per cent only due to the bad performance of agriculture sector (-0.1%). Afterwards, it was recouped to 6 per cent during 1998-99, despite the continued weak performance of industrial and service sectors. During the following year, 1999-2000, the economy is expected to grow by 5.9 per cent per annum in 1999-2000.[4]

Section II: Growth Rates of Saving and Investment

Saving is the backbone of any economy in the world and India is not an exception. Saving facilitates capital formation which in turn promotes productive capacity of the economy thereby accelerates the rate of growth of GDP. Of the total savings, savings from household sector constitutes an important source of saving. Next comes the public sector savings. The contribution of private corporate sector is the least.

Taking into account the information given in Table 4, the rates of savings and Gross Domestic Capital Formation (GDCF) showed a gradual increase from 20.4 per cent and 22.4 per cent in the pre-reform period to 24.3 per cent and 25.7 per cent respectively during the post-reform period. In addition, gross capital formation too increased from 23.0 per cent to 24.6 per cent during the same period.

The Table reveals that there has been a steady increase in the household sector savings from 15.7 per cent in the 1980s to 19.1 per cent in the 1990s. Of these savings, financial savings outstripped the physical savings in that the financial saving increased from 7.4 per cent to 10.3 per cent during the period under study. This is due to financial sector reforms.

On the other hand, there was a sharp jump in the private sector savings which remained below 2 per cent during the 1980s rose to 3.6 per cent during 90s. The GCF of this sector also increased. Contrary to this, the public savings declined from 2.8 per cent to 1.6 per cent during the period under study. The GCF of this sector also declined from 10.3 per cent to 8.4 per cent during the period under study.

Saving and Investment Gaps

Table 4 also reveals the extent of saving-investment gaps. The gap indicates the extent of an economy's dependence on foreign savings. In a growing economy, investment always outstrips domestic savings. During the period understudy, the dependence on foreign saving (saving-GDCF) was within 1.8 per cent of GDP. Such dependence was 2.1 per cent in 80s and declined to 1.4 per cent in the 1990s.

Regarding a sector-wise analysis of the gap, the decline in the overall gap was because of a surplus of household sector during the period under study. There was a deficit in the public sector gap which was higher privates sector increased from 2.4 per cent of GDP in 80s to sector was unaltered at 7.2 per cent of GDP from 1980-81 to 1997-98.

Section III: Inter-state Variations in SDP Growth Rates

Inter-State variations of socio-economic dimension do exist in any country. These include size, population, income, physical infrastructure, agro-climatic conditions, etc. As such, one can readily find variations in their rates of growth of State Domestic Product (SDP). The 'convergence' could not proved in these circumstances.

Table 5 provides the State level picture of Major States as regards income and population during 1996-97.[5] According to it, Maharashtra was a state with the largest income contributing 14.26 per cent of National Income in

1996-97.[6] It was also the third most populous state with an 8.8 crore population. Second to it was UP with a 9.44 per cent share of NNP but with a largest population of 15.32 crores, or 16 per cent of the total population. Next comes the middle-order States like AP (6.92%), West Bengal (6.56%) and Tamil Nadu (6.33%). These 5 states together contributed 43.52 per cent of NNP in 1996-97.

On the other hand, Bihar was the second most populous states, but its share of NNP was only 3.78 per cent during 1996-97. All the major states given in the table produced 79 per cent of NNP in 1996-97.

Growth Rates of Real S.D.P.

Table 6 provides information regarding growth rates real SDP and per capita real SDP during Period I and Period II. According to it, the combined growth rate of real SDP increased from 5.24 per cent in 80s to 5.94 in 90s. The real growth of SDP in 80s almost coincides with the real GDP growth of 5.5 per cent. Whereas the real SDP growth rate of 6.89 per cent in 90s. This difference in the growth rates was because of revision undertaken in respect of GDP data and which was not so in respect of SDP data.[7] In per capita terms, the real SDP grew from 3.03 in 80s to 4.02 in 90s.

The Table also explains about the performance of individual states, with some states growing faster and some others lagging behind. The range of variation in the growth of real SDP was from a low of 3.6 per cent per annum in Kerala to a high of 6.6 per cent per year in Rajasthan, nearly a factor of 2, in 80s. In the other part, the variation was much higher from a low of 2.7 per cent per year of Bihar to a high of 9.6 per cent per year for Gujarat, a factor of 3.5. As a result of reforms, the States of Maharashtra (8.01%) and Gujarat (9.57%) performed well even when compared to GDP in 90s. The second order states with 6 per cent growth are Rajasthan, MP, Tamil Nadu and West Bengal. The States—AP, Kerala, Karnataka and Haryana achieved more than 5 per cent growth in their SDP. The poor performers are UP, Bihar and Orissa.

In per capita terms, the variation in growth rates ranged from 2.1 per cent for MP to a high of 4 per cent in Rajasthan in 80s, a factor of 2. In the 90s, the ratio of variation is 1:7 with 1.1 per cent in Bihar and 7.6 in Gujarat. Hence, even in per capita terms, the performance of Gujarat and Maharastra was continued to be good.

Another interesting point is that the 6 best-performing States—Gujarat, Maharastra, Tamil Nadu, MP, Rajasthan and West Bengal—were fairly well distributed regionally in the country. Gujarat and Maharastra grew at rates normally associated with 'miracle growth' economics.

Section IV: Concluding Remarks

India witnessed sweeping changes in its economy during 1990s as a result of initiation of reforms in the form of 'L.P.G.' immediately after the Balance of Payments crisis in 1991. Since then, the economy never looked back and its recovery from the crisis is rapid and robust. The economy experienced a growth of 6.9 per cent per annum during 1992-93 to 1997-98 as against 5.5 per cent per annum growth during 1980s. Therefore, the economy was placed on a higher growth trajectory and has shown an improvement in a number of macro-economic indicators in a short span of time of less than a decade. This performance was backed by remarkable growth in the service sector followed by industrial sector. In fact, the service sector provided the necessary resilience to the economy particularly in times of adverse agriculture shocks. The fruits of GDP growth extended to the states in the form of rapid strides achieved by some of the states like Gujarat, Maharastra, Tamil Nadu, West Bengal, etc. With all these positive trends, the central importance in policy is now being given to the objective of achieving and sustaining a higher and overall growth rate in GDP. Therefore, a growth rate of 7 to 9 per cent per year is all the more important in the coming 10 years to sustain the higher growth trajectory.

Before concluding the paper, let us once again note that the present slogan is that 'when the country take a care of growth, poverty would be taken are of automatically.' Thus, there is no substitute for growth.

REFERENCES

1. Economic Survey, 2000, Government of India, New Delhi, pp. 3-4
2. Uma Kapita, (Ed.), Indian Economy Since Independence, Academic Foundation, Ghaziabad, 2000-2001, p. 741.
3. Ric Shand, S. Bhide, 'Sources of Economic Growth: Regional Dimensions of Reforms,' Economic and Political Weekly, October 14-20, 2000, p. 3747.
4. Economic Survey, 2000, op. cit.
5. Data regarding Population is taken from Ric Shand, S. Bhide, op. cit.
6. Economic Survey, 2000, op. cit.
7. Ahluwalia, M.S., 'Economic Performance of States in Post-Reform Period,' Economic and Political Weekly, May 6-12, 2000, p. 1638.

3

ECONOMIC SECTOR REFORMS: A FRESH LOOK OF AGRICULTURE SECTOR

V.V. Seshu Mohan

The economy of the country was at stake when the minority Govt., under the leadership of Sri P.V. Narasimha Rao was formed the Govt., was left with an option except take some satisfactory measures. At this function, India was running a current account default of $ 10 billion. Thus his credibility was very low and commercial borrowing impossible. Inflation was at an annual rate of 13% and the infield of foreign currency from non-resident Indian was reversed.

The Iraq of Kuwait aggravated the situation in 1990 when it resulted in the rise of oil. The later lame duck Govt. of V.P. Singh and of Chandra Sekhar failed to tackle of crisis.

A crisis is an opportunity for introduany, a new style of govt. pursuing a new model of development when the old style and the old model can convincingly be presented as having led to disaster. But in a democracy there must also be a sufficient body of influential opinion already convinced or very ready to be convinced, of the need for radical change. For nearly twenty years any mention of south Korea or Taiwan resulted in sign of amazement that any one might think that India could learn from such small economics. It was more than a decade once China's liberalization's reform could be seen to be highly successful. But, at last, the total collapse of the Russian Comme system must have convinced many people that a highly regulated economy with centralized planning was not still a model to copy.

One way or another the ground was sufficiently prepared to uses the crisis. As an occasion for embarking on a programme of reform where pursuit would result in a radical transformation of the Indian Economy.

Portfolio investment equities or bonds are another matter. There is no long-run advantage in influence these potentially disturbing movements, except by ortho macro-economic policy measures. But in the structure until the domestic banking and monetary systems are in good working order and inspire and monetary systems are in good working order and inspire confidence, and the large international portfolio disequilibria that are a hand over from a highly controlled part have been absorbed, there is a case for retaining administrate controls over private foreign borrowing and lending.

Medium terms stabilization has been achieved though inflation is higher than is desirable. But public sector deficits absorb too much of the savings urgently needed for private investment, and levels of borrowing that are unsustainable in the long run.

Tariff reforms has revenue consequences; this leads to an extended analysis of the whole fiscal scene. It is complicated because of the constitutional provision. The domestic indirect tax system is highly distorted, and direct taxes yield little. Subsidies have become a major recognized misuse of public finance there has been almost no success in redone there.

In July 1991, the Indian financial system was collapsing exploitation of the banks by Govt., and directed credit at subsidized interest rates had left many banks effectively bankrupt and incapable of properly fulfilling the many functions of a banking system. They were rescued by a massive in fusion of public capital the yield-designed interference led to their decay have been largely but not wholly reclined. A beginning has been made to institute sound prudential regulation of both banks and other financial institutions.

Another development relevant to the nexus between monitory and fiscal policy is the change in Govt., access to borrowing from RBI. In the mid 1950's an agreement was reached at between ROI and the Govt. of India that that whenever the cash balance of the Govt. fell below a certain limit they would be restricted by the creation ad hoc treasury bills. These arrangements in effect paved the way for automatic moneterization of large fiscal defaults.

The above arrangement is not an end to the moneterization of deficits. Any fiscal deficits. Any fiscal deficits are to be financed by printing money or by domestic borrowing. This forces the Govt. to borrow from the market in the first instance. This in turn increases the interest rates. It is now left to opinion of the Govt., to allow increase in interest rates are bring down the interest rates by back door with the help of print money. India, the central bank is not independent, so the opinion is left to the Govt.

The Reform of Agriculture's Incentives:

The central subsidy is only a small part of the total measure subsidization of agriculture inputs, much of which is the responsibility of state Govt. Agriculture trade is also subsidual the irrigation subsidy may be of the order of Rs. 10,000 crores that of electricity Rs. 4000 and credit subsidization Rs. 3000 crores.

The subsidies not only contribute the overall fiscal deficit both directly and indirectly but the also threaten the actual supply of irrigation and electricity as they undermine the financial viability of the state irrigation authorities and electricity bonds. Credit subsidies have also contributed to the weaknesses of the banks that threaten the whole financial system in India in 1990-91.

Directed Agricultural Credit: Financial Viability

Commercial banks have met directed credit targets by at the cost of cross subsidies and bad debts. Before 1991, the interest rate structure was enormously complicated in addition to being confessional. Since then, there has been significant rationalization but differentiation by six remains and cross subsidies continue on a substantial scale currently, loans smaller than Rs. 25,000 carry a stipulated interest rate of 12% and loans between the Rs. 2500 to 2,00,000 of 13.5%. Interest rates on loans larger than Rs. 2,00,000 are unregulated by the end of 1995. Prime lending rates are 16.5% and most borrowers pay around 20%. The maximum 2 year deposit rate is 12% higher unregulated rates are available for lower maturates. The arrange loan for agriculture is less than 10,000 and averages loans to small industries and transport operators is in between 25,000 to 2,00,000. The average loan to large-scale industry is larger than the ten lakhs. Thus it is dividend that loans to agriculture still carry a significant subsidy if allowance is made to administration and overheads for the greater risk.

The overdues with regard to commercial banks directed credit be also worth noting. In 1992, directed credit accounted for 35% in lending but 55% of overdues. In case of large-scale industry the directed credited accounted for 40% of lending and 29% of overdues. Thus the date shows that while overdues arrears and non-performing assets are a systematic problem, the performance of directed credit is worst than that of non-directed credit. Concessional directed has been an important factor in vitiating the financial performance of commercial banks and raising the cost of capital to non-priority sectors.

Regional Rural Banks

These were set up in 1976 as a result of disappointment with the progress of co-operative and commercial banks in extending credit or agriculture. RRB is capitalized to the tune of 65% by the central and relevant state Govt., and 35% by a sponsor bank. RRB were madated to lend solely to people below the poverty line at concessional interest rates applying to small loans, significantly below a Break Even rate. Their deposit rates were controlled. Their freedom of operation was severely restricted even with regard to providing incentives to borrowers to repay on time. They could survive only with refinance from the NABARD and their sponsor's commercial banks. Re-finance from NABARD is available at heavily subsidized rates of 6.5% to 8.5%. In 1994, re-finance from NABARD and sponsored banks were about 37% of advances. Even so 43 RRB's defaulted with respect to their payments to NABARD.

The network of RRB's grew rapidly and currently there are 146 RRB's with 15,000 branches. At the definition of 1994, 171 out of 196 banks were making losses and about three hundred of them had negative net-worth their overdues performance was even worse than that of commercial and co-operative banks, in 1992 RRBs is their total lack of commercial orientation. Their administration and wage costs are orientation. Their administrative and wage costs are high. Identification of borrowers and projects in both lacking and highly politicized. Over-dues are a pervasive problem with useful default playing a major rule.

Recently some steps have been taken to improve their function. They were given freedom both in the management of their funds and relocating of their loss making branches. Since the Govt., has not bitten the bullet of internet rate deregulation, the above change has led to RRB's reducing their lending to poor farmers and increasing their lending to the Govt. The budgets 1994-95 also announced that 100 RRB's would be taken up for clean-up and restricting with the Govt., contributing its share of Rs. 450 crores for the operation.

At the grass-roots level, co-operation banks are still very important and account for 37% of all rural advances in 1994. Unfortunately, their financial state is dismal except in few states. Their performance with regard to overdues is miserable. Overdues accounted for 34% of advances and about 50% of debt service in 1992. Surveys have found that a substantial proportion of default is useful. They are only co-operative in name. Their deposit mobilization is in adequate and their dependence on outside agencies such as NABARD very high. They are largely co-operatives of borrowers using their political misuse at state and local levels to secure subsidized credit.

Does Directed Agriculture Credit Promote Efficiency and Equity?

We have seen above that all the financial institution involved in agricultural lending are weak or insolvent. This shows that the system is unhealthy. But this is not a conclusive proof of the effects of directed credit. No study revealed that in the absence of directed concessional credit would deserve agriculture. Even the excellent econometric work of Binswanger and Khandker using date for 85 distincts proceeds on the assumption that directed credit has overcome credit constraints. Moreover the results of the study are favorable to directed credit. Directed credit has shown only a mildly positive effect on output and zero effect on employment.

The directed credit an events is not economic growing. Institutional credit to agriculture has expanded rapidly and rural households as an aggregate obtain 61% of their credit requirements from institutional sources. But there is a clear and dramatic correlation, between household wealth and reliance an institutional credit. For example, the poorest household wealth and reliance an institutional credit. For example, the poorest households meet only 9% of their credit requirements from institutional sources. It is a fact that only 30% of rural families have obtained access to institutional credit. The medium and large farmers have pre-empted a large part of such credit and consequently received large subsides. The incidents of overdues are just as bad among the large as among the small farmers. One of the main reasons for overdues among the large as among the small farmers. One of the main reasons for overdues among the large farmers is that they corner agricultural credit and re-lend it on the informal market.

IRDP was launched in 1979 whose aim is to enable households to cross an income-based poverty line by investing in income generating assets. The investment are financed by a financial package, half of which is a Govt., grant and the rest is a non-collectorised bank loan. The target of eligible households is done by local govt., officials while a commercial or regional rural bank co-operates with them and the recipient in selecting or purchasing the asset bought with the loan. Loan collecting is the responsibility of the lending bank the loan carry a concessional rate of interest. They are eligible for both refinance and insurance cover. The programme of IRDP is not a success.

4

PROBLEMS OF PRIVATISATION IN INDIA

M. Ramasomayajulu

The role of the state in the economic sphere continues to be a matter of controversy. The classical economists believed that all economic activities should be left to the market. However, by the 18th century, socialist thinking developed of many countries, and the state was given high importance in regulating the market.

This change in thinking was because of problems created by capitalism—trade cycles, income inequalities, worsening working conditions, regional disparities in development and also worsening poverty and unemployment.

Major Causes

The poor performance of the public sector is a major factor for the present tilt towards privatisation. The public sector in India could not achieve even the social objectives of planning like correcting regional imbalance in development.

In 1951, there were 5 central public sector units with an investment of Rs. 29 crores. By 2000, the number increased to 240, and the investment to Rs. 223050 crores.

The return on equity for the public sector as a whole is 17 per cent. But, what needs to be remembered is that an attempt is made to boost profits not by improving productivity but through the upward revision of administered prices for commodities like coal, steel, aluminium and petroleum products.

Due to political interference in the working of the public sector, it lacked functional autonomy. About the public sector, it is said, 'Its justification rests heavily on grounds of efficiency and its success on accompanying measures to promote a more competitive environment.'[1]

Of course, the failure of communism in the USSR and some East European countries has also led to the unpopularity of state role in the economic sphere.

Major Problems

In India, privatisation may create serious problems. According to the Human Development Report (HRD, 1993), privatisation has taken place for the wrong reasons, under the wrong conditions and in the wrong way.

Private investment is for profit anywhere in the world. Privatisation may increase the production of comforts and luxuries, neglecting the production of essential goods and services. This would further worsen the problem of poverty.

The unemployment situation in India is worsening. When capital and energy intensive technologies are adopted, unemployment situation worsens. There is the phenomenon of jobless growth, which developing countries cannot afford.

In the case of India, in 1999, employment in public sector declined by 0.015 per cent, in the private sector it declined by 0.57 per cent. The public sector shed off only 3000 from its workers pool during 1999, the private sector shunted out, in net terms 50,000.[2]

Foreign investment may enter into non-priority sectors. This would adversely affect national interests. Also, it is feared that the government is recklessly entering into foreign collaborations even in areas where domestic capabilities are well developed.[3] The free flow of director foreign investment in the consumer goods sector is inconsistent with out industrial policy as it permits foreigners to have control over the Indian economy.[4]

In India regional disparities in development are increasing. Private investors always invest in areas, which are well developed. The backward areas remain backward forever. In India, private investment under liberalisation is flowing mainly into four states: Maharashtra, Gujarat (high income states); Karnataka and Tamil Nadu (middle income states).

The backward states have to face a double disadvantage: fall in investment and lower tax collection.[5] Regional disparities in development cannot be corrected through market-oriented growth.[6]

The cost of service is also important. The private sector may provide good service, but the cost may be high, knot within the reach of ordinary people. A number of well-managed self-financed colleges are there but few students can afford the fees being changed by these colleges. Thus, privatisation would adversely affect social sectors like education, health and housing.

Privatisation is likely to produce adverse environmental affects. Air and water pollution and decline in forest cover are the results of profit-based investment. About 70 per cent of the industries in the country have failed to meet the pollution standards.

Conclusions

In most countries, the public sector has not been allowed to function on sound lines. The government has to concentrate on improving the performance of the public sector instead of allowing the private sector to dominate the economy. There should be professionalisation of management in the public sector.

In India, the Government is slowly withdrawing from the economic sphere. This is not desirable. Where competition is important and indispensable, private sector may be encouraged. In all other spheres where social objectives of planning are important, the public sector should be allowed to play its legitimate role. Extremes are always undesirable particularly in the economic sphere.

REFERENCES

1. *Finance and Development*, September 1988, p. 31
2. Alternative Economic Survey 2000-2001, Rainbow Publishers, Delhi-110092, p. 40.
3. Ruddar Datt: 'Multi-nationals Versus Swadeshi', *Mainstream*, Annual 1993, p. 65.
4. *Ibid.*, p. 67.
5. I. Satya Sundaram: 'Privatisation at the Crossroads', *New Quest*, January-March 2000, p. 82.
6. R.K. Roy: 'Unequal Development: Liberalisation Bypasses the Backward States', The Indian Express, February 4, 1994.

5

HEALTH CARE REFORMS—PAST, PRESENT AND FUTURE

Talluru Srinivas &
G. Prasad

Health is a rational asset and provides an essential means to social development and sound economic progress. The health of a nation can best be judged by the health status of its people. Experts consider general mortality, infant mortality and expectation of life at birth to be the primary determinants of improved health status. Health is considered to be absence of disease. Health is not perceived the same way by all members of a community including various professional groups. Health has evolved over the centuries as a concept from an individual concern to a worldwide social goal and encompasses the whole quality of life. Thus, Dubos[1] defined health as: "Health implies the relative absence of pain and discomfort and a continuous adoptation and adjustment to the environment to ensure optimal function." The holistic model of health recognises the strength of social, economic, political and environmental influences on health. It has been described as unified or multi-dimensional process involving the well being of the whole person in the context of environment. From the above discussion, it can be said that health is one of those terms which most people find it difficult to define although they are confident of its meaning. The Oxford Dictionary defines health as "Soundness of body or mind, that condition in which its functions are duly and efficiently discharged". The widely accepted definition of health is that given by the

World Health Organisation. In the preamble to its constitution is "a state of complete physical, mental and social well-being and not merely an absence of disease or infirmity."

In current times, a new philosophy of health has emerged which may be stated as follows:

1. Health is a fundamental human right.
2. Health is the essence of productive life and not the result of ever-increasing expenditure on medical care.
3. Health is intersectoral.
4. Health is an integral part of development.
5. Health is central to the concept of quality of life.
6. Health involves individuals, state and interval responsibility.
7. Health is worldwide social goal.
8. Health and its maintenance is a major social investment.

Historical Development of Health Care in India

In India, the history of Medicine and Surgeons dates back to the earliest of the ages. The brilliantly planned cities Mohenjodaro and Harappa are good examples of cities with sophisticated drainage system. Even in 6th century BC, during the time of Buddha, there were a number of hospitals to look after the handicapped and the poor. The outstanding hospitals in India at that time were those built by King Ashoka (273-232 BC). Books written by Arabian and European travellers (around 600 AD) reveal that the study of medicine in India was in its bloom. The invasion of foreigners in the 10th century AD brought with them their own physicians called Hakims. The use of Allopathic system of medicine commenced in the 16th century with the arrival of European missionaries. It was during the British rule that there was progress in the construction of hospitals. In 17th century, the European doctors employed by the East India Company played an important role in introducing modern medicine in India. At that time, Sir Thomas Roe introduced modern medicine in the court of Jahangir the Moghal

Emperor. During 18th century there was slow and steady progress in the growth of modern system of medical practice. During 1300-1800, although the knowledge of medicine was broadened, care in hospitals was not of high standard. Crowding and infection were prevalent in hospitals, till the middle of the 19th century. Florence Nightingale revolutionised the working of hospitals and this was the beginning of the era of 'Better Patient Care'.

Health Committees

After India attained freedom, there was rapid industrialisation in the country, but at the same time there was continuous growth of population which caused a number of medical and health problems. Special efforts were therefore made to solve those health problems and various committees are set up from time to time, a list of which can be given as under:

A committee under chairmanship of Sir Joseph Bhore was constituted to work out an integrated system of healthcare services in India in 1943. A Committee headed by Smt. Renuka Ray was set up in 1960 to examine various aspects of school health programmes. Mudaliar Committee was appointed in 1961 to review the progress made in medical relief and public health. A committee was appointed to chalk out the National Malaria Eradication Programme in 1963 under the chairmanship of Dr. M.S. Chadda. A committee to recognize family planning administration was appointed under the chairmanship of Dr. A.K. Mukherjee in 1965. The Govt. of India appointed the Jain Committee in 1968 to study the working of different classes of hospitals in the country to improve the standards of medical care. The Kartar Singh Committee was appointed on multi-purpose worker under health and family planning programme in 1973. Srivastava Committee was set up in 1975 to report on medical education and manpower requirements. A Committee under chairmanship of Dr. S.S. Sadhu was set up in 1977 to report on strengthening of accidents and emergency services in hospitals. The Bajaj Committee was set up in 1979 to lay down the guidelines for staff, equipment, space etc. for different size of hospitals. A Committee headed by Dr. Shantilal J. Mehta in 1981 was appointed to examine the status of medical education. Bajaj Committee was appointed in 1986 for health manpower and development with major emphasis on vocational training. The recommendations of the above-said committees were given in the Chart.

Health in Five Year Plans

The era of scientific planning was started with the establishment of Planning Commission in 1950. Health is fundamental to national progress. The planning of this field cannot be done in isolation. It has now been proved that health programme contribute directly to the socio-economic growth of the nation. Government of India has therefore been giving due attention to this matter ad has taken several important steps by opening training centres for all health related personnel. Health conditions in the country have improved considerably on account of sustained efforts towards the promotion of healthcare. Progressive increase in outlay of health plans can be observed from Table 1.

TABLE 1
HEALTH PLAN OUTLAYS DURING 1951-1997

Period	*Total Plan Outlay for Public Sector (Rupees in crores)*	*Health Plan Outlay including Family Welfare (Rupees in crores)*
1951-56	2356.0	164.0
1956-61	4800.0	307.0
1961-66	8098.0	341.8
1966-69	6756.5	215.3
1969-74	15902.0	749.0
1974-79	39322.0	1179.0
1979-80	12601.0	384.4
1980-85	71000.0	2028.0
1985-90	180000.0	6649.2
1990-92	137033.5	1934.5
1992-97	412000.0	8400.0

Source: Eighth Five-Year Plan, Vol. II.

First Five-Year Plan (1951-56) was a modest beginning towards development of different health programmes. A seven-point public health programme such as provision of water supply and sanitation, control of malaria, health services for mothers and children, education and training in healthcare etc. formed the basis for the plan. In Second Five Year Plan (1956-61) the Government aimed to expand existing health services to bring them within the reach of the people. In Third Five-Year Plan (1961-66) importance was given to expand health services to bring progressive improvement in health by ensuring a minimum of physical well-being. In Fourth Five Year Plan (1969-74) efforts were made to provide effective base for health services in rural areas for undertaking preventive and curative health services. Fifth Five Year Plan (1974-79) made an attempt to provide minimum public health facilities integrated with family planning and nutrition for vulnerable groups. Sixth Five-Year Plan (1980-85) emphasised on bringing qualitative medical education and training. In Seventh Five-Year Plan (1985-90) efforts were made to correct imbalances to improve quality and establishment of Universities of Health Sciences with an objective of linking training centres. Encouragement was given to states to participate fully in their own manpower development activities. During Eighth Five-Year Plan (1992-97) Plan period efforts were initiated to expand education facilities for those categories of healthcare providers. The incorporation of health related courses was pursued vigorously. Interest was shown in the bridging the gap between supply and demand of paramedical staff and nursing staff.

On close examination we find that health services component has been given less importance in total development. Only 16.18% of the total expenditure had been devoted to the sector in various plans. The outlay of health has been very little as it has been varying from 4% in first Five-Year Plan to 2 to 3% in fourth and fifth Five-Year Plans. This amount is not sufficient to solve problems of healthcare delivery system. In other countries of this region the health sector is being given a higher priority.

All the committees have contributed towards improving health services delivery in India. The reports of various committees are continued to guide the National policy.

National Health Policy

The Ministry of Health and Family Welfare, Government of India, evolved a National Health Policy in 1983 keeping in view the national commitment to attain the goal of Health for all by the year 2000. The policy lays stress on the preventive, promotive, public health and rehabilitation aspects of healthcare and points to the need of establishing comprehensive primary healthcare services to reach the population in the remotest areas of the country, the need to view health and human development as a vital component of overall integrated socio-economic development, decentralised system of healthcare delivery with maximum community and individual self-reliance and participation. In the context of size of the population, the socio-economic development and the existing health status of the people, the National Health Policy in India has the following notable elements:[2]

(a) A greater awareness of health problems and means to solve these, in and by the communities.
(b) Supply of safe drinking water and basic sanitation, using technologies that the people can afford.
(c) Reduction of existing imbalance in health services by concentrating on the rural health infrastructure.
(d) Establishment of a dynamic health management information system to support health planning and health programme implementation.
(e) Provision of legislative support to health protection and promotion.
(f) Concerted actions to combat widespread malnutrition.
(g) Research into alternative methods of healthcare developing and low-cost health technologies.
(h) Greater co-ordination of different systems of medicine.

The health policy is supported by components of wider socio- economic policies addressed to the reduction of regional disparities, full employment, elementary education, integrated rural development, population control, welfare of women and children, etc. The health strategies include restructuring the health infrastructure, developing health manpower, research and development. To translate these objectives into reality, the health policy laid down specific goals to be achieved by 1985, 1990 and 2000.

Various problems regarding Healthcare in India are given below:

The Population Explosion: Every year, in India, around 17 million people are added to the population. This creates a huge demand for additional resources of food, clothing, shelter, education, employment, health, and social welfare. With 2.4 per cent of the world's land area, India supports 16 per cent of the world's population. It has been reckoned that Net Reproduction Rate (NRR) of 1 may be obtained only by AD 2015. Yet, India's fertility and mortality rates and the age distribution of the population are such that even after attaining an NRR 1 by AD 2015, zero growth of the population may be achieved only after several further decades.

Communicable Diseases: The most important public health problems with their respective annual period prevalence estimates are as follows: malaria (16,86,179 cases), leprosy (1.3 million cases representing 42 per cent of the world total), tuberculosis (846.3 million cases and 5,00,000 deaths), diarrhoeal diseases (1.5 million deaths annually), kalazar (77,101 cases and 1,419 deaths), filariasis (396 million people living in 175 known endemic districts), Japanese Encephalities (2,432 cases and 888 deaths), blindness (12 million cases), iodine deficiency diseases (54.3 million cases), sexually transmitted diseases (11,41,740 cases) and enteric fever (3,54,143 cases, and 1,448 deaths).

Non-Communicable Diseases: The most important non-communicable diseases are: cancer—stomach, lung, breast, colon/rectum, cervis, oral (2.5 million total cases), and

TABLE 2
GOALS FOR HEALTH FOR ALL BY 2000 A.D.

Sl. No.	*Indicator*	*Current* *Level (1983)*	*1985*	*Goals set* *1990*	*2000*
1.	Infant morality rate (1978)				
	Rural	136	122	–	–
	Urban	70	60	–	–
	Total	125	106	87	Below 60
2.	Perinatal mortality	67	–	–	30.35
3.	Crude death rate	Around 14	12	10.4	9
4.	Pre-school child (1-5 years) mortality (1976-77)	24	20.24	15.20	10
5.	Maternal mortality rate (1976)	4.5	3.4	2.3	Below 2
6.	Life expectancy at birth (Yrs) (1976-81)—Male	52.6	55.1	57.6	64
	Female	51.6	54.3	57.1	64
7.	Babies with birth weight below 3,500 g(%)	30	25	18	10
8.	Crude birth rate	Around 35	31	27	21
9.	Effective couple protection rate (%) (March 1982)	23.6	37	42	60
10.	Net reproduction rate (1981)	1.48	1.34	1.17	1
11.	Annual growth rate (1977-81)	2.23	1.9	1.66	1.22
12.	Family size (1975)	4.4	3.8	–	2.8
13.	Pregnant mothers receiving anti-natal care (%)	40.5	50.6	60.75	100
14.	Deliveries by trained birth attendants (%)	30.35	50	80	100
15.	Immunisation status (% coverage)				
	-TT for women (Pregnant women)	20	60	100	100
	-TT for school children (up to 10 years)	–	40	100	100
	-(upto 16 years)	20	60	100	100
	-DPT (children below 3 years)	25	70	85	85
	-Polio (infant)	5	50	70	85
	-BCG (infants)	65	70	80	85
	-DT (new school entrants: 5-6 yrs)	20	80	85	85
	-Typhoid (new school entrants: 5-6 yrs)	2	70	85	85
16.	Leprosy: Percentage of disease arrested cases out of those detected	20	40	60	80
17.	TB: Percentage of disease arrested cases out of those detected	50	60	75	90
18.	Blindness incidence (%)	1.4	1	0.7	0.3

Source: Government of India, National Health Policy, 1983, New Delhi, Ministry of Health and Family Welfare.

diabetes (1.73 per cent of total population). Accidents are the cause of 60,000 deaths. India has a disability-adjusted life year (DALY) loss of 344 per 1,00,000 population for communicable diseases; 50.4 for non-communicable diseases; 40.4 for injuries and 9.1 for infant deaths. The overall DALY disease burden per 1000 population is 360.

Maternal Health: Since an overwhelming majority of deliveries are conducted by traditional birth attendants, and the extent of abortion-related maternal deaths is poorly understood. Nevertheless, deaths in pregnancy or within 42 days of giving birth can account for 36 per cent of female mortality in the reproductive age group. In addition, upto the age of fifty, mortality rates among women are higher than those for men, and women are less likely to seek medical care. It has also been estimated that in India, 2 maternal deaths and about 45 infant deaths would be averted for every 1000 girls provided with an extra year of primary schooling.

Child Health: The burden of largely preventable diseases or inexpensively curable diseases of children (diarrhoeal diseases, respiratory infections, measles, worm infestations, malaria) is still substantial in India—28 per cent of the total DALY's lost. It is estimated that about 1.5 million children die of diarrhoea every year and most of these deaths can be prevented if dehydration is checked in time.

Inequalities: It is widely known that people who live in disadvantaged circumstances have more illness, greater distress, more disability and shorter lives than those who are affluent. In India, 50 per cent of the population live below the poverty line and an equal number do not have access to primary health care. Yet, 75 per cent of the national health resources are spent on 25 per cent of the urban population and 25 per cent of the resources on 75 per cent of the rural poor. There is maldistribution and duplication of health care institutions even within the urban areas. Available health services, therefore, obviously lack comprehensiveness, equity and equality.

Rural Health Services: About 77 per cent of the country's

population resides in around 5,76,000 villages, more than half of which contain fewer than 500 people. Most doctors, on the other hand, are concentrated in the cities or major towns, and the majority of the population residing in rural areas is either uncovered or poorly covered by the health care system.

Urban Slums: Although urban health services absorb the major national health resources, the great majority of the under-privileged (slum dwellers) have limited access to health services. In Bombay alone, of its 8 million inhabitants, 2.8 million live in slums, the largest in Asia, without access to basic amenities. The living conditions in these slums are appalling and, in some cases, defy description. In them, women and children are at greater risk and exhibit higher morbidity and mortality rates.

In 1984, the Government of India and UNICEF together reviewed the Urban Basic Services Programme. It now emphasises priority area such as malnutrition, women's development activities, day care and early childhood development, responsible parenthood, family planning services, support for abandoned and disabled children, clean drinking water, and adequate sanitation. Following establishment of a community-based approach in 1984, the programme expanded rapidly to 295 towns by 1990.

Priorities for Improving the Current Situation

Human capital is increasingly considered one of the most important components of a nation's wealth. In a popular country like India the challenge lies in ensuring that human capital is developed to its fullest by enhancing the ability of the people to lead health and productive lives. By 2010, health indicators in India emphasis on disease prevention and control and on nutrition, sanitation, personal hygiene and fitness will sustain high levels of health. In future, it is the responsibility of policy-makers to provide basic health care services. In future, the poor will have to enjoy free health care both basic and specialised and other sections of the population will have to access these services through health insurance. For successful implementation of comprehensive health plan which provide both curative and preventive health care to all its people, the Government has to focus on the following key priorities.

- Providing universal access to primary healthcare.
- Promoting Indian systems of Medicine and Homeopathy.
- Encouraging private investment in tertiary healthcare.
- Focusing on specific programmes to promote family welfare, particularly the health of women and children, and family planning.
- Ensuring a strong prevention focus.
- Enhancing the performance of the public health system.
- Formulating a State IEC (Information, Education and Communication) programme.

Provision of Universal Access to Primary Healthcare: Health indicators show that health standards in the country have improved significantly over the last 20 years. However, the countrystill needs to significantly improve access to primary healthcare. Providing immediate access to basic healthcare—maternal and child healthcare, family welfare, and basic clinical services—throughout the country, particularly in villages and urban slums, will dramatically improve health standards. To do this, the Government will have to use two innovative approaches: a Community Health Worker programme and a system of mobile health centres. In addition, the Government will have to encourage the use of Indian systems of medicine as a source of effective, safe, and low cost healthcare. The Government has to develop a programme that uses voluntary Community Health Workers (CHWs) to deliver simple health services, backed by a system of referrals to Sub-Centres. CHWs are residents of villages or urban slums trained by the Government to provide such health services. They will need to provide 24-hour service on call and be compensated reasonably by the local community. The PHC/Sub-Centre/Health Post network (in the form of mobile units or otherwise) will back them up by treating more complex cases.

Promoting Indian Systems of Medicine and Homeopathy: India has a rich heritage of traditional systems of medicine, such as ayurveda and unani, that have now gained stature and popularity all over the world for their holistic approach for treating disease and ailments. Ayurveda is India's traditional, natural system of medicine and has been practised for more than 5,000 years. It provides an integrated approach to preventing and treating illness through natural therapies and better lifestyles. Unani is an ancient system of medicine practised in India since the 11th century. Unani medicine is effective in the treatment of chronic diseases. Its low cost therapies, using herbal and mineral substances, have made it a popular system of medicine in all parts of the country. Homeopathy can be used to treat acute and chronic health problems and to prevent diseases and promote health. It is a gentle and effective system of medicine, providing remedies prepared from natural substances that work by stimulating the body's own healing power. The Government has to encourage such systems of medicine since they provide safe, effective, and low cost solutions for most health problems.

Encouraging Private Investment in Tertiary Healthcare: Since the need for primary and secondary healthcare is paramount, the Government has to direct its spending towards these sectors. As a result, tertiary healthcare will have to make do with a small share of Government funding. Furthermore, this spending will be directed towards providing tertiary care for the poor and other vulnerable groups through existing teaching hospitals providing all specialities and super-specialities. At the same time, it cannot be denied that tertiary healthcare also needs augmenting. However, these investments will have to come from other sources, namely the private sector.

In the new environment, Government hospitals will increasingly have to create their own financial resources and match the service levels of private institutions. They will thus need to generate internal sources of revenue, mainly through selective user charges for those who can afford to pay.

Promoting Family Welfare and Population Control: A major component of the programme to achieve the objective of population control will require a three-pronged approach: improving female literacy; empowering women; and providing better healthcare and family planning services. Increasing female literacy will equip women with a better understanding of the social and economic importance of small families; improve their knowledge of sophisticated and safe family planning methods, and hence build their confidence in adopting them; encourage them to seek healthcare for themselves and their families; similarly, empowering women will give them more control over deciding the size and spacing of their families, create awareness about family planning among peer groups and the community, and increase the age at marriage of women. The third component of the approach to reducing population growth is family welfare. Most parents decide to have many children because of current high infant and child mortality rates. To address this concern, infant and child mortality rates must be brought down by safeguarding the health of women, infants and children. In addition, a new approach to family planning that remedies the defects of the traditional approach is also required.

To achieve these objectives, the Government has to focus on successfully implementing the Reproductive and Child Health (RCH) programme and one has to create awareness through IEC (Information, Education and Communication) programmes; ensuring decentralised, community-based planning; and strengthening managerial capacity.

Improve Maternal and Child Health: The major objectives of the RCH programme are to reduce illness and deaths of mothers and infants and ensure child survival. These will be achieved by providing essential and emergency obstetrics care and care of the new-born infant; increasing institutional deliveries; and managing reproductive tract infections, STDs and unwanted pregnancies. Infant mortality and child mortality can be reduced through immunisation coverage.

Promote Family Planning: The RCH programme also modifies the approach to family planning. The traditional approach was target and contraception-based. Government agencies decided the contraceptive method to be adopted and sought to popularise it. Predictably, this met with limited success. The new approach, client-based and more holistic, is to be introduced which includes innovative surgical methods. This programme will also provide advice on the proper age at marriage, the health reasons for spacing children, the need for both spouses to be literate, the health reasons for men to participate in the programme, and so on.

Strengthening Disease Prevention: Preventive efforts must emphasise mass immunisation and disease control, hygiene, sanitation, and the supply of safe drinking water. The Government has to initiate several mass programmes for immunisation and the control of communicable diseases like tuberculosis, malaria, leprosy, and gastro-enteritis (during summer and the rainy season) and non-communicable diseases such as blindness, iodine and nutrition deficiency. There is also the likelihood that HIV/AIDS, STDs, coronary heart disease and cancer will pose serious threats in the foreseeable future. The Government has to work actively to boost the effectiveness of disease prevention efforts, particularly for area-specific diseases, such as malaria in the tribal belts and leprosy.

Enhancing the Performance of the Public Health System: The current public health system is characterised by centralized structures and inadequate systems. Decisions on even minor operational issues (e.g., transfer of personnel) are taken in the State capital, Multiple Government Departments have authority over different, areas. For example, sub-centres are under the authority of the Family Welfare Department while PHCs are under the authority of the Health Department. Both Central and State Government programmes operate at various levels, sometimes resulting in duplication of work and inefficient use of resources. There are no information systems to track health results or control systems to monitor performance of personnel. Improving the effectiveness of the public health system is thus a mammoth task. It can be achieved only by moving to a decentralised management structure, supported by better information and incentive systems, and by involving the community in the management of health services.

Organisations conducting Central Government programmes at the PHC, sub-district, district and State Levels will have to be integrated to allow better coverage and co-ordination. To further strengthen the management of the public health system, information and incentive systems will need to be introduced. An effective way to improve the performance of the public health system is to involve the community in the management of services. To achieve this, Advisory Committees are to be set up to monitor the performance of the referral hospitals. Committee members would be the M.P. and M.L.A. of the area, other elected and prominent members of the local community and health officials.

Developing a Comprehensive Strategy to Enhance Health Awareness: As said earlier, a major part of improving health levels is increasing awareness of the importance of health, hygiene and sanitation. This will require the design and launch of many campaigns to publicise such issues. The Government has to use a mix of different media such as street plays, folk theatre, literacy programmes, interactive discussions, and so on, to build awareness. However, a major component of this strategy will be leveraging electronic media. In India, television and radio compaigns have often been used to publicise disease prevention and other health-related issues. Together with television and radio, the emergence of other electronic media will create enormous potential to conduct mass awareness compaigns.

6

TRENDS OF RURAL NON-FARM EMPLOYMENT IN INDIA

M. Koteswara Rao
P. Venu Gopal

The relevance of the concept of labour-force to developing countries of Asia and Africa continues to be debated by Social Scientists. In India, labour-force is increasing at a rapid rate along with population growth. The issue of providing employment to this increasing labour-force is a major problem. The problem of open unemployment, under-employment and disguised unemployment is becoming more widespread. Both agricultural and urban modern sector are not able to provide employment opportunities to the growing rural labour-force. The organized industrial sector, despite high rates of investment, absorbs only a small portion of the labour-force. It is observed that open unemployment is more in rural areas than in the urban areas. Hence, the major critical issue before most of the developing countries, like India, is the productive absorption of labour from rural areas. It is noticed from the existing literature that the shift of workers from agriculture to non-agricultural activities in rural areas is taking place.

The concept of rural non-farm employment (RNFE) is defined as employment in pursuits other than cultivation, livestock, forestry, fishing, hunting, plantations, orchards and allied activities. Broadly, it covers employment in mining and quarrying, manufacturing (manufacturing, processing, services and repairs in household industry and other than household industry), construction, trade and commerce, transport, storage and communications and other services. In the recent years, the rural non-farm sector employment acquired importance in the economic development. By providing gainful employment to the rural labour-force this sector is playing a positive role in the removal of poverty. It is a significant source of income to small and landless farmers during the slack season. It also facilitates structural transformation. There is a close relationship between employment generation in rural non-farm activities and the spread of prosperity from agricultural growth. Hence, it is pertinent to study the various issues relating to the rural non-farm employment in India.

Several attempts have been made in India to analyse the nature, character, growth and determinants of non-farm rural employment over time. For instance, the studies by Krishnamurthy (1984), Vaidyanathan (1986), Basant and Rakesh (1989), Kashyap and Desai (1990), Singh (1990, 1991), Basant and Kashyap (1992), Rayappa (1986), Unni (1991), Basu and Kashyap (1992) and Popala (1993) are some of the notable studies in this area of research.

In India the non-farm rural employment has witnessed a steady expansing during the last two decades, the work-force in rural areas is gradually moving out of agriculture. This process of structural change would lead to the emergence of problems of farm-non-farm relations especially from the point of employment for the rural household. An attempt is mace in this paper to study the changes in the pattern of employment in the non-farm sector in India over time.

Data Base

The data base for this study is various rounds of NSS on employment and unemployment. This data throw considerable light on the component of employment in non-farm sector in rural areas in India. In addition to NSS, Census data and some other published/unpublished data is also utilized for the purpose of comparison of work-force figures in rural areas.

The NSS estimates on employment are computed under three different approaches: the 'usual status' approach which has a reference period of 365 days preceding the day of survey, the 'current weekly status' approach under which the employment details are ascertained for a period of 7 days preceding the date of survey. The 'daily status' estimates are essentially in the nature of time flow, and are expressed in terms of number of persons days while the 'usual status' approach gives estimates in terms of number of persons.

Evidence on Non-Farm Employment

Like other developing countries in the world, the share of national income originating from the primary sector has been declining steadily while respective shares of secondary and territory sectors have been increasing steadily ever since the beginning of the planning era in idea. The pace of Rural Non-Farm employment will be seen from Table 1. We can observe a dynamism in the sectorial composition of rural work force at the national level from the past few decades. If we consider both the large sample and thin sample data of NSS which together provides a time series data on employment of rural workforce we can have an insight into the qualitative changes in the workforce structure. Table gives timé profile of data on sectorial composition of rural workforce. It can be observed from the table that the proportion of rural workforce employed in agricultural revealed a declining trend, while safe in the secondary and territory sectors have shown an increasing trend upto 1989-90 and 1990-91 respectively. In this connection we can say that, the occupational structure in rural India continued to move on a reverse gear such that the rural workforce hither employed in the secondary and tertiary sectors got dislodged and reverted back to agriculture for gainful employment.

The data presented in Table 2 based on usual status approach estimates supports the above statement for the period 1972-73 to 1999-2000. It is evident form the table in

TABLE 1
SECTORAL DISTRIBUTION OF THE RURAL WORKFORCE: INDIA

Sector	*Status*	*1989-90*	*1990-91*	*1992*	*1993-94*	*1999-2000*
Agriculture	UPS	74.2	74.5	78.5	76.9	75.1
	UPSS	75.1	75.5	79.4	78.4	76.3
Non-Agriculture	UPS	25.8	25.5	21.5	23.1	24.9
	UPSS	24.9	24.5	20.6	21.6	23.7
Secondary	UPS	12.3	11.0	9.7	10.6	11.6
	UPSS	12.2	10.9	9.5	9.6	11.4
Tertiary	UPS	13.5	14.4	11.6	11.9	17.3
	UPSS	12.7	13.6	11.1	11.4	12.4

rural India only 16.8 per cent of male workers were engaged in the non-agricultural activities in 1972-73, this increased steadily to 19.4 per cent in 1977-78, 22.5 per cent by 1983 to 25.5 per cent by 1987-88 and then 28.6 per cent by 1999-2000. A similar type of trend is applicable to female also. As against to this the inter-sectorial shifts among urban workers for both male and female are negligible. The type of shift in labour force in rural areas explains that the traditionally dominant agricultural sector is loosing its relative importance and gradually the work-force in the non-agricultural sector is increasing. The rural workers engaged in the primary sector declined form 83.2 per cent in 1972-73 to 80.6 per cent in 1977-78 while during the next 10 years, it registered a sharp decline to 74.5 per cent in 1987-88 and to 71.4 per cent by 1999-2000. The same changes in secondary sector provide the clear contrasts between the 1980s and 1970s. Interestingly it is found that upward trend in secondary sector for females is faster, i.e., from 6.0 per cent between 1972-73 and 1987-88. The same changes in secondary sector provide the clear contrast between the 1980s and 1970s.

Interestingly it is found that upward trend in secondary sector for females is faster, i.e., from 6.0 per cent to 9.0 per cent between 1972-73—1999-2000. The relative shift towards non-agricultural employment is faster and bigger in each sub-period as well as for the total period 1972-73 and 1999-

TABLE 2
INDUSTRY-WISE DISTRIBUTION OF RURAL NON-FARM WORKERS IN INDIA

State	*Male*				*Female*			
	1983	*1987-88*	*1993-94*	*1999-2000*	*1983*	*1987-88*	*1993-94*	*1999-2000*
Primary	77.5	74.5	74.1	71.4	87.5	84.7	86.2	85.4
Mining & Quarrying	0.6	0.7	0.7	0.6	0.3	0.4	0.4	0.3
Manufacturing	7.0	7.4	7.0	7.3	6.4	6.9	7.0	7.6
Utilities	0.2	0.3	0.3	0.2	–	–	0.1	0.0
Construction	2.2	3.7	3.2	4.5	0.7	2.7	0.9	1.1
Secondary	10.0	12.1	11.2	12.6	8.7	10.0	8.4	9.0
Trade hoteling	4.4	5.1	5.5	6.8	1.9	2.1	2.1	2.0
Transport Comn.	1.7	2.0	2.2	3.2	0.1	0.1	–	0.1
Services	6.1	6.2	7.0	6.1	2.8	3.0	3.4	3.7
Tertiary	12.5	13.4	14.7	16.1	4.8	5.3	5.6	5.8
All Non-Farm Activities	25.5	25.5	25.9	28.7	13.5	15.3	13.8	14.8

Source: Different Quinquennial Reports on Employment and Unemployment of NSSO, Gol.

2000. For instance, it is seen that for the entire period 1972-2000, the female workers showed an increase about 5.0 per cent for all non-agricultural activities against about 9 per cent for male workers.

Table 3 reveals that the proportion of rural workforce by a major groups of Industries over period. The states like Andhra Pradesh, Haryana, Punjab, Jammu and Kashmir, Tamil Nadu, West Bengal and Kerala the proportion rural male workforce engaged in non-farm activities remain above the same at national level. On the other hand majority of the states have achieved an increase in share in employment of female workforce. Kerela and West Bengal have been able to maintain a remarkable increase in the share in employment of female workforce in non-farm activities.

Conclusion

Broadly it can be concluded that rural non-farm sector in India have witnessed a steady expansion during the last two decades. The workforce in rural areas are gradually shifting from low productive agricultural jobs of various types partly in rural areas themselves and partly in urban areas. Nearly one-fourth of rural male and about one-sixth of rural female workers were engaged in different types on non-agricultural activities. The mode of employment is also undergoing significant changes. Further, the declining self-employment in agriculture as well as non-agriculture, increase in wage labour and its rising pace of caualisation are the emerging realities of past few decades. Further, the literature on non-farm sector in India do show that the growth of this sector depends upon agriculture development, infrastructure, urbanization rural incomes, population pressure, land-man ratio, commercialization of agriculture and so on.

TABLE 3

STATE-WISE DISTRIBUTION OF RURAL NON-WORKERS IN INDIA (1999-2000)

State	*Farm*		*Total Non-Farm*		*Manufacturing*		*Trade Hoteling*		*Services*		*Others*	
	M	*F*	*M*	*F*	*M*	*F*	*M*	*F*	*M*	*F*	*M*	*F*
Andhra Pradesh	74.4	84.3	25.6	15.7	5.3	6.0	5.8	3.0	7.1	5.1	7.0	1.6
Assam	64.7	79.4	35.3	20.6	20.9	8.3	9.9	1.5	16.6	10.4	5.9	0.5
Bihar	79.0	85.7	21.0	14.3	5.3	8.5	5.3	1.8	5.1	3.3	5.4	0.7
Gujarat	71.4	92.0	28.6	8.0	10.1	2.2	5.6	1.6	5.0	1.8	7.9	2.3
Haryana	59.6	92.1	40.4	7.9	9.2	2.0	7.3	2.6	8.7	2.5	14.2	0.8
Himachal Pradesh	53.8	95.1	46.2	4.9	6.7	1.1	6.1	0.6	9.9	2.6	23.2	0.6
J & K	66.9	93.5	32.1	6.5	4.4	3.9	5.4	0.4	9.9	1.9	13.4	0.4
Karnataka	78.5	87.8	21.5	12.2	5.2	5.7	5.8	2.5	5.1	2.9	5.5	1.0
Kerala	42.8	59.8	57.2	4.2	9.4	19.3	15.8	3.7	8.1	23.5	24.0	3.7
Madhya Pradesh	84.2	91.6	15.8	8.4	3.9	4.2	3.9	1.0	4.1	1.9	3.9	1.5
Maharastra	73.8	93.9	26.2	6.1	7.0	2.2	5.7	1.3	6.3	1.6	7.2	1.0
Orissa	77.0	80.4	33.0	19.6	5.6	12.9	6.1	1.9	5.0	2.8	6.5	2.0
Punjab	63.7	90.6	36.3	9.4	7.7	2.3	8.1	1.1	5.9	5.7	14.5	0.3
Rajasthan	67.3	91.9	32.7	8.1	5.4	2.8	5.6	0.6	4.6	1.4	17.1	3.2
Tamil Nadu	62.2	75.9	31.8	24.1	13.8	14.2	7.1	2.4	5.8	4.6	11.0	2.1
Uttar Pradesh	71.8	87.5	28.2	12.5	8.3	6.4	6.7	1.9	5.5	3.6	7.7	0.5
West Bengal	66.4	54.1	33.6	45.9	10.9	36.1	10.2	2.8	5.0	6.7	7.7	0.4
All Over India	71.4	8.54	28.6	14.6	7.3	7.6	6.8	2.0	6.1	3.7	8.5	1.5

7

THE ECONOMICS OF POWER SECTOR

A. Rajasekhar

Introduction

Economic growth and industrialization are contingent upon the adequate availability of inexpensive energy. The level of technology of a country and its rate of development hinge upon the nature and sources of available energy. The energy sector in India is marked by some areas of neglect. A vigilant and vigorous energy strategy is an essential requirement if economic growth and industrialization programmes have to proceed without obstacle due to scarcity of energy. An equally important area which needs to be strengthened in respect of policy is the inter-fuel substitution consistent with the long-term resource and represent economic development are mirrored patterns of sectorial energy consumption over time. In this connection an attempt is made in this paper to light on the energy sector contribution to economic growth of India and to suggest policy implications for future course of action.

Infrastructure and Economic Growth

The link between infrastructure and development is not a once for all affair. It is a continuous process and progress in development has to be proceeded, accompanied and followed by progress in infrastructure. Infrastuctural facilities often referred to as economic and social overheads consists of energy which includes coal, electricity, oil and non-conventional sources. Indian planners were fully aware of the link between infrastructural facility and general economic development and accordingly, they gave high priority to the expansion of these facilities right from the first plan itself. The first five-year plan devoted between 55 to 60 per cent of the total plan outlay on infrastructure development. The allocation on infrastructure in the sixth and the seventh plans is over 60 per cent. The same trend continues in the ninth plan also.

Energy Consumption and Economic Growth

The most important single factor which can act as a constraint on economic growth of a country is the availability of energy. There is a direct correlation between the degree of economic growth, the size of per capita income and per capita consumption of energy.

India is in the lower rank both in terms of per capita income (450 US Dollars) and per capita consumption of energy (479 kg of oil equivalent) while compared to other countries. Among the countries, USA ranks first because of higher per capita income (30,600 Dollars) and higher per capita consumption of energy (8076 kg of oil equivalent). It is understood from the above table that India is yet to increase the per capita income and per capita consumption of energy to achieve expected economic growth (Table 1).

TABLE 1
PER CAPITA INCOME AND CONSUMPTION OF ENERGY FOR SELECTED COUNTRIES IN 1999

Country	*Per capita Income (In US Dollars)*	*Per capita Consumption of energy (kg of oil equivalent)*
India	450	479
Indonesia	580	693
Egypt	1400	656
U.S.A.	30600	8076
U.K.	22640	3863
Japan	32230	4084
Canada	19320	7930

Source: World Development Report, 2000/2001.

Present Stage of Power Generation in India

As power plays an important role in economic development to know the situation in India it is appropriate to study the power generation in India. Power generation at 499.6 billion kwh in 2000-01 recorded a growth of 3.9 per cent. Power generation in April-December, 2001 at 383.2 billion kwh recorded a growth of 2.8 per cent over the generation during the corresponding period in 2000. Thermal and Nuclear generation grew by 3.5 per cent and 17.1 per cent respectively, while hydro generation decreased by 3.6 per cent (Table 2). Owing to heavy transmission and distribution (T&D) losses suffered by State Electricity Boards (SEBs), low user charges and operational and technical efficiencies. The power system in the country is experiencing great difficulty.

TABLE 2
TRENDS IN THE POWER SECTOR (UTILITIES ONLY)

	1990-2000 (Billion KWH)	2000-01*	April-December* 2000	April-December* 2001	Change over previous year 2000-01 (per cent)	Change over previous year 2001-02@ (per cent)
1 Power generation**	480.7	499.6	372.7	383.2	3.9	2.8
(i) Hydro-electric	80.6	74.5	59.8	57.6	–7.9	–3.6
(ii) Thermal	386.8	408.1	300.7	311.2	5.5	3.5
(iii) Nuclear	13.3	16.9	12.2	14.3	27.1	17.1
2 Plant load factor of thermal plants (per cent)	67.3	69.0	67.7	68.4	–	–

*Provisional. @ April-December.
** Excludes generation from captive & non-conventional power plants.
Source: Economic Survey, 2001-02.

The installed capacity of power generation in the country as on March 31, 2001 was 101,630 mw of which 72 per cent was thermal power generation, 25 per cent was hydro (including wind), and 3 per cent was nuclear. Installed capacity crossed 102,907 mw as on October 31,

2001. The capacity addition in 2000-01 was 3776 mw against a target of 4000 mw. A capacity of addition 2000-01 was 3776 mw against a target of 4000 mw. A capacity of 1375 mw has been added against a target of 3053 mw during April-October, 2001. Thermal plants at present account for 80 per cent of the total power generation, hydro electricity plants contribute 16 per cent and the nuclear plants account for the rest.

The Working Group on Power constituted by Planning Commission to formulate the 10th Five Year Plan has estimated a feasible capacity addition of 47,000 MW during the 10th plan. This is made up of 24,405 MW in Central Sector, 12,033 MW in the State Sector and 10,501 MW in the private sector. The funds requirement for these investments would be of the order of Rs. 5,66,000 crores.

Table 3 shows that the Plant Load Factor (PLF) is an important indicator of operational efficiency in thermal power plants. The average PLF in the Central Public Sector Undertaking (CPSUs) in the 2000-01 and during April-October, 2001 was appreciably higher than that achieved by the SEBs as a whole. Wide inter region variations are noticed in the average PLF of thermal power plants. Plants in the Southern and Western regions have shown better performance. The average PLF for Eastern and Northeastern regions continues to be much lower than the All-India level.

The recommendations of the Expert Group have been accepted with minor modification by High-Level group of Chief Ministers for implementation.

The financial health restoration of SEBs, and improvement in their operational performance continue to remain a critical issue in the power sector. Under Section 59 of the Electricity Supply Act, 1948, SEBs are required to achieve a rate of return (ROR) of not less than 3 per cent on their fixed assets in service, at the beginning of the year, after providing for interest and depreciation charges less consumers contribution. Despite this, in the following the accounting year 1985. Despite this in the following years there has been a continuing deterioration in the financial performance of SEBs.

TABLE 3
THERMAL PLANT LOAD FACTOR (Per Cent)

	April-December						
	1996-97	*1997-98*	*1998-99*	*1999-2000*	*2000-01**	*2001-02 (Target)*	*2001-02 (Actual)*
1. State Electricity Boards	60.3	60.9	60.7	64.3	64.3	66.4	65.1
2. Central Sector	71.0	70.4	71.1	72.5	72.2	70.5	72.7
3. Private Sector	71.2	71.2	68.3	68.9	76.4	73.1	77.2
4. Region:							
Northern	64.7	66.7	67.2	71.0	72.0	72.8	73.9
Western	70.2	70.3	70.5	72.3	72.1	73.1	72.1
Southern	75.8	77.1	75.4	79.6	79.7	79.8	89.9
Eastern	42.2	43.0	44.3	46.1	47.0	46.5	48.0
North Eastern	27.1	21.3	18.7	18.3	18.2	23.2	17.0
All India	**64.4**	**64.7**	**64.6**	**67.3**	**67.7**	**68.2**	**68.9**

*Provisional
Source: Economic Survey, 2001-2002.

Managerial and financial in efficiencies in State sector utilities have adversely affected capacity addition and systems improvement. Financial health of SEBs has been deteriorating over the years. In 1999-2000 only 7 SEBs had a positive ROR. The number of SEBs with a positive ROR of more than 3 per cent (without subsidy) has also fallen, in 1999-2000 only two SEBs (MSEB & TNEB) had a positive ROR of more than 3 per cent (without subsidy). In order to improve the profitability and financial viability of SEBs we need to tackle the key issues such as curbing of T & D loses, tariff rationalization, reducing gap between cost of supply and revenue/unit of electricity generated. All this will fetch more electricity revenue generating, and it will then be possible to generate more investment etc. The SEBs, have continued to suffer from high T & D losses which were at 24.8 per cent in 1997-98, and increased to 25.6 per cent in 1998-99.

The T & D losses are due to a variety of reasons, viz., substantial energy sold at low voltage, sparsely distributed loads over large rural areas, inadequate investment in distribution system, improper billing, and high pilferage. The hidden gross subsidy for agriculture and domestic sectors has increased from Rs. 7,499 crores in 1991-92 to Rs. 34,428 crores in 2000-01 and is projected to go up further to Rs. 38,836 crores in 2002-03 (Table 4).

TABLE 4
FINANCIAL PERFORMANCE OF THE STATE POWER SECTOR

(Rs. crore)

	1991-92	*2000-01**	*2001-02 (RE)*	*2002-03 (AP)*
A. Gross Subsidy involved				
1. On account of sale of Electricity to				
(a) Agriculture	5938	24075	25571	26959
(b) Domestic	1310	9968	10894	11651
(c) Inter-State Sales	201	386	247	226
Total	7449	34428	36713	38836
2. Subventions Received from State Governments	2045	8820	10099	7981
3. Net Subsidy	5404	25607	26613	30855
4. Surplus Generated by sale to other sectors	2173	3435	3615	7499
5. Uncovered Subsidy	3231	22172	22999	23356
B. Comercial Losses@				
1. Commercial Losses (excluding subsidy)	4117	25395	27306	24321
2. Commercial Losses (including subsidy)	NA	16575	17207	16340
C. Revnue Mobilisation				
1. Rate of Return (ROR)#	–12.7	–41.8	–39.5	–32.1
2. Additional Revenue Mobilisation from achieving				
(a) 3 per cent ROR	4959	27217	29404	26226
(b) from introducing 50 paise/unit from Agriculture/Irrigation	2176	1638	1350	1330

Source: Economic Survey, 2001-2002.

In 2000-01 the Government has initiated a new Plan Scheme namely the Accelerated Power Development Program (APDP) to provide financial assistance to the States for undertaking Renovation & Modernization Programs of Thermal and Hydro power stations and also for strengthening and improvement of Sub-transmission and Distribution network. Under this scheme, a focused investment program has been initiated in 63 identified distribution circles that would be developed as Centre of Excellence in the first phase of the APDP program. An amount of Rs. 978 crore was provided to SEBs/ED during 2000-01. An amount of Rs. 1,500 crores has been budgeted for release to States during 2001-02 under APDP, and proposals are under consideration for the sanction of funds.

The need to focus approach to address the issues afflicting states with special reference to their circumstance was realized by the government of India and the State Governments are thus being encouraged to sign MOU with the Government of India. So far the States of Karnataka, Uttar Pradesh, Madhya Pradesh, Gujarat, Haryana, Andhra Pradesh have signed MOUs with the Government of India. The MOUs are broadly joint commitments of the State Government and the Government of India to undertake reforms in a time bound manner.

The present situation of the power sector shows that Government of India is going to privatize the sector in the coming years. Hence, an attempt is made to observe the need and position of the sector after privatization has been observed in the following paragraphs:

Privatisation of Power Sector

The assumption that large-scale privatization is possible without reform, or delayed reform, of tariffs is questionable. Thus in most private power agreements (PPAs), private generating companies have (expectedly) insisted upon guarantees and counter-guarantees, and escrow accounts. The cash flow position of SEBs is, therefore, worsened, since the purchase price per unit of power by SEBs is much higher than the long-run marginal cost of generating the same internally. Profitability too is affected when this purchase price does not leave enough room to recover distribution costs. Equally important, the guarantees only mean that the contingent liability ceiling is either breached or under pressure. The limits of escrowability have already been reached in some SEBs. In this connection, the mitigation of Risk, the real solution to large-scale privatization, is hardly possible without basic reform of tariffs and collections and appropriate incentives for all involved parties.

In the era of near-exclusive state provision of electricity the risks were high, but the State had a comparative advantage to bear risk. It could also 'bear' the costs arising out of the weaknesses of the administration, protracted approval procedures and modes of tariff whetting, and other dysfunction emanating from political and legal processes. These risks and costs continue without much change. Basic risks emanating from environmental movements, wherein even the Supreme Court's verdict is not final, the softness of the state, and the dysfunctional and contradictory rulings of the environment bureaucracy have considerably increased.

Overcoming the Problem

Restructuring proposals cannot sidestep the agency problem. Any attempt at marketization, privatization, or regulatory reform, and especially restructuring would not be meaningful. Thus the problem of the SEBs is far more basic than the typical 'efficiencies of the public sector' noted worldwide. Indian bureaucracies are eminently capable of crafting institutions and rules that in form resemble success stories elsewhere, but in content and behaviour continue to remain dysfunctional.

No piecemeal or stop-gap arrangement that allows the continuation of the agency problem and does not rein in leakages is meaningful. Thus proposals to sell generation assets of SEBs, without a complete reform of distribution are of little use. Similarly, proposals to sell assets, when there is no regulatory or strategic clarity, to state-level public sector undertaking (PSUs) would amount to arm-twisting the few PSUs with the cash reserves to cough up these resources to allow the leakages within the SEB system to continue.

The dead-weight losses that are true social losses, and not just a transfer problem, are very large. They take the form of losses due to unutilized and underutilized capacity, both within the system (SEB) and outside (other power suppliers and captive generators). Allocative efficiency losses resulting from inappropriate technology choice, violation of merit order, and disincentives that prevent demand from responding appropriately to prices are even more severe, though difficult to estimate.

The independent regulators are already in place and would soon be working. The Gujarat Electricity Board (GEB), Maharastra State Electricity Board (MSEB), and the inheritor companies of the Haryana State Electricity Board have already asked for average tariff increases that are 20 per cent above current levels. In Maharastra, the Maharastra Electricity Regulatory Commission (MERC) has already disallowed the demand for tariff increases, pointing to the need for the Board to plug leakages and minimize the effect of 'sugar-coated' PPAs that have raised costs of purchased power unnecessarily. The Gujarat regulatory authority too is unlikely to grant the heavy tariff increase of 20 per cent asked for since it now has an idea of the vast inefficiencies and leakages. Similarly, the Haryana Electricity Regulatory Commission (HERC) is closely and critically examining the tariff proposals. In Andhra Pradesh, though, the regulatory authority has awarded rather steep increases in tariffs. Thus true reform of the SEB system cannot be further postponed.

Power network is the backbone of economic development. Being a key infrastructure, the availability of quality power in the required quantity would be one of the important determinants in the success of India's recently introduced, high growth oriented economic policy. Given the capital intensity of the sector and poor financial condition of the SEB's. Steps towards power sector reform taken by the Government of India are right on time. However, the success of the reform programme would largely depend on efficient management of the transition period and pursuance of a transparent. Problems of administrative, technical and political nature as experienced so far need to be tackled with great sincerity. Other countries experiences in power sector reform may be useful. The Government would have to monitor the transition and periodically review the status, so that midstream course correction can be made if necessary.

8

PROTECT RURAL POOR FROM URBAN EXPLOITATION

A. Ranga Reddy

I

Corruption is a universal phenomenon said Indira Gandhi. A.B. Vajpayee observed zero-tolerance towards corruption. "Kautilya's treatise Arthasastra said clearly that just as it is impossible for one dealing with government funds not to taste, at least a little bit, of the King's Wealth." British historian Lord Action observed that power tends to corrupt and absolute power corrupts absolutely. The Hydra-headed corruption had a position over global rankings. According to Transparency Internationals Corruption Perception Index (CPI), that India has found recently slipped to the 72nd rank from the 66th position in the year 1998. This has happened only because the base of countries has increased from 85 countries to 99 countries.[1] Infact, Money Lender had his own cup of woes. The World Bank has suspended loans worth $ 300 million to Kenya, saying that the country has failed to tackle high level corruption.[2] One of the sources of corruption is the comprehensive involvement of Government in business through public sector undertakings and the appointment of politicians to head them.[3] In early seventies, Gunnar Myrdal considered India as a soft state means easy going laws for rich, red tapism in bureaucracy and corruption attitude among all classes.[4] It can be called as government is jungle and privatization is a paradise. Nexus between Mafia dons, Police Bureaucracy and Politicians is a crude reality. The political economy is in bad shape. Criminals and politicians are two-in-one in a number of cases. The overall scenario is hostile towards market and investment. Consequently, development is the ultimate victim.[5] Further, the star hotels and picnic spots have become decision making centres. The "alcoholic linkages" is a new pattern of relationship. In fact, the battles have become to play effective role in removing the bottlenecks in administration.[6] Corruption is like a diseases—AIDS, which had no cure but preventable. Leading political party said that we will enact Lok Pal Bill with adequate powers to deal with corruption charges against anyone including the Prime Minister. In the administration of justice, we shall not allow discrimination between the rich and the poor, the empowered and the powerless; restore the majesty of law, and the objectivity of the state.[7]

This paper highlights the causes, cures and curbs of corruption.

II

Meaning of Corruption

It is defined as the abuse of public office for private gain. This includes bribery and extortion, which necessarily involves atleast two parties. In unbundling bribery, it is useful to consider what private parties can 'purchase' from a politician or bureaucrat.[8]

Widespread corruption is a symptom of a poor functioning State. It undermines the Economic growth, equity, social justice and International development. It further expropriates nation's wealth, leaving a very little for the poorest of the poor. Nonetheless, it directly affects the efficiency and honesty of economic systems. It pays to allow the unqualified person or Institution to obtain benefit. Corruption is like a theft. Such as rich students pay to alter the results of admission tests. Patients pay doctors for disability payments, firms that are not creditworthy pay to obtain loans, people least qualified for the service are often willing to pay a more. Many poverty alleviation programmes miserably failed, because greedy rich were taken the garb of poor in tapping the resources. Mafias pay money to police and judiciary, escapes from their net. Fixation of new pay scale needs a mammool.[9] Corruption may be presented as following in a formula:

$$C = M + D - A$$

Corruption equals monopoly (M) plus discretion (D) minus accountability (A).

Corruption undermines democracy and destroys the credibility of government. Corruption is stealing from the poor.

Classification and Levels of Corruption

By and large, corruption is classified in four categories:

(a) *Kleptocracy state:* Few recipients concentrated at upper levels of government. It is either extortionery state or a weak state or bilateral monopoly state. Bribers are found among very few.

(b) *Bilateral Monopoly:* A corrupt ruler faces a single major briber. Multiple recipients at lower level of government. It may be a mafia dominated state. Eg: Asia.

(c) *Freelance bribery states:* It is weak and disorganised with many officials engaged in freelance bribery. Private group dominates the state, buying the low level officials.

(d) *Competitive Bribery state:* Many corrupt officials deal with large number of ordinary citizens and firms. The situation is the potential for an upward spiral of corruption. The corruption of some officials can encourage others to accept bribes until all but the unreconstructed moralists are corrupt. Eg. India.

Of course, most developing countries fall somewhere between these two extremes.[10]

The truth is that in some parts of the country, a person

can get away even with murder if he has enough money to pay the police and if he has close contacts with the local heavy weights. On the other hand, false cases can also be registered against innocent people and can be pursued with the connivance of the police to harass or to extract money. In many localities, policemen are suspected of being in league with thieves and decoils. Apart from it a substantial portion of political class has thus become highly corrupted. Democratic institutions have become polluted. Corrupt India of today is their legacy.

Don't blame the politicians solely for all the ills of the country today. The bureaucrats are equally responsible for defiling India's administration. If all 5,067 IAS officers decide to use their enormous power to fight corruption in an unyielding manner and to run governmental administration honestly, efficiently and transparently, they will achieve amazing success. An honest index at district level is to be developed.

Results of Survey on Government Departments

(a) Findings

On the advice of Mr. N. Vittal[11], Chief Vigilance Commissioner, in the Vigilance Awareness Week' of Oct. 31-November 4, 2000, the exit poll was carried out in five cities—New Delhi, Lucknow, Chennai, Hyderabad, Pune and six departments—Electricity, Telephone, Civil Supplies, City Government, driving licence and local urban Development Office where a large number of people usually go. Out of 2,576 carefully selected sample visitors from each city not less than 500 visitors were covered as sample. The structured questionnaire was canvassed by local premier institutes like IIM Lucknow, symbiosis in Pune. The interview covered "perceptions" about corruption as well as first hand experience in availing the services of these public offices.

1. 50 per cent of visitors who avail the services had experience of giving bribe at one time or other.

2. 2/3 of people think that corruption is real.
3. In Lucknow and Hyderabad 60 per cent had given bribe against only 38 per cent in Chennai and 42 per cent in Pune.
4. In Chennai more than 60 per cent had named politicians as responsible for corruption. Middlemen menace seems to be far more in Hyderabad and Lucknow.
5. Road Transport Authority and Civil Supplies were viewed as most corrupt in all the five cities.
6. Relatively more among businessmen and self employed agreed giving bribe in all cities.
7. Interestingly, even among "government employees" more than 40 per cent agreed giving bribe at one time or other in all the cities covered.
8. A little over 40 per cent of people think that judiciary in the country is not able to tackle corruption cases. Recently a former Prime Minister, a former Chief Ministers and a few politicians were sentenced for corrupt practices. Whereas, Chief Justice S.P. Bharucha is reported that 20 per cent of judicial officers were corrupt and also expressed concern at the absence of an effective mechanism to deal with the allegations of corruption in respect of High Court and Supreme Court judges.

(b) Employment Generation and Poverty Alleviation Programmes

A number of specially designed poverty alleviation programmes are in operation in rural and urban areas in order to encourage self and wage employment for the year 2001-02 (BE) an outlay of Rs. 9,765 crores has been provided under plan provisions as compared to Rs. 9,270 crore (BE) made available in 2000-01 to the Ministry of Rural Development for rural development, rural employment and poverty alleviation programmes. The performance of the major anti-poverty and employment generating programmes is given in the Table 1.

TABLE 1
PHYSICAL PERFORMANCE OF SPECIAL EMPLOYMENT AND POVERTY ALLEVIATION PROGRAMMES

(in Million)

Sl. No.	Programmes	1999-2000 Achievement	2000-01 Target	2000-01 Achievement	2001-02 Target	2001-02 Achievement
	Programmes in Rural Areas					
1.	Jawahar Gram Samridhi Yojana (from 1999 April renamed from JRY). Mandays of employment generated	268.3	–	268.32	–	97.7
2.	Employment Assurance Scheme (Mandays of employment generated)	278.6	259.45	217.49	339.17	93.07
3.	Swarna Jayanthi Gram Swarozgar Yojana Families assisted	.94	–	1.09	–	.32
4.	Training of Rural Youth for Self employment	–	–	–	–	–
5.	DWACRA—Group formed, Membership	–	–	–	–	–
6.	Indira Awaas Yojana (House constructed)	.93	1.24	1.17	1.29	0.40
7.	Million wells schemes	–	–	–	–	–
8.	ARWSP—Habitation/villages	0.75	0.08	0.07	0.05	0.02
9.	Central Rural Sanitation Programme (CRSP)	1.08	1.26	0.62	–	0.20
10.	National Social Assistance Programme (NSAP) National Old Age Persion Scheme (NOAPS)	5.02	5.58	7.57	4.96	4.27
	Programmes in Urban Areas					
1.	Prime Minister Rojgar Yojana (PMRY)					
	(a) Micro enterprises	0.14	0.22	0.4	–	–
	(b) Employment generated	0.21	0.33	0.6	–	–

Sl. No.	Programmes	1999-2000	2000-01		2001-02	
		Achievement	Target	Achievement	Target	Achievement
2.	(i) Swama Jayanthi Shahri Rozgar Yojana (SJSRY) Urban Self Employment Programme					
	(a) Beneficiaries	0.13	–	0.1	–	0.08
	(b) Persons trained	0.10	–	0.09	–	0.11
	(ii) Urban wage employment programme (Mandays of employment generated)	10.14	–	15.87	–	3.63
3.	Beneficiaries covered under community structured component	26.05	–	28.73	–	29.59
4.	Beneficiaries assisted under DWCUA	0.008	–	0.007	–	0.18

Source: Economic Survey 2002, p. 242.

The employment generation for achieving the target of providing employment opportunities to 100 million people over that next 10 years, i.e., 10 million people per year. Much of the schemes and amounts are in the control of politicians and bureaucrats, who abuses the funds as middlemen and submits the reports and audit statements to the concern. Poverty has alleviated a little and mandays have not raised as anticipated, but many rural labourers are attending urban activities and made urbans as slums. Ignorance and illiteracy are the important factors among the beneficiaries not to get the right benefit from Government programmes.

Reform Programmes

Suppose reform minded government take to reduce corruption. The possibilities depend on the State's capacity and the Country's level of development. The honesty anti corruption officials efforts should limit public officials opportunities for corruption and increase the benefits of being honest and the costs of being corrupt. The incentives for corruption are influenced by:

(a) The benefits and costs are under the discretionary control of officials.
(b) The conditions of civil service employment and the incentive systems within the civil service.
(c) The ability of citizens to scrutinize government activities and file complaints.
(d) The level of press, freedom and freedom of individuals to form NGOs.
(e) The level of active political opposition.

The bulk of corruption in India originates in the realm of business an industry. Over the years, important business houses have made arrangements in through their contact men posted in New Delhi and state capitals for the discreet disbursement of cash funds. The Confederation of Indian Industry (CII) published in April, 1998, a document, entitled "Desirable Corporate Governance—A Code" Infact, the word 'ethics' does not appear at all in any of the 'CII recommendations.'

Reducing the Incentives for Payoffs

The most obvious approach is simply to eliminate the laws and programmes that leads to corruption. If the State does not have authority to restrict exports or license businesses, no one will pay bribes in those areas. If subsidy is eliminated, the bribes that accompanied it will disappear as well. If price controls are lifted, market prices will reflect scarcity values, not bribes. Privatization will eliminate the corruption. After a brief experiment with prohibition, United States repealed the Eighteenth Amendment to the Constitution, which outlawed the manufacture and sale of "intoxicating liquors." Gambling, once outlawed in many jurisdictions, has recently been legalized in many U.S. countries and States. The integrity of privatization is important in transition economies. The risk is not simply corruption and insider deals but dominant by organized crime groups, which, drive competitors, especially Western Firms, away. Thus the privatisation process should establish a transparent and reliable legal environment. Making rules more transparent also helps limit opportunities for corruption—as simple, non-discretionary tax spending and regulatory laws. Corruption is often embedded in the hierarchical structure of bureaucracies. Low-level officials collect bribes and pass a share on to higher level officials in the form of an upfront payment for the job itself. Conversely, higher-ups may organize the corrupt system to avoid wasteful competition among low-level officials—and to collect the spoils themselves. Breaking such pattern may require fundamental re-organization.

One way to lower officials bargaining power is to introduce competitive pressures within government. When bribes are paid for benefits that are not constrained by budgetary limits, such as licenses and permits, overlapping and competitive bureaucratic jurisdiction can reduce corruption. Since clients can apply to any of a number of officials and go to a second one if turned down by the first, no one official has monopoly power. Thus no official can demand a large bribe. A small number of honest officials can reform a corrupt system unless long queues develop in front of the honest officials. If those who pay bribes are unqualified, however, the honesty of some officials increases the gains to those who are corrupt, inducing more officials to become corrupt.

Needed Credible Law Enforcement

The key factor for controlling corruption is a viable legal framework that enforces the law without political favouritism or arbitrariness. Such a system deters those tempted to engage in corrupt acts and encourages the public to resist criminal conduct by officials. Tough laws are not sufficient but they are enforced. A country that is serious about reform must also have effective agencies to investigate and prosecute corruption and an independent judiciary that is not itself corrupt. An independent judiciary can be particularly effective in checking official malfeasance. In India, the Supreme Court pushed forward a corruption investigation that the government had wanted to quash (The times of India, 2 March, 1996). In Brazil the Supreme Court's insistence that the congressional vote on President Collor's impeachment be public helped keep the process honest. The first step in reform is improving pay and working conditions for judges and supporting personnel, but this must be accompanied by better monitoring of the system's performance, by both insiders and outsiders. For example, information on delays by court and type of case could be collected and made public. Laws should be modified and well written without arbitrariness. Judicial reforms will have little impact in the absence of an effective prosecutorial system. When ordinary law enforcement offices are ineffective or corrupt, an alternative is an independent anti-corruption Commission or an Inspector General reporting only to the Chief Executive or Parliament. The best known Commission is Hong Kong's Independent Commission Against Corruption (ICAC), which reported only to the Governor General and had extensive powers. Legal and judicial reforms may be beyond the reach of developing countries in which corruption is endemic. In such cases reform should focus on increasing the state's accountability to ordinary citizens. It is time to bring into focus not the bribe takers but the bribe givers.[12] India reached the position of 'dishonest corruption' whereas Thailand 'honest corruption.'

The best way to improve the quality of civil services may be to encourage strong private sector growth, so that it becomes politically possible to cut civil service jobs. To avoid adverse selection and continued corruption, wages will probably need to be raised as well but a reform that focuses only on pay levels will not succeed. Across the board pay increases with no link to productivity are exactly the wrong strategy. Yet they may be difficult for politicians to avoid. The role of state is to be reduced to a level of making legislation and monitoring than maintenance of Industries, service organisations.

Transparency and Accountability to Citizens

The private sector can be an important check on the arbitrary exercise of power by government—but only if citizens can find out what the state is doing and use this information to hold public officials accountable. At first step government should publish—budgets, revenue collections, expenditures, proceedings of legislative bodies. The financial data should be audited independently. Chief Executives and Ministers should not have access to secret funds.

Many scandals have occurred because top officials overruled the tender board or because sub-ordinate officials operated without formal controls. For example, the lowest bidder always win contract can lead to low quality work or facilitate bid rigging. Sometimes bribers are themselves losers, who would be better off in an honest world. Low level tribunals and ombudsmen that help ordinary citizens faced with routine bribery demands. An alternative is the creation of corrupt "hotlines" that citizens can call to complain directly to the government. Laws should be made to easy establishment of watchdog associations and non-profit organisations will be used to monitor their performance, surveillance and harassment.

Reduction of Powers of Politicians and Elections

If the problem is high-level corruption, it results from the way a political system functions and from the relationship between private wealth and political activity. Corrupt politicians might be more inclined to spend on fighter aircraft and large scale investment projects than on text books and teachers' salaries, even though the latter may promote economic growth to a greater extent than the former.[13]

In terms of campaign financing, it is hard to imagine that a democracy could survive without sources of funds to carry out elections. Still there is a need for transparency in those dealings. It involves large sums of money-big contracts, big concessions, big privatizations. *If a government structure is corrupt at the top, there is no way to restrain corruption at the bottom.* Thus different policies were needed to address different problems. On the micro-side a lack of internal and external monitoring of public institutions and complex and uncertain procedures are often to blame. Independent non-profit organisations, judicial institutions, social activists should monitor the behaviour of politician activities day in and day out.[14]

III

Measures for Checking Corruption

A meaningful civil liberties are a good starting point. An independent press, strong opposition groups and an active civil society are more likely to develop if they can express themselves publicly and are free from intimidation. Credible property and contract rights would help to increase investment. Broadened political alternatives also can weaken corrupt monopolies, such as courts, investigative agencies, Inspector Generals, ombudsmen. Political insecurity leads to voracious corruption. Bureaucratic corruption can become a factor in politics, as when agencies grant favours to the politically connected to maintain cover for their own corruption. Different connections between political and bureaucratic corruption produce different patterns of extended clientelism in society. Successful strategies begin by "frying a few big fish." A good rule of thumb is that to be credible, an anti-corruption campaign must achieve some tangible results. A collective political will is highly needed for developing countries.

Conclusion

Corruption is considered as just one of many-side problems in democracy. One that does not account for all that is wrong or over-whelm all that may be right in a developing country. Overall meaning of a government by J.M. Keynes was to solve all perennial problems of people—poverty, unemployment, depression, deficiency of demand. But what we observed, at present was government means public servants were looking for monopoly power for pocketing a part of development funds. By decentralisation of powers, bringing awareness among citizens, starting independent ethical enquiry institutions, stopping politician to poke nose at everywhere, action oriented judiciary could alleviate the corruption to a bottom level. A strong political will should be emerged among all political parties to check this social menace for ever lasting, like Denmark, Sweden.

REFERENCES

1. George Cherian (2000): India slips down to 72nd place on corruption index, **The Economic Times,** 21 June.
2. Rajmohan Gandhi (1997): Combating corruption: A National Agenda, Forum of Free Enterprise, Mumbai, Dec., p. 9.
3. Dr. P.V. Shenoi (1998): Corruption can be controlled, Forum of Free Enterprise, Mumbai, Jan.
4. Gunnar Myrdal: Asian Drama.
5. Ajit Kumar Sinha (2000): Organised Crime and Political Economy of Development: The Indian Panorama, **The Indian Economic Journal,** Vol. 47, Jan.-March, p. 9.

6. G. Haragopal & V.S. Prasad (1990): Social Bases of Administrative culture in India, The **Indian Journal of Public Administration,** July-Sept.
7. Cheryl N. Gray and Daniel Kaufmann (1998): Corruptions and Development, **Finance and Development,** March, p. 7.
8. Kadir Zaman, (1997): Bribery, Modern thought, Hyderabad.
9. Susan Rose-Ackerman (1997): Corruption and Development, Annual World Bank Conference on Development Economics.
10. Lubna Kably (2000): Feeding Corruption, **The Economic Times,** July 14.
11. N.K. Singh: Set back to fight against Corruption, The Hindu, March 22, 2002, p. 13.
12. N. Vittal, (1999): Ethics in Business, Industry and Public Life, Jan. 8, 1999, Free Forum Enterprise, Mumbai.
13. Paolo Mauro (1998): Corruption: causes, consequences and Agenda for further research, **Finance and Development,** March 1998, p. 12.
14. C.P. Srivastava (2001): India's enemy within, Macmillan.

9

A CRITIQUE OF ECONOMIC REFORMS IN INDIA

N. Sudhakara Rao

Introduction

The macro economic scenario in India at present is paradoxical in several respects. The country is passing through a difficult phase due to domestic shocks such as adverse security environment, natural disasters (cyclone in Orissa and earthquack in Gujarat) and social issues such as Ayodhya and terrorism and due to several external shocks such as East Asian crisis of 1997-98, oil price crisis in 2000-01, global economic slowdown, an external threat from Pakistan etc. Thus, there are many dangerous under currents beneath apparently placed water.

Planning Strategy and Role of Govt.

Planning in India is considered to be the first positive step in the path of progress. During five decades of development (1951-2001) Indian economy achieved a great degree of internal strength and resilience both in public and private sectors mixed economy to build a socialist pattern of society. India is an agrarian economy and agriculture being the primary sector is in the hands of the private individuals. The industrial sector and tertiary sector are also mostly in the hands of private individuals. Only a small section of the economy is in the hands of the Govt. 1950's and 1960's, the Government has assigned an important role both as a producer and as a regulator of economic activities.

The Government undertook several activities that are expected to be compensative for market failure. The emphasis was on production for the home market and important substitution for developing industries more especially heavy industries. Public policy was towards public sector undertakings mostly having investment-oriented industries. The liberalization of Government controls and that were started during late 1960's actually accelerated in 1980's it. But the reform process was slow and not self-sustaining. The initial planning strategy adopted in India was in sharp contrast to the strategy inherent in the economic reforms of the 1990's. The new economic reforms of 1991 seek to redefine the roles of State since four decades of development experience have shown that there can be Government failures as well. The situation prevailing before 1991 such as Gulf war, increased burden of imports of crude oil and petro-products, the sudden decline in rupee value lack of stable Government (minority grant), large-scale fiscal deficit and inflation led to economic crisis. The crisis in 1991 provided the context for the realignment of macro economic fundamentals through a programme of economic stabilization, structural reforms to accelerate growth potential. The new economic policy has not diminished the State's role, but redefined it expanding it in some areas and reducing it in some other areas. Disinvestments policy was initiated since many public sector undertakings are running losses (may be perhaps by the time the Govt. took over some of the private industries, they were running in losses). The trend is more on privatization reduce bureaucracy and develop competition between private and public sector and make Indian economy fit for the world economy.

Indian Economy in the Global Context

Globalization is considered as a dawn of new era. It brings critical transformation in economies. India at the end of 20th century witnessed gradual transformation influenced by global economic forces. Economic reforms are forced upon the nation and economic changes are taking place in

India as a result of liberalizatin and its integration in the world economy. The global economy experienced an overall deceleration during recent times especially after terrorist attacks in September 2001. Export growth suffered, industrial profitability has been affected by prevailing low commodity product prices globally.

India is no longer a country producing for the domestic market but also becoming a global player. As per the estimates of the Central Statistical Organization GDP growth rate in India during 2001-02 is 5.4 per cent, which is one of the highest growth rates in the world. The public perception is that India is not immune to slowdown phase of the global business cycle and remains as the best performing economies in the world. The country is rated as the 5th largest country in the world, measured in the purchasing power parity terms (other four being US, China, Japan and Germany). During 1990's, in terms of GDP growth rate, India is the 8th country in the world. It is the 16th country as far as consumption/income distribution (Gini coefficient) is concerned. It achieved lowest rate of inflation (2%) during recent times. (The lowest in the last three decades in India) India is considered as an island of stability amidst seas of turbulence, in International Currency Markets. India is the only developing country with a favorable debt GNP ratio. The country has experienced declining interest rate environment. Financial markets have remained stable. The external sector is clearly sustainable. Foreign exchange reserves are comfortable at US $ 50 billion. Business environment is less risky because of stable exchange rates. Food stocks have reached all time high rates. India is in the list of less indebted countries in the world. During last decade literacy, education, age of marriage, status of women had increased and fertility and mortality had declined. The India's population growth rate starts declining. Thus, the present state of the Indian economy reflects a combination of structural changes with different weights assignable to each one of them. What we have to do is restore confidence in the economy and try for all round development of the nation with unity, commitment, determination, and dedication.

Indian Economy—Retrospective

We shall examine the performance of Indian economy during pre-reform and post-reform period to assess the impact of liberalization on the economy, and to what extend the objectives of the new economic policy were realized. The year 1991 is an important landmark in the country's history. Country experienced severe economic crisis with serious balance of payments situation before 1991. A macro economic programme of economic stabilization and long-term structural reforms stipulated by IMF and World Bank were taken up in the areas of industrial licensing, foreign trade, foreign investment, exchange rate management, financial sector reforms were taken up to improve productivity, efficiency and accelerate growth potential of the economy and to come out from economic crisis successfully. Structural reforms were extended later to other areas. Reforms of 1990's removed entry barriers to investment, opened the new trade to other countries, provided free access to foreign technology opened up foreign investment and removed barriers that inhibit access to capital markets. The removal of restrictions expected to lead labour intensive economy with high growth potential. At present, we are talking about second-generation reforms, which implies depending of the existing reform process and bringing new areas with in its scope.

General Review

The country experienced wide an varied consequences brought by new liberalization programmes. Various modernizing forces are at work after this structural transformation. Even though there is no uniform opinion among the economists and policy-makers with regard to the success of these reforms, majority feel that area of success more than areas of failure.

Trends in GDP

Growth rate in gross domestic product is one of the important macro economic indicators through which one can judge the performance of an economy. The per capita NNP at 1993-94 prices was Rs. 3687 in 1950-51 and it increased to 5352 in 1980-81, Rs. 7321 in 1991 and Rs. 10254 in 2000-01. It implies that per capita NNP increased during 1990's as compared to 1980's, in spite of the fact that population growth is very high. As per 2001 census, India's population was enumerated 102 crores. The decadal growth of population is 21.34 per cent between 1991-2001. It is the sharpest decline in the rate of growth of population, witnessed since independence. The average exponential growth rate declined from 2.14% per annum during the previous decade to 1.93% per annum during 1990's. The declining trends indicate that the country is entering a phase of rapidly declining fertility in its process of demography transition.

TABLE 1
AVERAGE ANNUAL GROWTH RATES OF GROSS NATIONAL PRODUCTS, NET NATIONAL PRODUCTS AND PER CAPITA NET NNP

	Base Year 1993-94 and in per cent		
Year	*GNP*	*NNP*	*Per Capita NNP*
1	2	3	4
1951-61	3.9	3.9	1.9
1961-71	3.8	3.5	1.3
1971-81	3.2	3.1	0.8
1981-91	5.3	5.1	2.8
1991-01	5.6	5.5	3.5
1991-96	5.4	5.2	3.0
1996-2001	5.9	5.8	3.9

Source: Computed from Economic Survey, 2001-2002.

It is to be noted that NNP during First five-year plan was 3.7%. The maximum NNP growth rate observed during 8th Plan was 6.6%. During the period 1981-1991 average GNP growth rate was 5.3 per cent, and during 1991-2001 it was 5.6 per cent. The GNP growth rate was 5.4% during 1991-96 and 5.9% during 1996-2001. An analysis of Table 1 reveals that GDP growth rate fluctuated very widely during post reform period. The lowest growth rate (1.3%) was noticed in 1991-92 and highest (7.5%) in 1996-99. The estimated GDP growth rate in 2001-02 is 5.4%. The average GDP growth rate during 1991-202 was 5.5 per cent. If we exclude 1991-92 the average was 6%. The Finance Minister stated that the GDP is expected to raise at a rate of 6—6.5 per cent during 2000-2003 and expected to raise at the rate of 7 per cent the next four to five years to come. On the whole we can say that the performance of the Indian economy during post-reform period is better as compared to pre-reform period the performance is better during the second half of 1990's as compared to second half.

Sectoral Growth Rates

The sectoral growth rate in the various sectors of the economy is more important and concerned as compared to the overall growth rate of the economy, since the later gives an aggregate picture ignoring internal sectoral imbalances.

TABLE 2
AVERAGE ANNUAL GROWTH RATES OF REAL GDP AT FACTOR COST 1993-94 BY INDUSTRY ORIGIN (percentage)

S. No.	*Item*	*51-61*	*61-71*	*71-81*	*81-91*	*91-01*	*91-96*	*96-2001*
1	*2*	*3*	*4*	*5*	*6*	*7*	*8*	*9*
1.	Agri.	3.19	2.58	1.95	3.84	2.79	2.64	2.94
2.	Manufac.	6.33	5.61	3.98	6.98	5.86	6.30	5.42
3.	Transport	5.39	5.01	4.92	5.81	7.51	7.78	7.24
4.	Finance	2.97	3.43	4.09	9.88	8.46	9.02	7.90
5.	Pub. Ser.	3.65	5.30	3.98	5.88	6.78	4.36	9.20
6.	GDP	3.94	3.74	3.17	5.65	5.61	5.38	5.84

Source: Computed from Economic Survey, 2001-2002.

Table 2 provides information with regard to the distribution of plan outlays average annual growth rates of different sectors of the economy. The table reveals that the agricultural growth rate was 3.19% during 1951-1961 and this has declined to 2.79% during 1991-2001. As compared to 1980's it is low. In the year 1981-91 it was 3.84% during 1990's the second half had shown better performance than the first half.

TABLE 3
SECTORAL OUTLAYS DURING THE PLANS
(Per cent Distribution)

S. No.	Item	*Different Five-Year Plans* 1	2	3	4	5	6	7	8	9
1.	Agri. & ALI.	31	20	21	24	22	24	22	22	21
2.	Power	13	10	14	15	19	28	28	29	26
3.	Industry	06	24	23	23	24	16	13	11	08
4.	Tran. & Comm.	26	28	25	20	18	16	17	19	22
5.	Social Ser.	22	18	17	18	17	16	20	19	23
	Total	**100**	**100**	**100**	**100**	**100**	**100**	**100**	**100**	**100**

Source: Computed from Economic Survey 2000-2001.

An analyses of Table 3 reveals that the share of agriculture in the total plan outlay was 31% during first plan period and it declined to 21% during the 9th Plan period. As compared to 1980's the situation has worsened during 1990's.

Agriculture

The average annual growth rate of real GDP at factor cost 93-94 ravels that the share of agriculture, forestry and logging, fishing, mining and quarrying together was 3.19% during 1951-61. This has declined to 1.95% during 1971-81 and increased to 3.84% during 1981-91 and declined to 2.79% during 1991-2001. On the whole during the last five decades agriculture and allied sectors growth rate declined from 3.19% to 2.79%. The highest growth rate 3.84% was observed during 1981-91. As compared to 1980's the agriculture growth rate has declined during 1990's.

Production and Productivity

The annual compound growth of agricultural products is very high during 1991 to 2000-01 as compared to 1980-81 to

TABLE 4
PLAN OUTLAY BY HEADS OF DEVELOPMENT
1980-85 to 1997-2002 (Per cent Distribution)

	Head of Development	*Sixth Plan (1980-85)*	*Seventh Plan (1985-90)*	*Eighth Plan (1992-97)*	*Ninth Plan (1997-02)*
	1	*2*	*3*	*4*	*5*
1.	Agriculture	6.1	5.8	5.2	4.9
2.	Rural Development	6.4	7.0	7.9	8.7
3.	Special Area Program	1.4	1.6	1.6	0.4
4.	Irri. & Flod Control	10.0	7.6	7.5	6.5
5.	Energy	28.1	28.2	28.6	25.9
6.	Industry & Minerals	15.5	13.4	10.8	7.6
7.	Transport	13.0	13.5	12.9	13.9
8.	Communication & IB	3.2	3.9	5.8	5.5
9.	Science & Technology	0.9	1.4	2.1	2.1
10.	Social Services	14.5	16.0	18.2	2.3
	Education	2.7	3.5	4.5	N.A.
	Health & F.W.	3.1	3.1	3.2	N.A.
	Housing & U.D.	2.6	2.2	2.4	N.A.
	Other Social Services	6.1	7.1	9	N.A.
11.	Others	0.8	1.7	0.4	1.5
12.	Total	100	100	100	100
	Central Plans	52.9	58.3	57.1	57.0
	State Plans	45.3	40.0	41.5	43.0
	U.T. Plans	1.8	1.7	1.4	N.A.

Source: Economic Survey, 2001-02.

1989-90. But production growth rate is lower during 1990's as compared to 1980's. The productivity growth rate is lower during 1990's as compared to 1980's.

Public Distributions

Public distribution system is one of the welfare measures taken up by many Governments. In 1980-81, 13 m.ts were distributed and this increased to 20.8 m.ts in 1991, but it declined to 11.3 m.ts in 2001. The per cent of public distribution to total food grains was 11.4 per cent in 1981, 13.1 per cent in 1991 but only 6.6 per cent in 2001. So there is a decline public distribution during 1990's as compared to 1980's.

TABLE 5
ANNUAL COMPOUND GROWTH OF CROP AREA PRODUCTION AND PRODUCTIVITY

Sl. No.	*Crop*	*1980-81 to 1989-90*			*1990-91 to 2000-01*		
		Area	*Production*	*Yield*	*Area*	*Production*	*Yield*
1	*2*	*3*	*4*	*5*	*6*	*7*	*8*
1.	Rice & Wheat	0.43	3.59	3.15	0.84	2.27	1.42
2.	Rice	0.41	3.62	3.19	0.63	1.79	1.16
3.	Wheat	0.47	3.57	3.10	1.21	3.04	1.81
4.	Coarse	–	0.40	1.62	–	0.06	1.65
	Cereals	1.34			1.84		
5.	Pulses	–	1.52	1.61	–	–0.58	0.27
		0.09			1.02		
6.	Total	–	2.85	2.74	–	1.66	1.34
	Food grains	0.23			0.20		
7.	Non-Food Crops	1.12	3.77	2.31	0.84	1.86	0.59
8.	Oilseeds	–	5.20	2.43	0.44	0.66	0.61
		1.51					
9.	Sugarcane	1.44	2.70	1.24	1.72	2.62	0.89
10.	Cotton	–	2.80	4.10	2.21	0.92	–1.26
		1.25					
11.	All Crops	0.10	3.19	2.56	0.08	1.73	1.02

Source: Economic Survey, 2001-02.

Consumption

The consumption of edible oil was 3.37 kg. in 1961-71 and it increased to 7.04 kg during 1991-2001. All most gradually, it was 5.28 kg during 1981-91. Similar trend was observed for vanaspathi. Sugar consumption increased from 5.48 kg in 1961-71 to 14.19 kg during 1991-2001. It was 10.97 kg in 1981-91. Cloth consumption increased from 17.42 mts to 27.73 mts during 1961-2001. Tea consumption has doubled but the coffee consumptions had fallen during the same period. There is a lot of improvement in electricity domestic consumption. It increased from 5.57 KWH in 1960-61 to 5.29 KWH during 1991-01.

The production of milk increased from 17 m.t. in 1950-51 to 81. m.t during 2000-01. During 1981-91 it was 44.9 m.t and it increased to 67.98 m.t during 1991-2001. Similarly there is an improvement in the production of eggs, fish, meat, which is mostly used for domestic purpose.

There exist wild disparities in consumption expenditure between rural and urban areas. In 1972-73 (NSS 27th round) the share of food expenditure in total consumption was 72.9 per cent in rural and 64.5 per cent in urban. This declined to 59.4 per cent in rural and 48.1 per cent in urban during 1999-2000 (NSS 55th round). The decline the share of food grains expenditure to total consumption was more it declined from 46 per cent to 26.2 per cent in rural and 27 per cent to 15 per cent in urban during the same period. The expenditure on fruits and vegetables was 10.15 per cent in rural and 9.92 per cent in urban during 1972-73 and it increased to 14.48 per cent and 15.59 per cent in rural and in urban respectively during 1999-00. Similar consumption pattern was observed with regard to milk, meat, eggs, fish etc., thus we can say that the consumption expenditure the food has declined but with regard to fruits and vegetables.

TABLE 6
MONTHLY PER CAPITA FOOD AND FOOD GRAIN EXPENDITURE TO TOTAL CONSUMPTION EXPENDITURE (Per cent)

Sl. No.	*Year NSS Round*	*Expenditure Share of Food Consumption expenditures*		*Share of Food Grains Expenditure in total consumption expenditures*	
		Rural	*Urban*	*Rural*	*Urban*
1	2	3	4	5	6
1.	1972-73 (27th Round)	72.9	64.5	46.0	27.1
2.	1977-78 (32rd Round)	64.3	60.0	37.3	24.5
3.	1983 (38th Round)	65.6	59.1	36.3	22.9
4.	1987-88 (43rd Round)	64.0	56.4	30.6	18.7
5.	1993-94 (50th Round)	63.2	54.7	28.3	17.3
6.	1999-2000 (55th Round)	59.4	48.1	26.2	15.3

Source: Economic Survey, 2001-02.

Industry

The structural reforms in the early stages covered mostly in industrial front, such as industrial licensing, foreign trade, foreign investment, exchange rate management. It is observed that the share of industry was only six per cent in the first plan period this has increased to 24 per cent during 2nd plan and 8 per cent in the 9th plan period. There is an upward trend in the share of industry up to 1980's recording a maximum of 26 per cent in the 5th plan period. Then onwards it declined reaching 8 per cent during 9th plan period. As compared to 1990's, the share of industrial sector is higher during 1980's.

TABLE 7
SHARE OF EXPENDITURES OF FOOD GRAINS, FRUITS, MILK ETC., IN TOTAL FOOD EXPENDITURE (Per cent)

Sl. No.	*Year NSS Round*	*Expenditure on Food Grains*		*Expenditure on Fruits and Veg.*		*Expenditure on Milk, Meat, Egg and Fish*	
		Rural	*Urban*	*Rural*	*Urban*	*Rural*	*Urban*
1	*2*	*3*	*4*	*5*	*6*		
1.	1972-73 (27th Round)	63.10	42.02	10.15	9.92	13.44	19.53
2.	1977-78 (32rd Round)	58.01	40.83	9.95	10.67	16.17	21.67
3.	1983 (38th Round)	55.34	38.75	11.43	12.01	16.01	21.66
4.	1987-88 (43rd Round)	47.81	33.16	12.66	13.83	18.59	23.23
5.	1993-94 (50th Round)	44.78	31.63	14.40	14.99	20.25	24.13
6.	1999-2000 (55th Round)	44.11	31.81	14.48	15.59	20.37	24.53

Source: Economic Survey, 2001-02.

There has been significant decline in the growth rate of the industry. This may be attributed to various factors such as normal business and investment cycles, lack of demand both in consumer and investment sectors high interest rates, infrastructure constraints and power, and transports and delays in establishing credible institutional and regulatory frame work for private participation in key sectors. Investment in organized sector is very low. The market uncertainty is very high with the removal of quantitative restrictions on all most all imports. The key rigidity inhibit Indian industry from investing in labour using activities will to remove the hurdles, investment expansion. The list of industries reserved for public sector has been reduced. Equity in public enterprises is being divested. Access to foreign capital and technology has been made free. Quantitative restrictions on imports have been significantly reduced.

The industrial output shown halting growth rates over the entire decade of nineties. Large-scale industries are in recession since 1996, and small-scale industries are stagnant or even declining especially after dismantling of quantitative import restrictions and de-reservation of industries hither to reserved for manufacture of small-scale industries.

Manufacturing

Manufacturing construction, electricity, gas and water supply is concerned the average growth rate was 6.33 per cent during 1951-61 and 5.86 per cent during 1990-01. During 1980's the growth rate was 6.98 per cent. Thus there is a decline a growth rate during 1990's as compared to 1980's. During 1990's the performance in the first half is better than the second half.

Manufacturing goods can be classified into two categories. Labour Intensive and Capital Intensive. The rate of growth of output (value added) of labour intensive goods has been slow than that of capital-intensive goods. As a result the share of labour intensive goods have gone down during 1990-91 and 1997-98. But labour intensive goods have received more real investment during this period.

The reforms lead relatively more real investment in labour intensive goods but they could not transfer into intensity has gone down not only in capital-intensive goods but also in labour intensive goods.

TABLE 8
PER CAPITA AVAILABILITY OF CERTAIN IMPORTANT ARTICLES OF CONSUMPTION

Year	*Edible Oil (Kg)*	*Vanaspathi (Kg)*	*Sugar (Kg)*	*Cloth (Meters)*	*Tea (Grams)*	*Coffee (Grams)*	*Electricity Domestic (KWH)*
1961-71	3.37	0.74	5.48	17.42	356.3	80.9	5.57
1971-81	3.39	0.98	6.89	14.72	489	69.0	10.0
1981-82	5.1	1.3	8.2	17.1	466	79	15.1
1991-92	5.4	1.0	13.0	22.9	655	64	41.9
2000-01	8.0	1.4	15.8	30.7	638	58	N.A.
1981-91	5.298	1.21	10.97	20.18	560.7	73.3	25.28
1991-2001	7.04	1.1	14.19	27.73	648.6	58.4	50.29
1991-96	6.12	1.0	13.3	25.52	656.2	58	49.1
1996-2001	7.96	1.2	15.08	29.94	641	58.8	51.48

The value added growth in the registered manufacturing sector achieved since 1991 has not been able to surpass that achieved during 1980-81 and 1990-91. The growth record during the reforms of the 1990's has been worse than that of reforms of 1980's. Even when compared with the 1980's the situation in growth in consumer goods, capital goods and intermediate goods in the 1990's appears to be worse. Export growth has been found to be disappointing since the mid-1990's. the employment situation is worse than what we saw in the case of output. Labour intensity has gone down not only in the capital intensity goods but also in labour intensive goods.

As per the CSO, the compounded annual growth rate of registered manufacturing sector at constant prices show that the manufacturing growth rate was 17.03% during 1950-51 to 1955-56, 4.7% during 1955-56 to 1965-66, 7.66% during 1980-81 to 1990-91 and 5.91% during 1990-91 to 1998-99. Thus it is clear that the growth record during the reforms period has been worse than that of the previous period in the manufacturing sector.

The power sector has occupied an important place in the economy. Power sector was allotted 13 per cent share in the first plan, and it increased to 29 per cent during 8th plan and declined to 26 per cent in the 9th plan. The power sector out lay has doubled during last 50 years there is a marginal decline in the outlay during 1990's has compared to 1980's.

The gross energy generated increased from 6.6 billion KWH in 1950-51 to 20.1 billion KWH in 1960-61, 20.1 billion KWH in 1970-71, 119.3 billion KWH in 1980-81, and 289.4 billion KWH in 1990-91 and 532.2 billion KWH in 1999-2002. The performance of power sectors the remarkable during this period.

The share of transport and communications in total out lays was 27 per cent in the first plan and it declined to 22 per cent in the 9th plan. The share has remained more or less the other periods. The growth rate registered in this sector was very high. During 1951-61 it was 5.39 per cent and during 1991-2001 it was 7.51 per cent. During the first half of 1990's it was 7.78 per cent and the second half 7.24 per cent. We can say that there are impressive developments in the transport and communication sectors.

Public distribution defense and other services are concerned the growth rate was 3.65 per cent during 1951-61 and it increased to 6.78 per cent during 1991-2001. As compared to 1980's the growth rate is higher during 1990's. Especially in the second half of 1990's.

The share of social service was 22 per cent in the first plan but it declined to 16 per cent during 6th plan period and reached 23 per cent during 9th plan. The share increased from 15.3 per cent during 1980's to 21.1 per cent during 1990's. The increase is mor in the case of education.

Finance, insurance, real estates and business services are concerned the growth rate is very high. It was 2.97 per cent during 1951-61 and it increased to 8.46 per cent during 1991-2001, during 1981-91 it was 9.88 per cent. On the whole, we can say that the growth rate the service sector is very high. As compared to 1990's the rate is low during 1990's. The rate is high during the first half of 1990's as compared to the second half.

Electricity

The electricity consumption among the different sectors of the economy shows that during 1981-82 the domestic consumption was 11.6 per cent, commercial 5.8 per cent and industrial 58.8 per cent. The domestic consumption increased to 22.2 per cent during 1999-2000, commercial consumption 6.3 per cent, industrial consumption declined to 34.8 per cent during the same period. During 1990's domestic consumption had increased commercial consumption remain more or less the same. But industrial consumption has fallen which is reflected in low industrial growth. Electricity consumption in agricultural sector was 16.8 per cent in 1981-82 and it increased to 29.2 per cent in 1999-2000. Agricultural consumption was 21.24 per cent during 1981-91 and it increased to 29.93 per cent during 1991-2000.

Public Sector

The basic idea of the reforms is reduction in the size of public sector and the lifting of Government's controls and regulations on production, trade, and investment ushering new competitive environment by improving efficiency and hence growth.

Fisical Deficit

In 1990-91 the rate of capital expenditure ratio to GDP was 4.4%. Which has declined to 2.6% in 2000-2001. However, GFD was high because of high Revenue Deficit. Govt. should increased its capital expenditure behind current levels.

The most significant proportion of expenditure on social sector takes place on revenue account. Social sector spending is a must on health, education etc., Revenue deficits by detriment of inter play of expenditure and revenues. So, the ratio of tax collections (Net of State Share) to GDP had fallen i.e., 7.86% in 1989-90 to 6.52% in 1999-2000. So there is a need to raise it. India's fiscal scenario at present is about as bad as it was in 1991-92. The Government is unable to reduce expenditures and increase revenues. Today's fiscal deficit will result in tomorrow revenue deficit and hence fiscal deficit should be taken not only expenditure side but also from revenue side. In the sectors such as power, road transport, irrigation, the user charges are low or uneconomical there is need to increase taxes of high-income brackets and including user charge. There is reduction in gross fiscal deficit as a proportion of GDP from 7.4 per cent in 1981-91 to 5.0 per cent in 1991-2002. Similarly there is a decline in primary deficit. But revenue deficit had increased during 1980's and 1990's.

In spite of reductions in non-plan and non-capital expenditures gross fiscal deficit may exceed the budgetary target. The fiscal deficit growth rate was 6.6 during 1991 and 5.1 during 2001-02. Revenue deficit growth rate was 3.3 during 1991 and it reached 3.4 during 2001-02. However, primary deficit was reduced from 2.8 in 1991 to 0.2 in 2001-02.

TABLE 9
TRENDS IN DEFICIT OF CENTRAL GOVERNMENT AS PER CENT OF GDP 1980-81 TO 2001-02

Year	*Revenue Deficit*	*Primary Deficit*	*Fiscal Deficit*
1981-91	1.98	4.45	7.38
1991-2002	3.2	0.60	5.00
1991-96	2.9	1.95	4.96
1996-2002	3.4	0.28	5.00
2001-02	3.4	0.20	5.10

Source: Computed. Economic Surveys.

The table on deficit reveals that the revenue deficit had increased from 1.98 per cent in 1981-91 to 3.2 per cent during 1991-2002. As compared to first half the second half of the 1990's the revenue deficit had increased. There is tremendous decline in primary deficit 4.45 per cent in 1981-91 to 0.60 per cent during 1991-2002. The primary deficit at present is 0.2 per cent in 2001-02. The fiscal deficit in 1981-91 was 7.38 per cent and this had declined to 5 per cent in 1991-2002.

Savings

Saving is essential for investment. But the present savings are not diverted to investment. The gross domestic saving in household sector was 7.16 per cent during 1950-60 reached a maximum of 18.55 per cent during 1990-2000. During 2000-01 it is 20.90 per cent. As compared to 1980's the saving is very high during 1990's that too in the second half of 1990's.

The gross domestic saving in private sector was 1.01 per cent in 1950-60 reached a maximum during 1990-00. As compared to 1980's there is lot of improvement in GDS during 1980's especially in the second half of the 1990's. The gross domestic saving in public sector was 1.83 per cent during 1950-60 reached a maximum during 1980-90 and declined during 1990-2000. At present it is –1.7.

On the whole GDS increased during 1990's as compared to 1980's. The households sector is a major contributor for saving. The public sector's saving is meager and there is every need to increase it for better investment in the country.

TABLE 10
GROSS DOMESTIC SAVING

Year	*GDS Household*	*GDS Private*	*GDS Public*	*GDS Total*
1	2	3	4	5
1950-60	7.16	1.01	1.83	14.95
1960-70	8.4	1.49	2.76	12.65
1970-80	12.21	1.57	3.72	15.95
1980-90	15.15	1.87	2.79	19.83
1990-00	18.55	3.80	0.73	23.08
1990-95	18.16	3.54	1.58	23.24
1995-00	18.94	4.06	–0.12	22.92
2000-01	20.90	4.20	–1.70	23.40

Source: Computed.

The gross domestic saving in current prices was 23.3 per cent during 1991-2002 and 23.5 per cent during 1981-96 and 23.0 per cent during 1996-2001. With increasing shifts in distribution of national product in favour of the rich, personal savings keep increasing (time deposits) leading to savings, leading to hoarding, not invested in economic activities.

Capital Formation

Capital formation is very important for the growth of an economy. The gross fixed capital formation was 4.06 per cent during 1950-60 and it reached 10.54 per cent during 1980-90. As compared to 1980's it has declined in 1990's. At present it is 6.8 per cent (2000-01). The gross capital formation in private sector was 7.08 per cent in 1950-60 and it reached 10.59 per cent during 1980-90 and decreased to 14.58 per cent during 1990-2000. At present it is 15.10 per cent in 2000-01, on the whole gross capital formation increased during 1990's as compared to 1980's.

The gross domestic capital formation was 4.38 per cent during 1950-60 and increased to 10.07 per cent during 1980-90 and declined to 7.64 per cent during 1990-2000. At present it is 7.1 per cent in 2000-01. The gross domestic capital formation in the private sector was 7.04 per cent during 1950-60 and it increased to 15.23 per cent during 1990-2000. As compared to 1980's rate had improved and at present it is 15.8 per cent in 2000-01. the total gross domestic capital formation was 11.43 per cent in 1950-60 and improved overtime. And at present it is 22.9 per cent in 2000-01.

TABLE 11
GROSS FIXED CAPITAL FORMATION, GROSS DOMESTIC CAPITAL FORMATION (Percentage)

Year	*GFC*			*GDC*		
	Public Sector	*Private Sector*	*Total*	*Public Sector*	*Private Sector*	*Total*
1951-60	4.06	7.08	12.4	4.38	7.04	11.43
1960-70	6.52	7.52	14.04	6.96	8.45	15.42
1970-80	6.99	8.83	15.82	8.19	10.08	18.28
1980-90	10.54	10.59	20.22	10.07	12.50	22.59
1990-2000	7.71	14.58	22.26	7.64	15.23	22.89
1990-95	8.64	13.52	22.12	8.40	14.98	23.38
1995-2000	6.78	15.64	22.4	6.88	15.48	22.40
2000-01	1.80	15.10	21.9	7.10	15.80	22.90

Source: Computed.

Expenditure

Various economy measures were taken by the Govt. for reducing non-plan and non-capital expenditure. Expenditure management has kept total Central Govt. expenditure in the rage of 14-15.8% of GDP during 1990's. The total expenditure was 17.3 per cent in 1991 and reduced to 16.4 per cent in 2001-02. However, interest payments increased from 3.8 per cent in 1990-91 to 4.9 per cent in 2001-02. Major subsidies declined from 1.7 per cent in 1990-91 to 1.2 per cent in 2001-02. Defense share remained the same (2.7 per cent) during 1990-91 and 2001-02. Other non-plan expenditure reduced from 4.1 per cent during in 1991 to 3.2 per cent in 2001-02. The budget support for plan is reduced from 5.0 per cent in 1991 to 4.4 per cent during 2001-02. The total gross revenue percentage remained more or less the same (10 per cent). Direct tax contribution increased and indirect tax contribution reduced because of deceleration in industrial growth. Interest payments raised and major subsidies are reduced marginally. Non-plan expenditure was reduced considerably during 1990-91 to 2001-02. On the whole we can say that fiscal deficit was reduced marginally, primary deficit was reduced substantially, and there is an increase in revenue deficit.

Investment

Foreign investment as a per cent of the GDP was 1.05 during 1991-2002, 0.94 during 1991-96, and 1.14 during 1996-2002. Direct foreign (BOP) was 0.05 during 1991-92 and it increased to 1.0 during 2000-01. The foreign direct investment growth rate increased from 0.05 in 1991-92 to 0.4 during 2000-01. Portfolio investment, which was negligible during 1991-92, increased to 0.6 during 2000-01. Total capital growth rate increased from 1.7 in 1991-92 to 1.8 during 2000-01. Gross domestic investment growth rate was 22.6 per cent during 1991-92 and it increased to 24 per cent in the recent times. The growth rate in the Central Government's expenditure was 16.2 per cent during 1991-92 and it declined 15.3 per cent during 2000-01. The gross fiscal deficit of Central Government was 4.7 per cent in 1992 and it increased to 5.5 per cent 2000-01. Revenue deficit increased from 2.7 per cent to 3.4 per cent during the same period. Primary deficit declined from 0.7 per cent to 0.2 per cent.

Public borrowing for public investment is needed and justified provided; it is invested in projects yielding high reforms. As per RBI recent report investment in agriculture has not kept pace with demand. There is an absolute decline in real investment in agriculture after 1978-79. Even the Govt. investment on irrigation and other works in agriculture has taken a back seat after liberalization.

Taxation

Considerable progress have been made over the past 10

years in the reform of Indian Tax System in all its aspects, but tax revenue receipts have remained below 10% of GDP throughout the period. Collection from custom duties have fallen significantly, bringing certain tariffs in line with Asian levels. Excise duty collection not improved. Indirect tax depends on industry, which is weak. Direct taxes improved from 1.9% of GDP in 1990-91 to about 3.3 per cent of GDP in 2000-01. This share in grass tax revenue increased from 19% to 36% over the same period. Gross tax revenues contributed 10.1 per cent during 1991 and 9.9 per cent during 2001-02. Direct tax increased from 1.9 per cent in 1990-91 to 3.7 per cent in 2001-02 and indirect taxes declined from 7.9 per cent in 1991 to 6 per cent in 2001-02.

The tax reforms could not give desired benefits. As for the directions of central board of direct taxes. The recent times lot of promotions had taken place leading to the bulck of high level officials at apex and starting of new officers at deferent places increased the administrative budget tremendously. One of the main problems of taxation is the recovery. The recovery officers are not interested with full work and only with the help of better tax collections the situation will improve.

Inflation

The inflation (WPI) rate declined during 1990's. It was 8.04 per cent during 1991-02 and 11 per cent during 1996 and 5.57 per cent 1996-02. The inflation (WPI) rate was 13.6 per cent during 1991-92 and declined to 4.2 per cent during 2001-02. In terms of (CPI) it declined from 13.9 per cent during 1991-92 to 4.2 per cent during 2001-02.

Foreign Reserves

The foreign exchange crises of 1990-91 forced India to accept a substantial IMF bailout loan with severe conditions. The Indian Economy has been plagued by balance of payments problems late 1950's. After 1973, we adopted a system of flouting currencies. There is a creeping depreciation of rupee. Our merchandise exports achieved

TABLE 12
FIVE-YEAR AVERAGE INFLATION RATE (WPI) PER CENT

Sl. No.	*Period*	*52 week Annual Aveg.*	*Point (March End) to*
1.	1956-57 to 1960-61	6.3	5.2
2.	1961-62 to 1965-66	5.8	5.9
3.	1966-67 to 1970-71	6.7	5.7
4.	1971-72 to 1975-76	12.0	10.8
5.	1976-77 to 1980-81	8.5	11.0
6.	1981-82 to 1985-86	6.5	5.5
7.	1986-87 to 1990-91	7.8	8.5
8.	1991-92 to 1995-96	10.6	9.3
9.	1996-97 to 2000-01	5.0	5.3

rapid growth from 1993-94 onwards. During 1991-02 export rates increased by 8.87%. The export rate was 12.4% during 1991-96 and 5.95% in 1996-2001. Thus, exports improved a lot. The import growth rate was 6.82% during 1991-92. It was 9.12% during 1991-96, 4.9% during 1996-02. India's foreign exchange reserves have been growing steadly from US $ 9.2 billion during 1991-92 to US $ 49.5 billion by February 2002. The growth rate in foreign exchange was 2.6% during 1991-92 and 9.6% during 2001-2002.

External Debt

The external debt situation has improved because of external debt management by Govt. The external debt declined from 28.7% in 1991 to 21.0% in 2001. The debt service ration declined from a peak level of 35.3% in 1990-91 to 16.3% in 2000-01.

Subsidies

Subsidies on all services amount to 14.40% of GDP. Subsidies on merit goods amount to 3.69% of GDP. Subsidies on non-merit goods amount to 10.71%. In 1996-97 combined gross fiscal deficits was 9.5% of GDP. If the rate of subsidy on Non-Merit goods, drops to 50% the combined gross fixed deficits will fall to less than 2% of GDP. Though, eminently sensible reduction in subsidies seems inevitable to bring up crucial question of political economy. Governments are not able to reduced deficits because of the factors behind their control such as high oil prices slow down of the economy, group pressures, Political Manipulation for electrical gains. Subsidies remain as continuing problem of the Central Govt. The elimination of export subsidies in 1991 has not followed up by elimination of other existing subsidies. Food subsidy should also fall proportionately on a continuous basis. The continued high minimum support prices (MSP) applied for Wheat and Rice. It is estimated to maintain food security on one hand and more efficiency and greater investment of private trade on the other. Fertilizers subsidy is another problem. Most of the subsidies spent for poor are poorly devoted and do not really benefited the poor.

Trends in Poverty

During 1990's the slowing down of rural employment growth affected the pace of decline in rural poverty and widened rural urban disparities.

Rural per capita total expenditure per month at 1990-91 prices which was Rs. 158 in 1970-71, increased steadily to Rs. 213 by 1989-90 and declined sharply to Rs. 202 (1997) its annual trend growth fell to 1.2% during the 1990's from 1.5% during 1979-89.

In contrast there has been acceleration in the trend growth rate of the same in urban areas where the annual growth rate was 1.45% during 1970-89, which almost doubled to about 2.8% during 1990's. Clearly rural urban disparities widened during 1990's.

The growth rate of per capita expenditure of rural bottom 30% declined from 1.71% per annum during 1970-89 to 1.19% during 1990's the same for this urban counter part increased from 1.44% to 1.70%. Though all the urban classes gained during 1990's the top 30% gained the most.

Rural poverty declined at an annual rate of 2.5% during 1970's and 1980's. Most of it during the 1980's and 0.73% during 1990's. Poverty levels declined steadily from 57% in

TABLE 13
ESTIMATES OF POVERTY

Sl. No.	Year	All India Number *(million)*	Poverty Ratio *(per cent)*	Rural Number *(million)*	Poverty Ratio *(per cent)*	Urban Number *(million)*	Poverty Ratio *(per cent)*
1	2	3	4	5	6	7	8
1.	1973-74	321	54.9	261	56.4	60	49.0
2.	1977-78	329	51.3	264	53.1	65	45.2
3.	1983	323	44.5	252	45.7	71	40.8
4.	1987-88	307	38.9	232	39.1	75	38.2
5.	1993-94	320	36.0	244	37.3	76	32.4
6.	1999-2000	260	26.1	193	27.1	67	23.6

Source: Economic Survey, 2001-02

1970's to 44% in 1989-90 and 33% in 1997. During 1990's the absolute poverty increased.

Urban poverty declined at the rate of 2% during 1970's and 1980's and 3.05% during 1990's. The declined is due to higher income growth achieved during the period of liberalization. The widening rural urban disparity in incomes should be of great concern in a country like India.

The poverty rate is declined from 54.9 per cent in 1973-76 to 44.5 per cent in 1983 and to 26.1 per cent in 1999-2001. The poverty ratio is much higher in the rural areas as compared to urban. However, the obsolete number of people living below poverty line are high both in rural and urban areas i.e., 193 million in rural and 67 million in urban areas.

Employment

According to the planning commission overall employment is estimated to have grown by about one per cent per annum during the period 1993-94 to 1999-2000, compared with a growth of 2.43 per cent per annum during the period 1987-88 to 1993-94. The decline in employment growth is associated with the lowers growth of population (1.93 per cent during 1993-2000 as compared with 2.1 per cent during 1987-94) and labour force (1.03 per cent during 1993-2000 as compared with during 1987-94).

Public sector employment experienced an absolute decline of 0.03 per cent during 1994-2000, employment in the private sector grow by 1.87 per cent during the same period. This can be attributed to on-going process of restructuring of various public sector undertakings and ban on Government employment.

Employment in the agricultural sector is very slow at the first time in the country's history. However, employment sectors such as trades, constructions, financial services ranger between 5.7 per cent during 1990's. Thus employment generations in 1990's had undergone a structural transformation with jobs being increasingly generated in the non-government sector.

The rate of growth of population was 2.27 per cent per

annum during 1972-73 to 1977-78. And it declined to 2.14 per cent during 1983 to 1987-88 and 1.93 per cent during 1993-94 to 1999-2000. The labour force growth rate declined from 2.94 per cent to 1.03 per cent during the same period. The steep decline in employment growth rate from 1.73 per cent during 1972-73 and 1977-78 to 1.54 per cent during 1983-88 and 0.98 per cent during 1993-94 to 1999-2000.

TABLE 14
RATE OF GROWTH OF POPULATION, LABOUR FORCE AND EMPLOYMENT

Sl. No.	Period	*Rates of Growth of Population (per cent per annum)*	*Rates of Growth of Labour Force (UPSS) (per cent per annum)*	*Rates of Growth of Employment (UPSS) (per cent per annum)*
1	2	3	4	5
1.	1972-73 to 1977-78	2.27	2.94	2.73
2.	1977-78 to 1983	2.19	2.04	2.17
3.	1983 to 1987-88	2.14	1.74	1.54
4.	1987-88 to 1993-94	2.10	2.29	2.43
5.	1993-94 to 1999-2000	1.93	1.03	0.98

Source: Economic Survey, 2001-02.

Summary and Conclusion

The GDP growth rate is slightly higher during 1990's as compared to 1980's. The price level remained more or less the same. The exports are growing imports are reduced. Balance of payments position has been comfortable. The current account deficit to GDP ratio has remained below crises level. The rupee has weathered external disturbances. Debt service has been brought to very comfortable level. Poverty ratio has fallen from 36% in 1991 to 23.3% during 1991-2000. Population growth starts declining. Literacy levels had increased. Greater transparence and efficiency is observed in banking sector. People adopted consumerist values and global cultural norms. Women and child workers were brought under Global Scrutiny. Subsidies are gradual withdrawn. MNC's interred into agriculture. Thus, on the whole the Indian economy performed better in these areas during 1990's. However, in certain areas the performance is very poor. Agricultural and industry showed deceleration competitive forces did not work. Infrastructure growth is very low. High physical deficits exists. There exists unsustainable imbalance between Govt. revenue and expenditure. High growth rate achieved is attributed to the cost of Govt. Finances. Govt. expenditure used to full-fill political needs. Revenue deficits have been financed by surpluses on capital account, which is harmful to the economy. Employment generation has slowdown. The significant structural change is the fall in the agricultural employment that has occurred for the first time because for agricultural diversification.

The Indian economy responded to the economic reforms of 1990's with a high growth performance than in previous decades. It may be able to achieve higher growth rate by deepening economic reform process. Second generation reforms have been initiated already.

Economic reforms are continuous process, which need to be adopted as the economic environment changes both domestically, and Internationally. The continued implications of reforms along with this upturn in the economic environment is likely to help in regeneration of economic activity in the years to come. Indian Economy needs a change in direction. We must be prepared to face the new challenges since the world is changing so fast. We have to meet the new challenges in the context of high population growth rate, poverty, illiteracy, ignorance, and gainful employment for all able-bodied people.

10

FINANCIAL SECTOR REFORMS—SOME ASPECTS & ISSUES RELATING TO NON-PERFORMING ASSETS IN COMMERCIAL BANKS

D.N.M. Raju &
G.N. Brahamanandam

The main objective of any banking industry is grating of credit facilities for economic development. The banks meet their credit requirements by raising resources through fresh deposits, borrowings, etc. However, their major source of funding credit is through recycling of funds recovered from borrowers. Non-recovery of loans granted negates the effectiveness of this process of credit cycle. Non-recovery not only affects the profitability of banks but also force the banks to maintain more owned funds by way of creating provisions and reserves to act as cushion for the loan losses. Therefore, the bank managements should try to keep the loan losses at low level as elimination of such losses is not possible in toto. Mounting NPA's may have widespread repercussions. It is due to mounting NPA's in Long Term Credit Bank of Japan, that Government of Japan was forced to nationalise it to avoid a major melt down of the financial system.

In India, the Non-Performing Advances are at higher levels when compared to other advanced countries. The seriousness of the problem not only attracted the attention of the public but also the International Financial Institutions. This has gained further prominence in the wake of Financial

Sector Reforms. It is these developments that prompted us to undertake this subject, to understand the problem and influence on the banking Industry.

What is NPA?

Non-Performing Advance is an advance where payment of interest or repayment of instalment of principal (in case of Term Loans) or both remains unpaid for a period of two quarters or more. An amount under any of the credit facilities is to be treated as past due when it remains unpaid for 30 days beyond due date.

NPAs in Indian Banks Vis-a-Vis Other Countries

Comparison of NPAs in Indian Banking system with that of other advanced countries is made only in context of the opening up of our Financial Sector Reforms. Certainly, the level of NPAs in Indian Banks is more than that of countries like USA, Japan, Hong Kong, South Korea and others.

The practices relating to NPAs in advanced countries are quite different from that of Indian Banks. In some countries, all or bulk of banks provisions are general provisions and identified losses are written off at an early stage. Banks in these countries carry very little NPAs in their balance sheets. Their recovery measures are also expeditious in view of bankruptcy and foreclosure laws. Moreover, the concept of Gross and Net NPAs is not in practice. Their practices with regard to the securities also differ. In certain countries, an advance is considered 'un-collectible' and classified as loss asset only after it remains as 'past due' or 'doubtful' for a certain period of time, whereas in India, an advance is to be classified as 'loss' the moment it is uncollectible. The concept of collateral also differs. Other countries adopt norms as per their requirements. Stringent prescriptions do not exist in a number of Third World countries. Therefore, the comparison of norms in India with the best practices of the Third World Countries would be reasonable.

Prudential Norms on Income Recognition, Asset Classification and Provisioning

In order to ensure greater transparency in the borrowal accounts and to reflect actual health of banks in their balance sheets, RBI introduced prudential regulations relating to income recognition, asset classification and provisioning as recommended by Narasimham Committee (1991) in a phased manner over a three-year period beginning 1992-1993. These regulations brought in the necessary quantification and objectivity into the assessment of NPAs and provisioning in respect of problem credits.

GROSS & NET NPAS OF SCHEDULED COMMERCIAL BANKS—BANKs GROUPWISE

(As at end March) *(Rs. in Crores)*

	SCS				*PSB*				*All Pvt. SB*				*Foreign Banks*			
	1	*2*	*3*	*4*	*1*	*2*	*3*	*4*	*1*	*2*	*3*	*4*	*1*	*2*	*3*	*4*
1998	14.4	6.4	7.3	3.0	16.0	7.0	8.2	3.3	8.7	3.9	5.3	2.3	6.4	3.0	2.2	1.0
1999	14.7	6.2	7.6	2.9	15.9	6.7	9.1	3.1	10.8	4.5	7.4	2.8	7.6	3.1	2.9	1.1
2000	12.7	5.5	6.8	2.7	14.0	6.0	7.4	2.9	8.2	3.6	5.4	2.3	7.0	3.2	2.4	1.0
2001	11.4	4.9	6.2	2.5	12.4	5.3	6.7	2.7	8.5	3.7	5.4	2.3	6.8	3.0	1.9	0.8

Source: Trend & Progress of Banking, 2000-01.
1—Gross NPA% to Gross advance; 2—Gross NPAs to Total Assets
3—Net NPA% to Net Advance; 4—Net NPAs to Total Assets.

The above statistical data reveals that the ratio of gross and net NPAs to total assets as well as gross and net advances, however, declined for all bank groups other than private sector banks.

Causes for NPAs

1. Global Recession.
2. General Recovery climate which encourage willful defaults.
3. Lack of expertise on the part of the loan purveyors.
4. Failure to render dedicated and honest service by bankers.
5. Inadequacy of professional skills in assessing business risks.

6. Scandalous siphoning off funds by corporate racketeers without any fear of legal action.
7. Political interference and unstable political scenario in the country.
8. Herd mentality of the borrowers in respect of Stock Market.
9. Lack of proper publicity for the RBI scheme OTS.
10. Delay in legal system.
11. Frequent rotation of duties of bank staff dealing with NPAs.
12. Absence of reward and punishment system in banks.
13. Braindrain of qualified personnel due to market competition.
14. Slowdown of industrial activity and the dumping of goods from abroad under liberalised economy.
15. Lack of remunerative prices for agricultural sector.

Suggestions to Overcome the Problem of NPAs

1. Urgent reforms of the antiquated legal system and the laws prevalent in the country are necessary to enable banks to recover their dues.
2. Branches which are continuously making losses and found unvibale can be shifted to better locations.
3. Members of the staff may be used aggressively to recover old dues.
4. The top management should give active guidance to the branch personnel for a turn around. The branch functionaries should have easy access to the senior functionaries for advice and support.
5. Rehabilitation programmes can be drawn up expeditiously in respect of sick units. Nursing programmes to be properly implemented so that revival is faster with timely back up support.
6. In India, bankers first decide on the assessment and then go for appraisal, which is not the correct way. It should always be appraisal first, where the decision is taken as regards to giving the loan or not, which depends on the character, integrity of the borrower.

7. Supervision and follows-up are two sides of the same coin. It is a proven fact that, regular supervision during the initial stages of any kind of advance and suggesting remedial measures to the borrower will have a lasting effect on the borrower and the account. This helps to reduce NPAs in the long run.
8. The government must come out with clear cut policies on the matters of speedy loan recovery process. Recovery team should be formed at each branch and its performance be reviewed at periodic intervals.
9. In-Branch Training, Forum should be formed at all the branches having a staff strength of 15 and above and all the officials be made responsible to fill in the knowledge gaps of other employees in specific areas of NPAs.
10. Cosmetic changes like recovery tribunals will not produce the required results unless far reaching changes in the legal system and provisions are introduced. Taking banks out of the review of external surveillance is not easy. But it can be achieved if some urgency is shown to speed up the reforms.
11. Compromises and write-off of loans are lefts to the courts of law. Infact, compromises enable bankers to make better recoveries than awaiting a court verdict. So, proper steps should be taken in this direction.
12. Lethargy in higher ups should be dealt with seriously. All the persons from top to bottom dealing with NPAs should be made responsible for the recovery.
13. The procedure in granting loans must be liberalised. Borrowers must be protected from the unscrupulous officials who make secret dealings while granting loans.
14. Cut-throat competition among the banks in reaching the target set is another major reason for loans

turning NPAs. In anxiety the bankers may violate the three 'C's of the customer. i.e. Character, Capacity and Capital. It results in mounting NPAs.

15. Special Acts should be enacted exclusively for the bankers to deal with defaulters without any delay. The properties of the entire family of the borrower should be brought under guarantee. Freedom must be given to the banks to recruit qualified personnel and to decide the compensation package in order to reduce NPAs.
16. Banks should be given freedom to dispose off the assets of the borrower without the intervention of the legal system on the lines of Revenue Recovery Act.
17. Above all, the banks should act as a friend, philosopher and a guide to the corporate borrowers and advise them through counselling to sell the assets, which are either unproductive or inefficient.

However, credit risk is a major risk in the working of banks and the elimination of NPAs in total is not possible. Hence, all possible measures should be taken by all concerned to minimize the NPAs in banks.

The above measures not only help the banks to minimize the NPAs in general but give a face-lift to banks in International arena. It is all the more the need of the hour for banks, which are opting for overseas expansion.

11

INDIAN ECONOMY—ITS EFFECT ON THE CHALLENGES OF THE 21ST CENTURY

K. Sarada Devi

Impact of Indian Economy on the Political Structures

The economic reforms in the recent has delinked the relationship between the community and the state and widened the freedom of corporations further eroding the powers and freedoms of the people. In the process, the State itself is undergoing a major transformation, becoming more one-side in representing corporate interest and failing to represent citizen and community interest. The globalisation, which is a form of economic reform had undermined community protectionism, is now itself being undermined to corporate protectionism. This undermining is the heart of the globalization process. The power is vested in the hands of corporations. It does not give power downwards into the hands of communities but moves upwards into the boardrooms of corporations. Globalization has caused massive environmental damage, and the competition of resources between states, capital and people resulting in conflicts and territorial disputes left with ecological and political refugees.

Constraints on the Local Economies

The result of increasing domination of market forces in the food sector and reduced public policy intervention for food security, food prices increased by 63% between 1989-90 and 1993-94, leading to a decline in per capita food consumption. Liberalisation of agricultural exports have also led to the exports of cotton and yarn. Export of cotton has led to a doubling and tripling of the cost of yarn and the creation of massive unemployment in the decentralised handloom weaving sector. The handloom sector employs 9 million workers, largely in home based production. The main reason for the destitution of the weavers was that between 1991 and 1994 the prices of yarn had more than doubled from Rs. 226.30 to Rs. 415 per bundle of 40's count (New Wave, September 15, 1996).

Poverty

Poverty is not a phenomenon. Poverty in this era of Globalization has assumed new dimensions. Libralisation and marginalisation go hand in hand. What prospects are there for the millions of poor peasants, rural labourers, urban unemployed, slum dwellers, the 23 million refugees, 100 million street children and the millions displaced by "development" projects under the new globalization regime? In the words of the Human Development Report 1995, "the poorest 20% of world's people have benefited little from the increased globalization of economies. In world trade, their share is only 1% and in world commercial lending a scant 0.2%. More than three-fourths of world's people live in developing countries, but they enjoy only 16% of the world's income while the richest 20% have 85% of global income." The reality is more sharply focused when it is noted that 70 per cent of the 1.4 billion absolute poor (their number has swelled form 1.05 billion in 1985 to 1.4 billion in 1995) as measured by the world Bank using an absolute poverty line of $ 31 per person per month.

Poverty is defined as the minimum level of consumption expenditure which is determined on the basis of calorie nutrition requirement for physical subsistence—"the poverty line." According to the World Bank, more than a quarter of the world's population—i.e., between 1.2 and 1.3 thousand million human being—live in absolute poverty. The clearest index of this is hunger, which is the sheer lack of access to food. Another is ill health, often due to such elementary needs as clean water (it is estimated that nearly two thousand million people lack safe drinking water). Absolute poverty is a breach of the most basic human right to the gift of life itself.

Similar sources (e.g. Human Development Report, 1990, UN Development programme) suggest that some 900 million people cannot read or write, that one out of every three children born alive is undernourished, at some time within its first five years, and that at least 14 million of those children die of hunger every year.

One out of every four humans on the earth is absolutely poor, and lives in a condition of malnutrition, illiteracy, disease, high infant mortality or low life expectancy. More than half are small farmers, and between one-fifth and one quarter are landless labourers. Of these, 80% live in India, Pakistan and Bangladesh. Their poverty is self-sustaining, self-generating, and the women suffer the most.

In India, 1.5 per cent of the population, numbering about 12 million hold about 65% of the nation's private wealth. 30% of the population amounting to the total population of all western European countries live below the poverty line at a meagre Rs. 195.50 per capita month.

To quote a few alarming facts and figures of India. In India, about 250 millions of people at the bottom of the society share about 1.5 to 2% of the national income. Therefore, they are permanently poor, from generation of generation, exploited, starving and insecure; hunger, ill health and ignorance are their constant companions. Another 600 millions of people just above the poorest of the poor, also live in poverty. Perhaps only about 200 millions—not now, but in the future—may have access to means of better life although just today it is only about 10% of the population that seem to be quite comfortable.

Unemployment

After one year of the implementation of a SAP in India, 6.6 million additional people were rendered jobless as a result of the privatization of public companies, the application of new technologies and the several of state discrimination in favour of backward areas.

Flow of Human Capital—The Braindrain

Another form of resource transfer form East to West is the migration of highly skilled manpower contribution "intellectual technology" to the West. Through the brain drain, the East loses economic resources in two ways. First, a substantial amount of money (usually public money) had been expended to educate and train professional or skilled personnel in the expectation that they would in turn contribute their skills towards the nation's development; when the personnel migrate, the funds expended on their training are thus lost to the country. Secondly, the country also suffers a cost in terms of the loss of future economic benefits that could have arisen from the application of skills of the migration personnel.

Globalization and Food Insecurity

Trade liberalisation has been generating food insecurity at three levels. Firstly, it is transferring the resources from peasants to industry. Secondly, shifting the land use from the production of staple for exports. Thirdly, it is removing food subsidies, thus lowering domestic consumption and increasing food export. The resource and livelihood insecurity linked to land alienation, the production insecurity linked to decline of food production, the consumption insecurity linked to decline in consumption are all contributing to food insecurity for the people in India.

India has the second largest population in the world. The country has low incomes compared to world standards and the per capita availability of calories and food grains (the main staple food of the poor) are among the lowest in the world. It has been shown that the proportion of people below the poverty line has not declined significantly over the year. This is sufficient show that while food deficit at the national level has been contained, food insecurity for the poor still exists.

The area under food crop production in India is on the decline, from 100.7 to 97.3 between 1990-91 and 1994-95, while the index for the area under non-food crops increased from 120.0 to 125.7 during that period. Production of course cereals and pulses, the main food for the poor has shown as declining trend.

The agricultural exports increased by about 71% from Rs. 21.98 billion in 1988-1989 to Rs. 377.66 billion in 1992-93. The India prices of staple food grains are lower than world prices. Indian rice prices are about 54% lower than world prices, the wheat are 17% lower. These crops get exported. Thus the domestic price rice taking the staple food grains beyond the reach of poor people.

The freedom to export food grain under liberalised trade has already benefited the giant grain traders Cargill and Continental. They bought wheat at $ 60 to $ 100 per tonne from India and sold it at $ 230-240 per tonne at the international market in 1996, making a neat $ 130-170 profit per tonne, while India lost $ 100 m in exports because of the concentration of power in the hands of five merchants of grain.

Declining Economies

A survey of 69 countries over the past decade shows that, in 46 countries which recorded economic growth only 27 saw employment increase while 19 experienced 'jobless growth.' The latter group include India. We learn that the world has 358 billionaires and that their combined assets exceed the total annual income of the world's 2.3 billion poorest people that is, 45 per cent of the global population. If the process generating such inequalities is not held in check, the HDR warns that it will generate a world's gargantuan in its excesses and grotesque in its human and economic inequalities.

The "Human Development Report 1997" places India at 138 in this ranking of 175 countries on a composite index based on life expectancy, adult literacy and the GDP per capita. Over 170 million Indians—one in every six—don't have access to safe drinking water. Nine Indians are born every ten seconds. 71% of national income or consumption is shared by 30% Indians and 12% is shared by the low 30% Indians. In India, irrigated area devoted to produce jowar, bajra, maize and ragi combined is 4.8% while 5.4% irrigated land is devoted to produce cash crops like sugar and tobacco. 53% of India's population barely lives less than 1 dollar a day. Out of every 100 Indians, 16 Indians enjoy electricity, safe drinking water and toilet facilities. Value of a poor Indian is estimated to Rs. 10,000 (250 USD). In the fifty first year of independence, India finds itself a misfit in the world's hierarchy: a subcontinental nation, almost a billionaire in population, but with more citizens in poverty and illiteracy than any other country (Politics India—Feb.'98 Steering Steady in the Post-Cold War World—A Madhavan).

When the British lift India in 1947, our resources were already depleted by the exploitative colonial regime. The process of globalization since 1991 continues and intensifies the anti-people process of development that has been going on since Independence. The aims are neither to reduce poverty and unemployment nor to provide basic need's (The World Bank and Globalization of Indian Economy—Dalip S. Swamy).

Education

The Indian government, in its 1992-93 budget, cut support for community village schools by 80%, non-formal education programs by 17%, and technical education by 15%. Uniforms, books, and notebooks, as well as school fees, became more expensive, forcing parents to keep children, particularly girls, out of school. About 75 million children (of which 54 million are girls) are not in school. Some 10 million are not of school. 19.4 of world's adult males and 33.6% adult females are illiterate. More than half the world's 842 million illiterates are Indians.

Deterioration of Health Care Systems

The Indian government began withdrawing public support for health care for the poor in 1992, with fees rising of nursing home charges up to five times, and the price of essential drugs rising 50-400%. For every three TB patients worldwide one lives in India. Indian Government spends 1.3% of GDP on Health. 75% of health budget goes towards staff salaries. The statistics recently released by National Council of Applied Economic Research (NCAER) showed that about 40% of India's population remains under the poverty line. According to an other surgery by the NCAER, 37% of the country's rural population is landless. This is the poorest section, which cannot grow enough food, cannot find other means to ward off hunger and unable to cope up with health needs. In the 1992-93 Indian Government budget on mother and child-care programs, as well as government dispensaries, and 11% from vaccination programs, while 40% was also cut from water and sanitation programs. To the contrary, 95% of worldwide spending on health research is devoted to health problems of the industrialised countries.

Women in India

World Development Report 1995 has reported a fall in the percentage share of women in the labour force in India from 30% in 1970 to 25% in 1993 (The Economic Times—18 April 1996). Female literacy is at a poor 38% as compared to male literacy at 66%. Average real wage of a woman in India for every 100 rupees in real wages earned by a man, is only Rs. 51. Average number of women raped or killed for dowry every hour in India is 2. Statistically, the participation of women in the workforce has increased, from 8.31% in 1981 to 9.74% in 1991 (Deshpande). In 1981, there were 139 women to 1000 men workers in urban areas, the figure rose to 178 in 1991. Three-fourths of these have insecurity of income and employment.

Out of every 10 days that women find employment is only for 3 days. Average number of times women cry every week is 3 times. Number of Russian women killed by their husbands in 1994, were 15,000. Chances that a married women in rural India in the age group 13-16 is already a mother: 1:3.

Share of women in India's adult labour force in 1970 was 34 and today it is 31. Number of girls in the age group 0-6 years that are missing from India's population due to gender discrimination, is 14 lakhs girls. Average number of hours a week women work in India is 69 hrs. Number out of every 3 female agricultural labourers that are below poverty line is 2. Number out of every 3 female—headed households that constitute rural poor is 1. Proportion out of every 10 women lodged in Indian jails that are under trials are 7. 150 million women living below the poverty line constitute our female workforce. More than 90% of these women work in the unorganised sector. 16% of the rural population earns less than Rs. 3 per day and another 18% less than Rs. 5. 60 million children under six years belong to a group whose mothers have to work for their survival (Seminar—462 February 1998).

Children

Every third household in India has a working child and they all contribute over 20% of GNP of India. India has the world's largest malnourished children of about 53% of total under fives, exceeding even the sub-Saharan countries at 31%. 50% of children in the age group 5-15 years do not go to school. Child abuse through tourism has victimised thousands of children in Asia. Fifteen per cent out of an estimated 2 million prostitutes in India are children.

Human Rights

Today, the dominant force of economic development is not aid but trade and investment. Development is defined as "a comprehensive economic, social, cultural and political process, which aims at the constant improvement of the well-being of the entire population and of all individuals" and "in which all human rights and fundamental freedoms can be fully realized." The Global, have become important in their impact on human rights and the quality of life all around the world to be ignored or given only peripheral attention by those struggling to build a more just and sustainable future for humanity.

Conclusion

Any reformation whether it be economic, social, political or cultural should aim at the welfare of the public—more so ever should meet the basic needs of the common man. Are economic reforms of Indian Economy benefited the poor? Or the rich? When there had been reasonable growth in technological sector and increase in GDP why not the agriculture sector and the Public Distribution System have not developed at a proportionate growth rate?

12

AN ASSESSMENT OF THE REFORMS IN SMALL INDUSTRY

J. Revathy

ABSTRACT

Small Industry has been given an indispensable role in the development of nations by almost every government. The Presence of Small Business Unity cannot be easily ignored by the policy-makers. In the context of our country, Small Units have a significant presence in terms of their number value addition and contribution to the generation of employment. In the planned development process, small units were provided with policy support, incentives, concessions and even finance. The situation appears to be changing to the disadvantage of small units now. There is an all-round liberalization and integration effort at the national and international levels, small units, be set with a wide variety of problems are experiencing a rough weather.

Against this background, an attempt has been made in the present paper to highlight the several reforms taken by the government of India for the development of small industry in India. More specifically the paper focuses on the reforms of the Nayak Committee, Abid Hussain Committee, Kapur Committee and the report of the study group on development of small scale enterprises.

Significance of Small Industry in India

Small business units (SBUS) are viewed increasingly as an important vehicle for meeting both the growth and equity objectives of developing economics. The contribution of SBUS to the industrial growth is significant. Viewed in terms of turnover, value addition and exports, the share of

SBUs is relatively high. For example: in Malaysia, SBUs constitute the majority of all industrial establishments, accounting for at least one half of industrial employment and value added.[1] In Singapore SBUs in manufacturing, commerce and the service sectors constitute approximately 87 per cent of businesses, 42 per cent of employment, 25 per cent of value added and 16 per cent of direct exports.[2] Taking India as an example, small business units in India accounted for about 40 per cent of the gross turnover in the manufacturing sector, about 45 per cent of the manufacturing exports and 35 per cent of total exports.[3] Similarly, employment generated by this sector stood at 167.2 lakh which constitutes 59.8 per cent of the total employment in the organised sector of the country.[4]

SBUs, being labour intensive, are believed to provide more employment and earning opportunities for unskilled workers. As unskilled workers may often underemployed or unemployed, small scale industry therefore contributes towards reducing poverty and inequality. Research in six developing countries shows that, collectively, small establishments account for most industrial employment. That may be true of many countries, if not most.[5] In developing countries much manufacturing employment is found in rural areas. Further, SBUs tend to be more dispersed then larger enterprises and can thus contribute to the promotion of a more balanced development process.

They have the ability to accelerate rural industrialisation by forgoing linkages between the more organised industrial sector in the urban areas and the rural manufacturing enterprises that often produce a variety of inputs for industries located in urban areas. In this way, SBUs also provide employment for a large section of the rural population, especially in the off-season, thus smoothening out variations in rural incomes and consumption.[6] Further, there is also evidence that SBUs can create jobs for a relatively lower level of investment and are particularly suitable for an economy with a surplus of low-skilled labour. The number of small units, value of production and employment have gone up quite substantially. The total number of SBUs have increased to 31.21 lakh in 1998-99 from just 20.8 lakh in 1991-92, and the output has increased from 1,78,699 crore to 5,27,515 crore in 1998-99. Further, the value of employment has gone up to 171.6 lakh persons from 129.8 lakh persons during the same period.[7]

Inspite of phenomenal growth in the SBUS, sickness in the industry is growing year after year. Of the total number of cases referred to BIFR expansion include Board for Industrial and Financial Reconstruction cases pertaining to SBUs are substantial. As per the provisional data compiled by RBI, the total number of sick/weak units financed by scheduled commercial banks increased to 3,09,013 as at the end of March 1999 from 2,24,012 as at the end of March 1998.[8] The SSI sick units constitute 99 per cent of total number of sick/weak units, they accounted for 22.2 per cent of the total outstanding bank credit. The studies sponsored by RBI have identified factors like deficiencies in the project appraisals, shortage of raw materials, power crisis, transport and financial bottlenecks as the reasons for growing sickness in the small industry. The independent research studies undertaken by individual researchers have also identifies several factors like the above being responsible for the failure of SBUs. An International planning team invited to suggest measures for the development of SBUS as early as in 1954 that there was a severe lack of capital as well as credit largely because of low productivity and over population. S.P. Mathur on the basis of his study in Agra Region reported that finding adequate fixed and working capital was the greatest bottleneck in the growth of small industry.[10]

POLICY RECOMMENDATIONS OF VARIOUS COMMITTEES

General problems faced by SSIs, certain sector groups, such as, tiny sectors, micro enterprises, women entrepreneurs etc., require special attention. Undertaking continuous reviews of the credit policies and evolving new ones in the changing economic scenario for meeting emerging conditions has been the corner stone of the credit policy so far. A brief description of the major Committees set up to review the credit availability to the sector after the introduction of economic reforms, is given below:

Nayak Committee—1991

The Nayak Committee set up by the Reserve Bank of India in December 1991 (Report submitted in September 1992) mainly dealt with the question of adequacy and timeliness of credit made available to SSIs. The Committee found that small scale sector was getting working capital to the extent of 8.1% of its annual output which was less than the normative requirement of 20%. Accordingly, the Committee recommended that the SSI sector should obtain 20% of its annual projected turnover by way of working capital. Based on these as well other recommendations of the Nayak Committee, the RBI issued a number of guidelines advising the banks to grant working capital finance to SSI units to the extent of 20% of the projected annual turnover, timely disposal of loan applications and setting up of specialized bank branches for SSI financing in areas where there was a large concentration of SSIs.

As a follow-up of the Nayak Committee recommendations, the Finance Minister in Budget speech for the year 1995-96, announced a Seven Point Action Plan for improving the flow of credit to small scale sector. This included-setting up of specialized SSI bank branches; adequate delegation of powers at branch and regional levels; conducting sample surveys of the banks performing SSI accounts; sanction of composite loans as far as possible; regular meetings with SSI entrepreneurs; sensitisation of bank managers towards working of SSI sector; and simplification of procedural formalities by banks. The banks have initiated necessary steps for effective implementation of the points of the Action Plan.

Steps Taken by Reserve Bank of India to Improve Credit Flow to SSI Sector in Accordance with the Nayak Committee Report

(a) In order to ensure credit availability to tiny segments of the SSI sector, the RBI has issued instructions that out of the funds normally available for SSI sector, 40% be made available to units with investment in plant and machinery up to Rs. 5 lakhs; 20% of units with investment between Rs. 5 lakhs to Rs. 25 lakhs and remaining 40% for other units.

(b) Public sector banks have been advised to operationalise more specialised SSI branches to provide focussed attention at centres where there is a potential for financing many SSI borrowers. As on March 2000, 389 specialised SSI branches were working in the country.

(c) The 'Single Window Scheme' of the SIDBI has been extended to all districts to meet the financial requirements (both term loan & working capital) of SSIs.

(d) With a view to moderating the cost of credit to SSI units, banks have been advised to accord SSI units with a good track record, the benefit of lower spreads over the prime lending rate.

(e) In order to facilitate expeditious decision on credit proposals of SSI units, banks have been advised to delegate enhanced powers to the branch managers of the specialised SSI branches so that majority of the credit proposals are decided at the branch level itself.

Abid Hussain Committee on Small Enterprises—1997

The Abid Hussain Committee reiterated the recommendations of the Nayak Committee in general and recommended introduction of innovative finance. The Committee also recommended higher earmarking of credit for tiny sector units among SSI Units.

Kapur Committee—1998

In spite of the detailed instructions/directions issued by the Reserve Bank of India in accordance with recommendations of the Nayak Committee, the problems earlier faced by SSIs still persisted. Alarmed at the continuing problems and non-adherence of its guidelines on flow of credit to SSI sector, the RBI set up High Powered Committee under the Chairmanship of Sh. S.L. Kapur, Member, BIFR and former Secretary (SSI & ARI) to review the working of credit delivery system for the SSIs. The Committee submitted its report on 30th June 1998. The Report contained 126 recommendations. Some of the major recommendations of the Committee were:

1. Special treatment should be accorded to smaller among small industries.
2. The quantum of limits of composite loans should be enhanced.
3. The procedural difficulties in obtaining loans by SSIs should be removed.
4. The issues relating to mortgages of land including removal of stamp duty and permitting equitable mortgages should be sorted out.
5. The Small Industries Development Bank of India (SIDBI) should be allowed access to low-cost funds for refinancing SSI loans.
6. The obtaining of collateral for loans up to Rs. 0.2 million should be dispensed with.
7. A collateral reserve fund to provide support to first party guarantees should be set up.
8. With a view to developing industrial areas in/around metropolitan and urban areas, a Small Industries Infrastructure Development Fund should be put in place.
9. The definition of SSI units require appropriate changes in the emerging scenario.
10. The State Level Inter-Institutional Committees (SLIICs) should be armed with statutory powers.
11. A separate guarantee organization and 1,000

additional specialised bank branches should be set up.

12. The role defined for and the status accorded to SIDBI should be so as to match with that of National Bank for Agriculture and Rural Development (NABARD).

Out of the various recommendations of the Committee, the RBI has accepted 64 recommendations and accordingly has advised the banks to implement 48 of these recommendations. The remaining 16 recommendations pertaining to their respective sphere of activities have been implemented by SIDBI/NABARD. The important guidelines issued to the banks by the RBI pertain to the following:

1. Enhancement in the limit of composite loans.
2. Special programmes for training Branch Managers for sensitising them with the requirement of SSIs.
3. Delegation of more powers to Branch Managers to grant ad-hoc facilities to the extent of 20% of the limit sanctioned.
4. Strengthening of the recovery mechanism.
5. Opening of more specialised SSI branches by banks.
6. Adoption of Committee Approach for sanction of applications and disposal of loan applications in a time bound fashion.
7. Meticulous following of instructions issued by the RBI on implementation of Nayak Committee Recommendations.
8. Permitting use of prescribed application form for higher limits.

The rest of the recommendations are under examination by the RBI and the Government of India (Ministry of Finance).

Further, the Government of India has taken several steps under the Planning Commission in 2000 and 2001 for the development of small enterprises in India. It has developed a new package for small scale Industrial Sector in which several new changes were brought into effect from 30th August 2001.

NEW PACKAGE FOR SSI SECTOR

Policy/Support

The investment limit for the tiny sector will continue to be Rs. 25 lakh and for the SSI sector it will be Rs. 100 lakh. The Ministry of SSI, A&RI will being out a specific list of high-tech and export oriented industries which would require the investment limit to be raised up to Rs. 5 crore to admit suitable technology upgradation and to enable them to maintain their competitive edge. The Limited Partnership Act will be drafted quickly and got enacted.

Fiscal Support

To improve the competitiveness of Small Scale Sector the exemption on excise duty limit raised from Rs. 50 lakh to Rs. 1 crore.

Credit Support

Composite loans limit raised from Rs. 10 lakh to Rs. 25 lakh. The Small Scale Service and Business (Industry Related) Enterprises (SSSBEs) with a maximum investment of Rs. 10 lakh will qualify for priority lending. In the National Equity Fund (NEF) Scheme, the project cost limit will be revised from Rs. 25 lakh to Rs. 50 lakh. The soft loan limit will be retained at 25 per cent of the project cost subject to a maximum of Rs. 10 lakh per project. Assistance under the NEF will be provided at a service charge of 5 per cent per annum, and 30 per cent of the investment will be earmarked for the tiny sector. The eligibility limit for coverage under the Credit Guarantee Scheme has been revised to Rs. 25 lakh from the present limit of Rs. 10 lakh. The Department of Economic Affairs will appoint a Task Force to suggest revitalization/restructuring of the State Finance Corporations. The Nayak Committee's recommendations regarding provision of 20 per cent of the projected turnover as working capital is being recommended to financial institutions and banks.

Infrastructural Support

The Integrated Infrastructure Development Centre (IIDC) Scheme will progressively cover all areas in the country with 50 per cent reservation for rural areas. Regarding upgrading the industrial estates, which are languishing, SSI Ministry will draw up a detailed scheme for consideration of the Planning Commission. A plan scheme for cluster development will be drawn up. The funds available under the non-lapsable pool for the North-East will be made use of for industrial infrastructure development, setting up of incubation centers, for cluster development and for setting up of IIDCs in the North-East including Sikkim.

Technological Support and Quality Improvement

Capital Subsidy of 12 per cent for investment in modernization and upgradation technology in selected sectors. An inter-ministerial committee of experts will be set up to define the scope of technology upgradation and sectorial priorities. To encourage total quality management, the scheme of granting Rs. 75,000 to each unit for getting ISO 9000 certification will continue for the next six years, i.e., till the end of the 10th Plan. Setting up of incubation centers in sunrise industries will be supported. The Technology Bureau for Small Enterprises (TBSE) set up by SIDBI will be strengthened so that it functions effectively as a Technology Bank. It will be networked with NSIC and SIDO. SIDO's Small Enterprises for Information Resource Centre Network (SENET) Programme and Asia Pacific Council for Technology Transfer (APCTT) in association with NSIC would be utilized for this. SIDO, SIDBI and NSIC will jointly prepare a compendium of available technologies from R&D institutions in India and abroad and circulate among the industry associations for dissemination of the first technology related information. Commercial banks are being requested to develop schemes to encourage investment in technology upgradation and harmonise the same with SIDBI. One time capital grant of 50 per cent will be given to small scale associations who wish to develop and operate testing laboratories, provided they are of international standards.

Marketing Support

SIDO will have a Market Development Assistance (MDA) programme, similar to the one obtaining in the Ministry of Commerce. It will be a Plan scheme. The vendor development programme, buyer-seller meets and exhibitions would be organized more often and in dispersed locations.

Streamlining Inspections/Rules and Regulations

To minimize harassment to small scale sector a Group will be set up to recommend within three months, means of streamlining inspections. This will include repeal of laws and regulations applicable to the sector that have since become redundant. Self-certification will be progressively encouraged in lieu of inspections, which should be prescribed under the following three conditions: (i) On receipt of specific complaint, (ii) Selection of unit for sample check (say, 10 per cent of total units), and (iii) For audit and safety purposes.

Entrepreneurship Development

Capacity building in the SSI sector, both for entrepreneurs as well as workers will be given top priority. SSI Ministry and Labour Ministry will jointly work out a strategy.

Facilitating Prompt Payment

The Reserve Bank of India is being requested to appoint a Task Force to go into the question of how to strengthen and popularize factoring services and how to encourage bills culture, without recourse to the SSI suppliers. The Task Force shall give its report within six months of its constitution. RBI is being requested to take up with the banks the question of sub-allocating overall limits to large borrowers specifically for meeting the payment obligations in respect of purchases from the SSIs, either on cash basis or on bills basis.

Rehabilitation of Sick Units

RBI is being requested to draw up revised guidelines for rehabilitation of currently sick but potentially viable SSI units. Such guidelines should be detailed, transparent and non-discretionary.

Promoting Rural Industries

To support the Handloom Sector, "Deendayal Hathkargha Protsahan Yojana" has been announced. The scheme has a total financial implication of Rs. 447 crores and will provide comprehensive financial and infrastructural support to the weavers. The government is working out a new comprehensive package to strengthen Khadi and Village Industry that will further upgrade the skills of Khadi workers.

Improving Data Base

A fresh census of small scale industries will be conducted covering, interalia, the incidence of sickness and its causes.

Policy Package for Tiny Sector

The investment limit for the tiny sector will continue to be Rs. 25 lakh. Under the Prime Minister's Rozgar Yojana, which finances setting up of micro enterprises and generate employment for educated unemployed youth, the family income eligibility limit has been revised from Rs. 24,000 to Rs. 40,000 per annum.

Credit Support

The Nayak Committee's recommendations regarding provision of 20 per cent of the projected turnover as working capital is being recommended to the financial institutions and banks. In respect of tiny units also twenty per cent of the projected annual turnover of the tiny units would qualify for working capital loan, as indicated for SSI units. The national Small Industries Corporation will continue to give composite loans upto Rs. 25 lakh to the tiny sector and continue to charge one percent concessional interest rate. SIDBI will continue to give concessional rate of refinance to the tiny sector which is now at 10.5 per cent, as compared to 12 per cent for the SSI sector. This policy will continue. In the National Equity Fund (NEF) scheme, the project cost limit will be raised from Rs. 25 lakh to Rs. 50 lakh. The soft loan limit will be retained at 25 per cent of the project cost, subject to a maximum of Rs. 10 lakh per project. Assistance under the NEF will be provided at a service charge of 5 per cent per annum, and 30 per cent of the investment will be earmarked for the tiny sector.

Infrastructural Support

The IID scheme will progressively cover all areas in the country with 50 per cent reservation for rural areas. Under this scheme, 50 per cent of the plots will be earmarked for the tiny sector as against 40 per cent at present. Under the National Programme for Rural Industrialization (NPRI), cluster development is being taken up by KVIC, SIDO, SIDBI and NABARD. The major beneficiaries of cluster development programme will be tiny sector units. The sponsoring organization for each cluster will provide for design development, capacity, building, technology intervention and consortium marketing. A cluster development fund will be created under the Plan.

Technological Support

Capital Subsidy of 12 per cent for investment in technology in select sectors, preference will be given to the tiny sector for loans for technology upgradation.

Marketing Support

Preference will be given to the tiny sector while organizing buyer-seller meets, vendor development programmes and exhibitions.